WORK MOTIVATION

SERIES IN APPLIED PSYCHOLOGY

Edwin A. Fleishman, George Mason University
Series Editor

WORK MOTIVATION

Edited by

Uwe Kleinbeck
Bergische Universität

Hans-Henning Quast
Rohrer, Hibler & Replogle
International (Europe) Company

Henk Thierry
University of Amsterdam

Hartmut Häcker
Bergische Universität

LEA LAWRENCE ERLBAUM ASSOCIATES, PUBLISHERS
1990   Hillsdale, New Jersey   Hove and London

Lawrence Erlbaum Associates, Inc., Publishers
365 Broadway
Hillsdale, New Jersey 07642

Library of Congress Cataloging-in-Publication Data

Work motivation / edited by Uwe Kleinbeck . . . [et al.].
      p.   cm.
    Papers from a symposium held in 1987 in Leichlingen, West Germany
and sponsored by the German Research Foundation.
    ISBN 0-8058-0452-8
    1. Employee motivation—Congresses.   2. Goal setting in personnel
management—Congresses.   I. Kleinbeck, Uwe.   II. Deutsche
Forschungsgemeinschaft.
    HF5549.5.M63W67   1990
    658.3 '14—dc20   89-17142
                                                                        CIP

Printed in the United States of America
10 9 8 7 6 5 4 3 2 1

Contents

Series Foreword

There is a compelling need for innovative approaches to the solution of many pressing problems involving human relationships in today's society. Such approaches are more likely to be successful when they are based on sound research and applications. This *Series in Applied Psychology* offers publications that emphasize state-of-the-art research and its application to important issues of human behavior in a variety of societal settings. The objective is to bridge both academic and applied interests.

The application of psychological principles to improve working conditions can only be successful if the knowledge underlying the development and the use of these principles is compatible with the results of empirical research. Both the productivity of organizations and the well-being of individuals and groups can be increased by the application of sound research findings. This volume, *Work Motivation*, illustrates how theoretical concepts and techniques in organizational psychology are related to the solution of practical problems of work performance in organizations.

This book includes contributions from leading scientists in the field of work motivation. They have provided contributions especially prepared for this volume. These contributions deal with issues of work motivation at several conceptual levels. The first section deals with concepts, such as goal-setting and feedback, that aid our understanding of fundamental motivational structures that are important for work effectiveness. The second section emphasizes the applications of theoretical and methodological advances from research on motivation in the design of programs in organizations to improve performance and organizational effectiveness and to make work more interesting. Issues related to training and self-management and organizational design are dealt with. The third section evaluates psychological states and processes that influence work motivation over time. Relevant issues dealt with include the work motivation of young people entering the labor force, the effects of unemployment on work values, and the experience of organizations in implementing programs concerned with improving higher order need fulfillment.

The book brings together material related to work motivation, which has not been integrated previously. An important aspect of this book is its international perspective. The authors come from different countries, and the common themes from different cultural settings strengthen the impact of these research findings and extend their generality.

The book should be a valuable text for psychologists interested in work motivation, as well as for those individuals concerned with the improvement of productivity and well-being in organizations. The book is appropriate for professionals and students in organizational psychology.

Edwin A. Fleishman, Editor
Series in Applied Psychology

General Introduction

If psychology is to be used to solve problems in an important area of life as the one of work in organizations, we need to have good applied research. In the case of work motivation a solid foundation has been achieved already, the general and experimental psychology of work motivation has always been oriented towards practical issues in its development. Currently, we have reached a level, that can be considered as a model for other areas in Applied Psychology.

Therefore, the first part of the book represents current topics of research and the discussion of a central issue in the field: the relationship between motivation and performance. In focusing on the mechanisms of transforming motivation into performance the book does justice to major concerns of work psychology: understanding and promoting productivity of organizations from the perspective of performance capacities (cognitive abilities, skills) on the one side and understanding the functional processes of human motivation so that they can be used in work re-design. The second part contains practical examples of building and strengthening the motivating potential with regard to productivity and the health of employees. The development of work motivation over time and the change of the relative importance of central variables are the content of the last part of the book.

This volume developed out of a symposium on "Work Motivation" end 1987 in Leichlingen, West Germany. The symposium was sponsored by the German Research Foundation (DFG) and brought together industrial and organizational psychologists from Australia, Japan, USA and Europe. The fruitful and inspiring discussion of the presentations led to the conception of this book, in which current issues of research as well as future trends and developments in Applied Psychology are outlined.

The Editors
U. Kleinbeck, Wuppertal
H. H. Quast, Brussels
H. Thierry, Amsterdam
H. Häcker, Wuppertal

Part I

Motivation, Performance, and Effectiveness

The chapters in the first part of the book deal with the motivational conditions of performance at work. They aim at an understanding of fundamental motivational structures of achievement behavior that are crucial for the efficiency and effectiveness of work.

To characterize the motivational structure and dynamic of the achievement behavior, Locke and Latham have conceptualized a high performance cycle in the introductory chapter. They have outlined a theoretical framework in which the central variables of successful performance in organizations can be placed. Goal setting, feedback, mechanisms, and moderators of the transformation of goals into action constitute the focus of the discussion. The chapter by Kleinbeck and Schmidt demonstrates how one can get to empirical findings in the context of this theory. To analyze the differential effects of goals in information processing, determining performances, the technique of multiple goals in dual-task conditions was used. The authors have described a way to look at motivational and cognitive processes and the interaction between both.

On the background of a field study Antoni and Beckmann have looked at the effects of goal setting and feedback from the perspective of European action theory in the sense of W. Hacker and J. Kuhl. The authors stimulate further thoughts on modifying, adding, or refining concepts within the high performance cycle. Erez has addressed a classical theme of performance theory that traditionally was a topic of cognitive psychology: the relationship and exchange between quantity and quality. On the basis of a motivation approach to the problem she can show that the quantity-quality relationship and exchange can be explained in terms of motivation variables. At the end of the first part, Thierry has summarized the discussion on extrinsic and intrinsic motivation with respect to the behavior in organizations. His analysis of the contrary views led him to conclude that the distinction between extrinsic and intrinsic motivation can no longer be made.

1
Work Motivation: The High Performance Cycle

Edwin A. Locke
University of Maryland

Gary P. Latham
University of Washington

Industrial-organizational psychologists have been studying motivation and satisfaction in the workplace for some five decades. For at least three reasons, however, progress in understanding these phenomena has been slow. First, it turned out that the motivation to work (exert effort) and satisfaction are relatively independent outcomes; thus somewhat different theories are required to understand them (Locke, 1970). Connecting the two types of theories has proven to be especially difficult (Henne & Locke, 1985). Theories that have tried to explain both phenomena with the same set of concepts generally have been unsuccessful. Second, theories within each domain, especially motivation–performance theories, have focused only on a limited aspect of the domain such as needs (Maslow, 1970), perceived fairness (Adams, 1965), or managerial motives (Miner, 1973). Third, the phenomena themselves are highly complex; thus extensive research has been required to understand them irrespective of any attempts to connect them.

It is now possible, however, to piece several of these theories together into a coherent whole. This integrated model cannot only explain, in terms of broad fundamentals, both the motivation to work and job satisfaction; it can specify key interrelationships between them. For purposes of simplicity we describe this model in terms of a single, interrelated sequence of events. We call this sequence the high performance cycle. It is outlined in Fig. 1.1. This model is restricted primarily to the individual level of analysis, though there is evidence that the same principles apply to groups and organizations (Latham & Lee, 1986; Locke & Latham, 1984; Smith, Locke, & Barry, in press). For purposes of simplicity, the model omits other possible causal paths as well as possible bidirectional causal relationships.

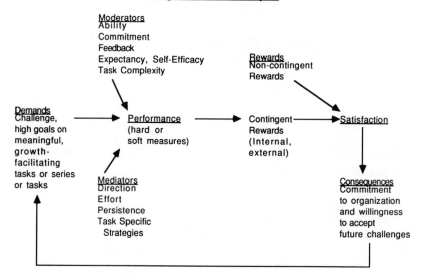

FIG. 1.1   The High Performance Cycle.

DEMANDS (CHALLENGE)

The model starts with demands being made of or challenges provided for the individual employee or manager. The theoretical base for this part of the model is goal-setting theory (Locke, 1968, 1978; Locke & Latham, 1984; Locke, Shaw, Saari, & Latham, 1981). This theory (based on earlier work by Ryan, 1970 and others) asserts that performance goals or intentions are immediate regulators or causes of task or work performance. Goal-setting research has shown repeatedly that people who try to attain specific and challenging (difficult) goals perform better on tasks than people who try for specific but moderate or easy goals, vague goals such as "do your best," or no goals at all. This finding, replicated in close to 400 studies (Locke & Latham, 1990), has been verified by both narrative or enumerative reviews (Locke et al., 1981) and meta-analyses (Mento, Steel, & Karren, 1987; Tubbs, 1986). These findings have shown external validity across a wide variety of tasks from simple reaction time to scientific and engineering work, as well as across laboratory and field settings, hard and soft performance criteria, quantity and quality measures, and individual and group situations (Latham & Lee, 1986). The findings also generalize outside North America (Erez, 1986; Punnet, 1986; Schmidt, Kleinbeck, & Brockmann, 1984).

The finding of goal-setting theory, that performance is a positive function of goal difficulty (assuming adequate ability), is at odds with achievement motivation theory. Achievement motivation theory (Atkinson, 1958) asserts that maximum motivation will occur at moderate levels of difficulty where the product of probability of success (PS) and the incentive value of success (assumed to be 1–PS) is highest (assuming the motivation to succeed is stronger than the motivation to avoid failure). However, the curvilinear, inverse-U function originally obtained by Atkinson (1958) has proven quite difficult to replicate (Arvey, 1972; Locke & Shaw, 1984; McClelland, 1961; Mento, Cartledge, & Locke, 1980). Two problems with that model are the failure to include an explicit goal-setting stage and/or the failure to measure commitment to succeeding. These factors are crucial to predicting the individual's response to subjective probability estimates (Locke & Shaw, 1984).

Goal-setting theory is also seemingly at odds with expectancy theory, which was first introduced into industrial-organizational psychology by Vroom, (1964). This theory asserts that, other things being equal, expectancy of success (which is inversely related to goal difficulty) is positively related to performance. However, as shown later, goal-setting theory and expectancy theory can be fully reconciled.

Challenging goals are usually implemented in terms of specific levels of performance to be attained (e.g., 50 assemblies completed in 8 hours; 10% improvement in sales in 6 months). There are, however, alternative forms in which to present a challenge, e.g., a specific amount of work to be completed (White & Locke, 1981); the frequency with which specific job behaviors are to be engaged in (Latham, Mitchell, & Dossett, 1978); a deadline to be met (Bryan & Locke, 1967); a high degree of responsibility (Bray, Campbell, & Grant, 1974); or a budget to be attained (Stedry, 1960).

There are several different sources of job demands or challenges. They may come from authority figures such as supervisors, managers, or the CEO (Bray et al., 1974). They may come through a joint decision on the part of the boss and a subordinate (participation). Demands may also come from peers either as direct pressure to perform at a certain level or in the form of role models (Earley & Kanfer, 1985; Rakestraw & Weiss, 1981). Direct peer pressure to restrict output has been observed frequently, including in the famous Hawthorne studies (Roethlisberger & Dickson, 1939). However, there can also be peer pressure to not produce below a certain minimum or to produce at a high level (Seashore, 1954). Goals, deadlines, and high workloads can also be chosen by the individual employee in the form of self-set goals. Research on "level of aspiration" in the 1930s and 1940s found that self-set goals were affected by past successes and failures and by personality factors (Lewin, 1958). More recently it has been argued that Type A personalities, specifically those high in job involvement, are especially likely to put high demand on themselves (Kirmeyer, 1987; Taylor, Locke, Lee, & Gist, 1984). Finally, demands can stem from forces external or partly external to the organizations such as unions, bankers, stockholders, competitors, or customers.

Goal-setting theory approaches the explanation of performance quite differently from that of motive or need theories such as those of McClelland and

Maslow. Whereas needs and (subconscious) motives are crucial to a full understanding of human action, they are several steps removed from action itself (Locke & Henne, 1986). Goal-setting theory was developed by starting with the situationally specific, conscious motivational factors closest to action: goals and intentions. It then worked backwards from there to determine what causes goals and what makes them effective. In contrast, need and motive theories started with more remote and general (often subconscious) regulators and tried to work forward to action, usually ignoring situationally specific and conscious factors. Generally the specific, close-to-action approaches (including goal-setting theory; social-cognitive theory, Bandura, 1986; turnover intentions theory, Mobley, 1982) have been far more successful in explaining action than the general, far-from-action approaches that stress general, subconscious needs, motives, and values (Locke & Henne, 1986; Miner, 1980; Pinder, 1984).[1] The interrelationship between the two types of theories and sets of concepts is highly complex and not yet fully understood. For example, need for achievement (measured as a subconscious motive using the TAT) has been found to be unrelated to goal choice (Roberson-Bennett, 1983). But the value for achievement, a conscious motive that is not correlated with n ach, has been found to be significantly related to goal choice (Matsui, Okada, & Kakuyama, 1982; Steers, 1975).

We could hypothesize that one way that general needs, motives, and subconscious values could influence behavior is through their effects on situationally specific, conscious goals and intentions in conjunction with perceived situational demands.

In summary, the precursor of a high level of work motivation will be present when the individual is confronted by a high degree of challenge in the form of a specific, difficult goal or its equivalent. We say precursor because being confronted by a challenge does not guarantee high performance. There are at least five known factors or moderators that affect the strength of the relationship between goals and action.

MODERATORS

Ability

It is obvious that ability limits the individual's capacity to respond to a challenge. Goal-setting research has found that the relation of goal difficulty to performance is curvilinear after the limit of ability has been reached (Locke, 1982; Locke, Frederick, Buckner, & Bobko, 1984a). Fur-

---

[1]It is worth noting that attitude theory has recently gone through the same metamorphosis as work motivation theory in that theories that predict behavior from generalized attitudes have been supplanted by far more successful theories that focus on situationally specific attitudes and intentions to act (e.g., see Fishbein & Ajzen, 1975).

ther, there is some evidence that goal setting has stronger effects among high- than among low-ability individuals, and that ability has stronger effects among high-goal than among low-goal individuals (Locke, 1965a, 1982). One reason for the latter finding is that, when goals are low and people are committed to them, output is limited to levels below the individual's capacity.

Commitment

Challenging goals will lead to high performance only if the individual is committed to them. The effect of variation in goal commitment on performance is shown in phase II of Erez and Zidon's experiment (1984); it was found that, as commitment declined in response to increasing goal difficulty, performance declined rather than increased.

At least four classes of factors affect goal commitment (Locke, Latham, & Erez, 1988). The most powerful of these appears to be what French and Raven (1959) termed legitimate power or authority. Authority in the form of the experimenter in the laboratory or the manager at the workplace has been sufficient to guarantee high goal commitment in the overwhelming majority of goal-setting studies. The "demand" aspect of the experimental setting has been documented by Orne (1962). Goals that are assigned by authority figures typically become the individual's personal goal. Instructions to try for a certain goal even carry over to later trials in which the individual is free to choose his or her own goal (Locke, et al., 1984a, 1984b). The power of authority to produce commitment has surprised many people, but it should not shock those familiar with the potent demand effects obtained in the controversial Milgram experiments (Milgram, 1974). In those studies, experimenter-authority figures were able to convince some people to take actions that were far more extreme than simply trying for a goal. Field studies have shown that direct pressure for performance is effective in raising performance as long as it is not viewed as excessive (Andrews & Farris, 1972; Hall & Lawler, 1971).

Related to the preceding is the finding that setting goals participatively does not lead to greater goal commitment or productivity than having the authority figure simply assign the goals (Latham & Lee, 1986; Schweiger & Leana, 1986; Tubbs, 1986; Wagner & Gooding, 1987).

An apparent exception to these conclusions are several recent experiments by Erez and her colleagues (Erez, 1986; Erez & Arad, 1986; Erez, Earley, & Hulin, 1985), which found that participative goal setting led to higher commitment and performance than assigned goals. Latham, Erez, and Locke (1988) conducted four jointly designed experiments to resolve this apparent contradiction. There were a member of methodological differences that accounted for the different results. But the main difference was that Erez and her colleagues used very brief, curt, "tell" instructions in the assigned goal-setting conditions, whereas Latham and his colleagues, who had obtained null results, used somewhat more lengthy "tell and sell" instructions. In the jointly conducted experiments, no difference was found between the tell and sell and participative styles, but both were more effective than the tell style. Thus assigned goal setting is as effective as participative goal setting, providing the goals are accompanied by a reasonable explanation and the experimenter or manager is supportive.[2]

A second factor affecting goal commitment is peer influence, specifically peer pressure and modeling. As noted earlier, peer pressure has long been known to induce commitment to low goals in the form of restriction of output (Mathewson, 1931; Roethlisberger & Dickson, 1939; Taylor, 1967). Strong group norms also may produce commitment in the form of low variance in production among group members (Seashore 1954). Commitment to high goals will occur when the group norms are high (Seashore, 1954) and when there are peer models performing at a high level (Bandura, 1986; Earley & Kanfer, 1985). Assigning both individual and group goals for a group task produces higher commitment to the individual goals than assigning individual goals alone (Matsui, Kakuyama, & Onglatco, 1987). Another peer factor is the degree to which the commitment was made publically (Hollenbeck, Williams, & Klein, 1989).

A third factor affecting commitment is the individual's expectancy of being able to reach the goal or perform at a high level. Expectancy theory, a subjective-expected-utility model (e.g., see Porter & Lawler, 1968; Vroom, 1964), states that the force exerted towards a given act will be a product of the individual's belief that he or she can perform at a certain level, the instrumentality of that level for attaining various outcomes, and the (value) valence of those outcomes. In general, goals that are and/or are perceived as difficult are less likely to be accepted than goals that are moderate or easy, although in a laboratory setting a high degree of commitment can be obtained for a short time to goals that are impossible to reach (Locke, 1982). Individuals usually *prefer* goals in the moderate range of difficulty, but their choices can be influenced by previously as well as currently assigned goals (Locke et al., 1984a, 1984b).

Related to, but broader than, the concept of expectancy is the concept of self-efficacy, a key concept in Bandura's social-cognitive theory (Bandura, 1986). Bandura (1982) defines it as one's judgment of "how well one can execute courses of action required to deal with prospective situations" (p. 122). Like expectancy, self-efficacy is related to goal commitment and to choice of goal difficulty level (Locke et al., 1984b).

A fourth factor known to affect commitment is the use of rewards or in-

---

[2]There may be important cognitive benefits of participation in terms of getting better ideas of how to perform a task by asking for subordinate input (Campbell & Gingrich, 1986), but this issue is not directly pertinent to the motivational (commitment) effect of participation.

centives. Numerous work motivation theories predict this either directly or by implication including: expectancy theory (rewards promote high valences), behavior modification (rewards act as reinforcers), and social-cognitive theory (rewards as information cues). Goal commitment is high when working to attain the goals is perceived as instrumental in gaining other valued outcomes (Mento et al., 1980; Yukl & Latham, 1978). Specific outcomes that have been studied include winning in a competitive situation (Locke & Shaw, 1984) and money (Oldham, 1975). In another study verbal self-congratulations were especially powerful in motivating children working towards goals (Masters, Furman, & Barden, 1977). The commitment concept may also explain why incentives sometimes fail to work. For example, Mowen, Middlemist, and Luther (1981) found that offering a bonus only for reaching a very difficult to impossible goal led to lower performance than assigning the same goal but paying people for performance (on a piece-rate basis) rather than for goal success as such. Although commitment was not actually measured in this study, it was presumably higher when a reward was offered for partial success (difficult goals with piece rate) than when only full success was rewarded (difficult goals with bonus); the instrumentality of effort was presumably higher in the former case.

Feedback

Both laboratory and field research have shown that knowledge of one's overall score on a task (knowledge of results or KR) does not lead to improved performance when differential goal setting by KR and NoKR groups is controlled (Locke, Cartledge, & Koeppel, 1968). Thus KR by itself is not a sufficient condition for improved performance (Latham et al., 1978)[3]. Frequent positive findings reported for the effects of KR (Ammons, 1956; Annett, 1969; Kopelman, 1986) probably stem from the deliberate or inadvertent confounding or combining of KR with other factors such as goal setting, information regarding better task strategies, recognition, and reward (e.g., Locke, 1980).

Other research, however, has shown that goal setting in the absence of feedback is also ineffective (Erez, 1977; Locke et al., 1981). Goals and feedback together lead to higher performance than either one alone (Reber & Wallin, 1984). The joint benefit of goals and feedback may be due to their fulfilling different but crucial functions: Goals direct and energize action whereas KR allows the tracking of progress in relation to the goal.

Matsui, Okada, and Inoshita (1983) found that, when individuals working toward a goal were told that they were behind the pace required to at-

---

[3]Knowledge of performance can affect subsequent performance if it promotes learning (e.g., of better techniques). This discussion is confined to the motivational effects of feedback.

tain their goal, they subsequently improved their performance, whereas those told that they were "on target" did not. Bandura and Cervone (1983, 1986) found that self-efficacy moderates the individual's response to feedback indicative or below target performance. Maximum improvement following negative feedback occurs when there is high self-efficacy (Bandura, 1988).

Expectancy and Self-Efficacy

Expectancy and self-efficacy play a ubiquitous role in the high performance cycle. As previously noted, high expectancy and self-efficacy lead to high levels of goal commitment. They also lead to high goal levels when goals are self-chosen (Locke et al., 1984b). Further, they affect the individual's response to feedback concerning progress in relation to goals and may even affect the efficiency of their task strategies (Bandura, 1988). Finally, they have a direct effect on performance independently of goals.

The apparent contradiction between expectancy theory and goal-setting theory has been resolved in two different ways by Locke, Motowidlo, and Bobko (1986), based on the ideas of Garland (1984) and Bandura (1982). Garland (1984) found that *within* any given goal group, where the expectancy measure has the same referent for all subjects, there was positive association between expectancy and performance (see Locke et al., 1984b); only *between* groups did high goals with low mean expectancies lead to higher performance than low goals with high mean expectancies—the opposite of the within-group pattern. The between-group finding was an artifact of the different reference points for measuring expectancy of success.

Another resolution by Locke et al. (1986) is based on Bandura's self-efficacy concept. Self-efficacy is measured by having individuals rate their confidence in attaining each of a number of different performance levels; it is not measured in relation to goal levels. Thus the measures are directly comparable between as well as within groups. Locke et al. (1984b) found that self-efficacy is related positively to performance both within and between groups; subjects with higher goals have higher self-efficacy on the average than those with lower goals. The higher the efficacy, the higher the performance.

Task Complexity

Wood (1986) defined task complexity in terms of three dimensions: component complexity (number of elements in task), coordinative complexity (the number and nature of the relationships between the elements), and dynamic complexity (the number and types of elements and the relationships between them over time). Wood, Mento, and Locke (1987) rated the tasks used in 125 goal-setting studies on the basis of these dimensions and related these complexity ratings to the size of the goals-setting effect obtained. The meta-analysis results confirmed a significant moderating role for task complexity. The average effect size was significantly larger on the simpler than on the more complex tasks, although the effects were significant on both types.

An explanation for this finding is that on simple tasks the effort induced by the goals leads relatively directly to task performance. In more complex tasks, however, effort does not necessarily pay off so directly. One must decide where and how to allocate effort. For example, setting a goal for high grades may not actually lead to higher grades unless the student uses proper study habits and an appropriate course strategy based on knowledge of what the professor is looking for. Thus in more complex tasks, the plans, tactics, and strategies used by the individual play a larger role in task performance than they do in simpler tasks where the number of different strategies is more limited and is generally known to all performers.

There is some evidence that on complex, heuristic tasks where the individual has no previous experience with the task and is pressured to perform well immediately, specific, hard goals may not lead to better performance than "do best" goals and may even lead to poorer performance (Earley, Connolly, & Ekegren, 1989; Huber, 1985). Under these conditions hard goal subjects seem to choose less than optimal strategies. We will say more about task strategies in a later section.

In summary, a specific challenging goal has maximum effect when the individual has high ability, there is commitment to the goal, there is feedback showing progress in relation to the goal, the individual has high self-efficacy or expectancy of performing well, and the task is simple. Now let us consider the mechanisms by which goals affect performance.

MEDIATING MECHANISMS

Given that the individual has a challenging goal and the moderating variables facilitate goal attainment, what are the mediators or mechanisms by which goals actually affect performance? There are three relatively direct mechanisms that Wood and Locke (1986) have called *Universal Task Strategies* (UTS's). These are direction of attention, effort, and persistence. They correspond to the three attributes of motivated action: direction (choice), intensity, and duration. We call them UTSs because virtually every individual learns at an early age that you perform better on a task if you pay attention to it, exert effort on it, and persist at it over time than if you do not do so.

When acted on, goals direct attention to the activity specified by the goal and simultaneously away from goal-irrelevant activities. Locke and Bryan (1969), for example, gave individuals six types of feedback on car-driving performance but goals for only one of them. Performance improved only on the performance dimensions for which a goal was set. Similarly, if an individual reads a prose passage and is told to look for information about man-eating sharks in an article about sea creatures, he or she will (given goal commitment) focus on content relevant to sharks and pay less attention to information not related to sharks (e.g., see Rothkopf & Kaplan, 1972). Goals will direct attention most effectively when they are specific (e.g., look for three facts about sharks) rather than vague or general (e.g., look for information about sea creatures). More specific goals regulate action more closely than more general goals (Locke, Chah, Harrison, & Lustgarten, 1989).

The effort aroused and expended in response to a goal depends on the perceived difficulty of the goal (Locke, 1968); the greater the demands, the greater the expended effort (Locke, 1967), assuming the goal is accepted. For example, the individual who tries to do 40 push-ups will expend more energy than the one who tries to do only 4, other things (e.g., ability) being equal.

Finally, goals affect task persistence in that, given goal commitment, people will continue working at the task until the goal is reached. Persistence is really directed effort extended over time. Thus, if there are no time limits, people will work longer for a harder goal than for an easier goal. They also will spend more time preparing to perform if a high-performance standard is involved than if there is a low standard involved (LaPorte & Nath, 1976). There can be a tradeoff between speed and time so that people with low demands and a long time limit, or no time limit, may work more slowly than those with high demands in order to fill the time available (Bryan & Locke, 1967; Latham & Locke, 1975). The excess time in such a case, however, is the result of a slower pace rather than of greater persistence.

Goals can also affect performance indirectly by motivating the individual to develop task-specific strategies or plans. Wood and Locke (1986) have suggested that there are, broadly speaking, two types of task-specific strategies: Stored Task Specific Strategies (STSS's) and New Task Specific Strategies (NTSS's). Stored strategies are learned through practice and instruction on the task (e.g., how to hit the basic strokes in tennis) and may become automatized in the form of skills. Such strategies will be brought into play automatically when the individual works on the relevant task. If STSS's fail to work either because the task is actually new or because certain aspects of the task situation are different (e.g., a businessman faced with changing market or new competitors), the individual may develop NTSS's to cope with the new circumstances. Creative thinking and problem solving will come into play. There is no guarantee that the individual will always discover or choose appropriate task-specific strategies when confronted with a goal on a task, but goals may promote the search for and adoption of strategies (e.g., Latham & Baldes, 1975; Shaw, 1984; Terborg, 1976). Challenging goals also motivate people to *use* task strategies provided to them through training (Earley, Connolly, & Lee, 1988).

PERFORMANCE

To the degree that the demands are challenging, the facilitating moderators are present, and the mediators are operative, task performance will be high on whatever dimensions the goal specifies as important (quantity, quality, etc.). In work settings there are three basic types of "hard" or objective outcome measures that can be used to index performance (Locke & Latham, 1984): units of production or quality (amount produced, number of errors); dollars (profits, income, sales); and time (job attendance, lateness in meeting deadlines).

When objective outcome measures are not available or not appropriate, various behavioral measures are recommended (Latham, 1986). An example would be the frequency with which various suitable or critical behaviors are performed by employees or supervisors. For example, does the supervisor explain to his or her subordinates the reasons for a pending organizational change? Does the sales clerk smile when approaching a customer? The frequency of such behaviors can be measured by an observer, thus making it a more objective measure, or they may be estimated by supervisors, subordinates, customers, or others, thus making it a more subjective measure. If critical behaviors, derived from a job analysis, are demonstrated frequently, they will lead to or help lead to desirable outcome measures such as productivity, sales, and profits (Latham & Wexley, 1981).

REWARDS

Rewards are placed toward the end rather than at the beginning of our model in contrast to behaviorist theory that would put them, at least in terms of causal importance, at the beginning—in the form of past reinforcements. The instrumental response in behaviorist theory is assumed to be emitted at the initial stages more or less randomly; when the response is regularly reinforced, the reinforcement schedule becomes controlling.

Bandura (1986) has identified many flaws in this theory. For example, responses are made not just on the basis of past outcomes but also on the basis of anticipated future outcomes, observations of models, internal standards, and self-efficacy. Past rewards can be an incentive to act under certain conditions but they are not controlling. Furthermore, rewards will not necessarily encourage high performance in the future unless such performance is first emitted—which may never happen in the absence of high demands.

Once high performance has been demonstrated, rewards can become important as inducements to continue, but not all rewards are external. Internal, self-administered rewards that can occur following high performance include a sense of achievement based on attaining a certain level of excellence, pride in accomplishment, and feelings of success and efficacy. The experience of success will depend on reaching one's goal or level of aspiration (Lewin, 1958) or making progress toward the goal. Satisfaction will also depend on the perceived instrumentality of performance in attaining longer term goals (Locke, Cartledge, & Knerr, 1970). The self rather than others is typically given credit for successful actions (Locke, 1976). Higher satisfaction is experienced if the success is attributed to the self rather than to external factors such as luck (Weiner, 1986).

High goals may lead to less experienced satisfaction than low goals because they are attained, by definition, less frequently. Satisfaction with performance is positively associated with the number of successes experienced (Locke, 1965b). Thus some compromise on goal difficulty may be necessary to maximize both satisfaction and performance. However, there are sources of satisfaction associated with simply trying for hard goals, such as the satisfaction of complying with a respected authority figure, the satisfaction of responding to a challenge, the satisfaction of making some progress toward the goals, and the belief that future benefits may accrue in terms of skill development (Matsui, Okada, & Mizuguchi, 1981). Of course, it is possible to reward partial success. Furthermore, goal difficulty can be increased incrementally thus allowing temporary success before the goal is raised.

Success and failure (depending on how they are appraised) can affect subsequent self-efficacy. Bandura (1988) has noted that high self-efficacy itself can have positive consequences for affect just as low self-efficacy can lead to negative affect, including anxiety and depression.

Another issue to consider with respect to the effects of goal attainment is the nature of the task. Hackman and Oldham's (1980) job characteristics theory states that the degree to which the work is seen as rewarding is dependent on the degree to which the task possesses four core attributes: (personal) significance; feedback; responsibility/autonomy; and identity (as a whole piece of work). In general, empirical studies support this theory with regard to work satisfaction (Locke & Henne, 1986). These core attributes are growth producing, and they may fulfill important needs. An extensive review of the literature on the relation of job scope to satisfaction also supports the Hackman–Oldham theory (Stone, 1986).

The external rewards that are most likely to be tied to performance are pay, promotion, and recognition. Expectancy theory (Dachler & Mobley, 1973; Vroom, 1964) states that the motivational power of pay in producing high performance will be a function of the belief that high performance can be attained, the belief that high performance will lead to outcomes, and the degree to which those outcomes are valued.

Equity theory (Adams, 1965) asserts that pay will bring satisfaction to the degree that it is seen as fair or equitable. Equity judgments will be based on the judged ratio of the individual's outputs and inputs in comparison to the output/input ratio of people to whom the individual compares himself or herself. If pay is seen as inequitable, thus producing dissatisfaction, people will take steps to restore equity by, for example, modifying the quantity or quality of their output (Locke & Henne, 1986).

Perceptions of equity will depend on who the comparison person is. Consider, for example, Park Jin Kean (Halberstam, 1986), who works 12 hours a day, 6 days a week as a foreman in an auto factory and makes $9,600 a year. Park is very proud of his job and his salary. Park is from Korea, where the average wage is $2,000; furthermore, he grew up on a farm where he worked even harder for less return. Clearly Park's adaptation level (Helson, 1964) is radically different from that of most Americans and even of most Japanese workers.

An important reward for most employees is that of recognition (Herzberg, Mausner, & Snyderman, 1959; Locke, 1976). A recent survey of public-sector employees who performed staff work for a state legislature (Locke, 1987) found that the most important forms of recognition were: personal thanks and credit from the recipients of the work; being given responsibility for a new project; being sent to a professional meeting as an expert representative on a topic; and seeing one's work have an impact (in this case an impact on actual legislation).

Peters and Waterman (1982) have noted that the most effective American organizations make heavy use of recognition not only in the forms previously mentioned but also in the form of badges, pins, plaques, buttons, notices on the bulletin board, and membership in high performance "clubs."

In addition to contingent rewards, virtually all employees receive various noncontingent rewards based simply on the fact that they hold the job. These may include, for example, fringe benefits, base pay, seniority awards, job security, flexible hours, good equipment, considerate supervision, congenial co-workers, and association with a prestigious or reputable organization. Although such rewards may not serve directly to motivate high performance, they do encourage the employee to remain with the organization rather than leave.

SATISFACTION

If internal and external rewards provide the individual with what he or she wants or values or considers appropriate or beneficial, the individual experiences satisfaction with the job (Locke, 1976). Job satisfaction can be viewed as the result of a positive appraisal of the job against one's value standards (Locke, 1984). This appraisal model is also congruent with Lazarus and Folkman's (1984) appraisal approach to stress. Job satisfaction is not a result of the person alone nor of the job alone but of the person in relation to the job—that is, the job as appraised by the person. Thus, if the job is appraised as a fulfilling or facilitating the attainment of one's values, satisfaction is experienced; if the job is appraised as blocking or negating one's values, dissatisfaction is experienced.

More important values have a greater impact on affective reactions than less important values (Locke, 1976; Locke, Fitzpatrick, & White, 1983; Mobley & Locke, 1970). The work itself is usually a more important aspect of the job for professional and skilled people than for others. Thus as a category, the work itself is usually the job aspect most strongly related to overall job satisfaction for people at the higher job levels (Locke et al., 1983). As noted earlier, having challenging and meaningful work leads to high work satisfaction and, if rewarded by the organization, to high satisfaction with rewards as well. For more extensive discussions of job satisfaction see Gruneberg (1979) and Locke (1976).

CONSEQUENCES OF SATISFACTION AND DISSATISFACTION

The most difficult problem for industrial-organizational psychology researchers has been to determine what happens after the individual employee becomes satisfied or dissatisfied. It was originally assumed that high satisfaction would lead to high productivity out of gratitude to the employer (Locke, 1986), but this association has failed consistently to be supported in the literature (Iaffaldano & Muchinsky, 1985; Podsakoff & Williams, 1986). At best, when the reward system is clearly tied to performance, satisfaction results from productivity (Henne & Locke, 1985; Podsakoff & Williams, 1986)—the opposite of the original assumption. However, even this relationship does not hold if the tie between rewards and performance is loose. Nor does the reverse model specify what satisfaction *does* lead to.

Recent theoretical and empirical work has suggested two important modifications of the simplistic assumption that satisfaction causes performance model. First, it has been recognized that satisfaction and dissatisfaction can have many different consequences (Fisher, 1980), depending on subsequent choices that the individual makes. Second, it has been found that a number of processes intervene between the experience of satisfaction and the taking of action.

Henne (1986, based on Henne & Locke, 1985) found through asking people to list their responses to dissatisfaction that there were at least six possible categories of responses: (1) avoidance (come late, be absent, quit job); (2) complaint (complain to boss, company); (3) formal protest (grievance, lawsuit); (4) illegal acts (steal from company, sabotage); (5) passive-aggressive response (lower output or quality, withhold information); (6) substance abuse (alcohol, drugs). The category most frequently related to dissatisfaction was the first, avoidance, especially quitting the job.

Mobley (1982) developed a turnover model that starts with dissatisfaction but posits a number of intervening steps before the individual actually quits, such as thinking of quitting, considering alternative jobs, and job search. The key step before actually leaving, however, is the formation of the intention to quit. The latter is the best predictor of actual turnover. It intervenes between the experience of dissatisfaction and quitting (Mobley, 1982).

The other side of the coin of the intent to leave is organizational commitment. Williams and Hazer (1986), in a reanalysis of data collected by others, found that job satisfaction affected organizational commitment that in turn affected the intent to stay. Lee and Mowday (1987) obtained similar findings. O'Reilly and Chatman (1986) found significant correlations between commitment and the intent to stay. Curry, Wakefield, Price, and Mueller (1986) found strong associations between satisfaction and commitment but claimed these were due to both variables being associated with exogenous variables such as the nature of the work.

Mowday, Porter, and Steers (1982) reported consistent evidence for an association between commitment and turnover across a number of studies. Further, they found that work experiences of the type that would lead to satisfaction (job scope or challenge, considerate supervision, compatible work groups) were associated with commitment.

Mowday et al. (1982) actually *defined* commitment as entailing three aspects: (1) the acceptance of the goals and values of the organization; (2) willingness to exert effort on behalf of the organization; and (3) a desire to stay with the organization.

If we assume, in line with at least some research evidence, that positive job experiences conducive to satisfaction are a crucial factor in bringing commitment about, and that commitment is a key factor in getting people to stay with the organization and cooperate with its members, then presumably committed employees will be prone to accept organizational demands. In sum, individuals who are both satisfied with and thus committed to the organization should be more likely to stay with the organization and to accept the challenges that it presents to them. This link brings us back full circle to the beginning of our model (see Fig. 1.1).

We have not attempted to specify the time span of the high performance cycle. Substantial aspects of it are repeated daily: The individual goes to work, is confronted by the day's challenges, takes action in response to them, experiences certain consequences as a result of that action, and increases, maintains, or decreases the degree of satisfaction and commitment experienced. The decision to quit when the individual becomes dissatisfied is not typically a decision that is made quickly but rather one that evolves gradually, incrementally, out of day-to-day experiences. Mowday et al. (1982) found that lowered commitment may precede actual quitting by several months. The final decision may be the sum total of accumulated experiences considered in conjunction with an estimate of the outlook for the future.

Discussion

The high performance model has important implications for the management of organizations. Effective organizations must expect a lot from their employees and must try to insure that they gain a sense of satisfaction in return for their efforts. Employee satisfaction will derive, in part, from giving employees personally meaningful work that they are capable of handling and, in part, from taking pains to reward good performance. Peters and Waterman (1982) have argued, consistent with this model, that the best American organizations in the private sector have organizational philosophies that place a high premium on excellence in performance and on respect for employees.

It is important to note that our model posits no *direct* connection between satisfaction and subsequent productivity. The lack of such a connection has long puzzled researchers. Our model shows two ways in which these processes are connected. First, consistent with the evidence (Henne & Locke, 1985), high satisfaction is shown to be the *result*, not the cause, of high performance when rewards are commensurate with performance. Second, the model shows that satisfaction relates to subsequent performance *indirectly* by keeping the individual committed to the organization and by making him or her willing to cooperate. By implication this means that the employee is willing to become committed, in some form, to its goals. If the goals of the organization are low, however, high satisfaction will be followed by low rather than high satisfaction. Thus it is not satisfaction alone that is the key to high performance, but *satisfaction in conjunction with other factors* (White & Locke, 1981). To repeat, the effect of satisfaction on performance is indirect, not direct.

The model specifies the moderator variables that managers should take into account to ensure both high performance and satisfaction among the people they manage. Managers must ensure that their people are thoroughly trained before a high performance cycle can impact performance and satisfaction positively. Training is especially important for goal commitment. If the person does not believe that goal attainment is possible, goal commitment will be low if not zero. Goal commitment will be high to the extent that the manager models the high performance cycle by making subordinates' goals clear and giving support and recognition to them. Feedback to subordinates regarding their progress toward goal attainment is especially critical to the effectiveness of a high performance cycle. Without it, goals have little or no effect on subsequent performance (Locke et al., 1981). From a learning standpoint, feedback helps the employee to develop effective task strategies. From a motivational standpoint, feedback, if positive, builds self-efficacy and, if negative, pinpoints the need to improve by revealing a discrepancy between the goal and present performance.

The high performance cycle also has implications for self-management, a concept that has been studied for at least two decades in clinical settings (Kanfer, 1970) and only recently in organizations (Frayne & Latham, 1987, see also chapter 11 in this volume). Again, feedback plays a critical role. Goals are set in relation to feedback. A behavioral contract is written to oneself, specifying the strategies that one will take to attain the goal, and the rewards that one will self-administer for both goal approximation and attainment. Rewards self-administered for goal approximation facilitate perceived self-efficacy and ensure continuing goal commitment. In addition, they increase self-monitoring. The outcome is not only high performance but satisfaction derived from a sense of achievement. This has recently been demonstrated among union employees who increased their job attendance in a climate where peers encouraged absenteeism (Frayne & Latham, 1987).

Because task complexity influences the effects of goals on performance and hence satisfaction, managers need to work with their people to enrich their jobs and then formulate effective task strategies. To the extent that this is ongoing, people should remain committed to the organization in which they work because of the degree of satisfaction that they continually experience. A concomitant finding of self-management in industry is that peers seek one another's input for ways of accomplishing tasks and derive pleasure from helping one another do so (Mills, 1983).

The high performance model also might be extended beyond work organizations to the field of education. For example, American education has in recent years been compared unfavorably with the educational system of the Japanese. Much more seems to be demanded of Japanese students (in terms of amount of homework, number of courses, etc.) especially in mathematics, than of American students. The result is that the average Japanese worker is very competent in math, a factor that helps Japanese organizations to use sophisticated quality control techniques very successfully. This, in turn, makes their goods highly competitive in the international marketplace.

This is not to deny that many factors have contributed to the success of the Japanese, but there seems to be little doubt that the Japanese educational system is one factor responsible for the remarkable growth of their economy over the last 40 years. On the other side of the same coin, the American system with its lower demands may not bode well for our future.

Perhaps the high performance cycle should be made part of our schools as well as our work organizations.

ACKNOWLEDGMENTS

The authors would like to thank Tom Lee and Robert Wood for their helpful comments on this chapter.

REFERENCES

Adams, J. S. (1965). Inequity in social exchange. In L. Berkowitz (Ed.), *Advances in experimental social psychology* (Vol. 2, pp. 267-299). New York: Academic Press.

Ammons, R. B. (1956). Effects of knowledge of performance: A survey and tentative theoretical formulation. *Journal of General Psychology, 54,* 279-299.

Andrews, F. M., & Farris, G. F. (1972). Time pressure and performance of scientists and engineers: A five-year panel study. *Organizational Behavior and Human Performance, 8,* 185-200.

Annett, J. (1969). *Feedback and human behavior.* Penguin: Baltimore.

Arvey, R. D. (1972). Task performance as a function of perceived effort–performance and performance–reward contingencies. *Organizational Behavior and Human Performance, 8,* 423-433.

Atkinson, J. W. (1958). Towards experimental analysis of human motivation in terms of motives, expectancies, and incentives. In J. W. Atkinson (Ed.), *Motives in fantasy, action and society* (pp. 288-305). Princeton, NJ: Van Nostrand.

Bandura, A. (1982). Self-efficacy mechanism in human agency. *American Psychologist, 37,* 122-147.

Bandura, A. (1986). *Social foundations of thought and action: A social-cognitive view.* Englewood Cliffs, NJ: Prentice-Hall.

Bandura, A. (1988). Self-regulation of motivation and action through goal systems. In V. Hamilton, G. Bower, & N. Frijda (Eds.), *Cognitive perspectives on motivation, and emotion* (pp. 37-61). Dordrecht: Kluwer Academic Publishers.

Bandura, A., & Cervone, D. (1983). Self-evaluative and self-efficacy mechanisms governing the motivational effects of goal systems. *Journal of Personality and Social Psychology, 45,* 1017-1028.

Bandura, A., & Cervone, D. (1986). Differential engagement of self-reactive influences in cognitive motivation. *Organizational Behavior and Human Decision Processes, 38,* 92-113.

Bray, D. W., Campbell, R. J., & Grant, D. L. (1974). *Formative years in business.* New York: Wiley.

Bryan, J. F., & Locke, E. A. (1967). Parkinson's law as a goal-setting phenomenon. *Organizational Behavior and Human Performance, 2,* 258-275.

Campbell, D. J., & Gingrich, K. F. (1986). The interactive effects of task complexity and participation on task performance: A field experiment. *Organizational Behavior and Human Decision Processes, 38,* 162-180.

Curry, J. P., Wakefield, D. S., Price, J. L., & Mueller, C. W. (1986). On the causal ordering of job satisfaction and organizational commitment. *Academy of Management Journal, 29,* 847-858.

Dachler, H. P., & Mobley, W. H. (1973). Construct validation of an instrumentality-expectancy-task-goal model of work motivation: Some theoretical boundary conditions. *Journal of Applied Psychology* (Monograph), 58, 397-418.

Earley, P. C., Connolly, T., & Ekegren, G. (1989). Goals, strategy development, and task performance: Some limits on the efficacy of goal setting. *Journal of Applied Psychology, 74*, 24–33.

Earley, P. C., Connolly, T., & Lee, C. (1988). Task strategy interventions in goal setting: The importance of search and strategy development. Unpublished manuscript, Department of Management, University of Arizona.

Earley, P. C., & Kanfer, R. (1985). The influence of component participation and role models on goal acceptance, goal satisfaction and performance. *Organizational Behavior and Human Decision Processes, 36*, 378–390.

Erez, M. (1977). Feedback: A necessary condition for the goal-setting performance relationship. *Journal of Applied Psychology, 62*, 624–627.

Erez, M. (1986). The congruence of goal-setting strategies with sociocultural values and its effect on performance. *Journal of Management, 12*, 585–592.

Erez, M., & Arad, R. (1986). Participative goal-setting: Social, motivational and cognitive factors. *Journal of Applied Psychology, 71*, 591–597.

Erez, M., Earley, P. C., & Hulin, C. L. (1985). The impact of participation on goal acceptance and performance: A two-step model. *Academy of Management Journal, 28*, 50–66.

Erez, M., & Zidon, I. (1984). Effect of goal acceptance on the relationship of goal difficulty to performance. *Journal of Applied Psychology, 69*, 69–78.

Fishbein, M., & Ajzen, I. (1975). *Belief, attitude, intention and behavior: An introduction to theory and research*. Reading, MA: Addison-Wesley.

Fisher, C. D. (1980). On the dubious wisdom of expecting job satisfaction to correlate with performance. *Academy of Management Review, 5*, 605–612.

Frayne, C. A., & Latham, G. P. (1987). Application of social learning theory to employee self-management of attendance. *Journal of Applied Psychology, 72*, 387–392.

French, J., & Raven, B. H. (1959). The bases of social power. In D. Cartwright (Ed.), *Studies in social power* (pp. 150–167). Ann Arbor, MI: Institute for Social Research.

Garland, H. (1984). Relation of effort–performance expectancy to performance in goal-setting experiments. *Journal of Applied Psychology, 69*, 79–84.

Gruneberg, M. M. (1979). *Understanding job satisfaction*. New York: Wiley.

Hackman, J. R., & Oldham, G. R. (1980). *Work redesign*. Reading, MA: Addison-Wesley.

Halberstam, D. (1986). The Korean challenge. *Parade Magazine, Nov. 2*, 4–7.

Hall, D. T., & Lawler, E. E. (1971). Job pressures and research performance. *American Scientist, 59*, 64–73.

Helson, H. (1964). *Adaptation level theory*. New York: Harper.

Henne, D. (1986). *Thoughts and actions as consequences of job dissatisfaction*. Unpublished doctoral dissertation, College of Business and Management, University of Maryland.

Henne, D., & Locke, E. A. (1985). Job dissatisfaction: What are the consequences? *International Journal of Psychology, 20*, 221–240.

Herzberg, F., Mausner, B., & Snyderman, B. B. (1959). *The motivation to work*. New York: Wiley.

Hollenbeck, J. R., Williams, C. R., & Klein, H. J. (1989). An empirical examination of the antecedents of commitment to difficult goals. *Journal of Applied Psychology, 74*, 18–23.

Huber, V. L. (1985). Effects of task difficulty goal setting, and strategy on performance of a heuristic task. *Journal of Applied Psychology, 70*, 492–504.

Iaffaldano, M. T., & Muchinsky, P. M. (1985). Job satisfaction and job performance: A meta-analysis. *Psychological Bulletin, 97*, 251–273.

Kanfer, F. H. (1970). Self-regulation: Research issues and speculations. In C. Neuringer & J. L. Michael (Eds.), *Behavior modification in clinical psychology* (pp. 178–220). New York: Appleton-Century-Crofts.

Kirmeyer, S. L. (1987). *Job demands, productivity, and type A behavior: An observational analysis*. Paper presented at American Psychological Association meeting, New York.

Kopelman, R. E. (1986). Objective feedback, In E. A. Locke (Ed.), *Generalizing from laboratory to field settings* (pp. 119–145). Lexington, MA: Lexington.

LaPorte, R. E., & Nath, R. (1976). Role of performance goals in prose learning. *Journal of Educational Psychology, 68*, 260–264.

Latham, G. P. (1986). Job Performance and appraisal. In C. L. Cooper & I. T. Robertson (Eds.) *International review of industrial and organizational psychology* (pp. 117–155). Chichester, England: Wiley.

Latham, G. P., & Baldes, J. J. (1975). The "practical significance" of Locke's theory of goal setting. *Journal of Applied Psychology, 60*, 122–124.

Latham, G. P., Erez, M., & Locke, E. A. (1988). Resolving scientific disputes by the joint design of crucial experiments by the antagonists: Application to the Erez-Latham dispute regarding participation in goal setting. *Journal of Applied Psychology.* (Monograph) *73*, 753–772.

Latham, G. P., & Lee, T. W. (1986). Goal setting. In E. A. Locke (Ed.), *Generalizing from laboratory to field settings* (pp. 101–117). Lexington, MA: Lexington.

Latham, G. P., & Locke, E. A. (1975). Increasing productivity with decreasing time limits: A field replication of Parkinson's law. *Journal of Applied Psychology, 60*, 524–526.

Latham, G. P., Mitchell, T. R., & Dossett, D. L. (1978). Importance of participative goal setting and anticipated rewards on goal difficulty and job performance. *Journal of Applied Psychology, 63*, 163–171.

Latham, G. P., & Wexley, K. N. (1981). *Increasing productivity through performance appraisal.* Reading, MA: Addison-Wesley.

Lazarus, R. S., & Folkman, S. (1984). *Stress, appraisal, and coping.* New York: Springer.

Lee, T. W., & Mowday, R. T. (1987). Voluntarily leaving an organization: An empirical investigation of Steers and Mowday's model of turnover. *Academy of Management Journal, 30*, 721–743.

Lewin, K. (1958). Psychology of success and failure, In C. L. Stacey & M. F. DeMartino (Eds.), *Understanding human motivation* (pp. 223–228). Cleveland: Allen.

Locke, E. A. (1965a) Interaction of ability and motivation in performance. *Perceptual and Motor Skills, 21*, 719–725.

Locke, E. A. (1965b). The relationship of task success to task liking and satisfaction. *Journal of Applied Psychology, 49*, 379–385.

Locke, E. A. (1967). Relationship of goal level to performance level. *Psychological Reports, 20*, 1068.

Locke, E. A. (1968). Toward a theory of task motivation and incentives. *Organizational Behavior and Human Performance, 3*, 157–189.

Locke, E. A. (1970). Job satisfaction and job performance: A theoretical analysis. *Organizational Behavior and Human Performance, 5*, 484–500.

Locke, E. A. (1976). The nature and causes of job satisfaction. In M. D. Dumnette (Ed.), *Handbook of industrial and organizational psychology* (pp. 1297–1349). Chicago: Rand McNally.

Locke, E. A. (1978). The ubiquity of the technique of goal setting in theories of and approaches to employee motivation. *Academy of Management Review, 3*, 594–601.

Locke, E. A. (1980). Latham versus Komaki: A tale of two paradigms. *Journal of Applied Psychology, 65*, 16–23.

Locke, E. A. (1982). Relation of goal level to performance with a short work period and multiple goal levels. *Journal of Applied Psychology, 67*, 512–514.

Locke, E. A. (1984). Job satisfaction. In M. Gruneberg & T. Wall (Eds.), *Social psychology and organizational behavior* (pp. 93–117). Chichester, England: Wiley.

Locke, E. A. (1986). Job attitudes in historical perspective. In D. Wren (Ed.), *Papers dedicated to the development of modern management* (pp. 5–11). Chicago: Academy of Management.

Locke, E. A. (1987). How to motivate employees. *State Legislatures, 13* (1), 30–31.

Locke, E. A. & Bryan, J. F. (1969). The directing function of goals in task performance. *Organizational Behavior and Human Performance, 4*, 35–42.

Locke, E. A., Cartledge, N., & Knerr, C. S. (1970). Studies of the relationship between satisfaction, goal setting and performance. *Organizational Behavior and Human Performance, 5*, 135–158.

Locke, E. A., Cartledge, N., Koeppel, J. (1968). Motivational effects of knowledge of results: A goal setting phenomenon? *Psychological Bulletin, 70*, 474–485.

Locke, E. A., Chah, D., Harrison, S., & Lustgarten, N. (1989). Separating the effects of goal specificity from goal level. *Organizational Behavior and Human Decision Processes, 43*, 270–287.

Locke, E. A., Fitzpatrick, W., & White, F. M. (1983). Job satisfaction and role clarity among university and college faculty. *Review of Higher Education, 6*, 343–365.

Locke, E. A., Frederick, E., Buckner, E., & Bobko, P. (1984a). Effect of previously assigned goals on self-set goals and performance. *Journal of Applied Psychology, 69*, 694–699.

Locke, E. A., Frederick, E., Lee, C., & Bobko, P. (1984b). Effect of self-efficacy, goals, and task strategies on task performance. *Journal of Applied Psychology, 69*, 241–251.

Locke, E. A., & Henne, D. (1986). Work motivation theories. In C. Cooper & I. Robertson (Eds.), *International review of industrial and organizational psychology* (pp. 1–35). Chichester, England: Wiley.

Locke, E. A., & Latham, G. P. (1984). *Goal-setting: A motivational technique that works.* Englewood Cliffs, NJ: Prentice-Hall.

Locke, E. A., & Latham, G. P. (1990). *A theory of goal setting and task performance.* Englewood Cliffs, NJ: Prentice-Hall.

Locke, E. A., Latham, G. P., & Erez, M. (1988). The determinants of goal commitment. *Academy of Management Review, 13*, 23–39.

Locke, E. A., Motowidlo, S. J., & Bobko, P. (1986). Using self-efficacy theory to resolve the conflict between goal-setting theory and expectancy theory in organizational behavior and industrial/ organizational psychology. *Journal of Social and Clinical Psychology, 4*, 328–338.

Locke, E. A., & Shaw, K. N. (1984). Atkinson's inverse-U curve and the missing cognitive variables. *Psychological Reports, 55*, 403–412.

Locke, E. A., Shaw, K. N., Saari, L. M., & Latham, G. P. (1981). Goal setting and task performance: 1969–1980. *Psychological Bulletin, 90*, 125–152.

Maslow, A. H. (1970). *Motivation and personality.* New York: Harper & Row.

Masters, J. C., Furman, W., & Barden, R. C. (1977). Effects of achievement standards, tangible rewards, and self-dispensed achievement evaluations on children's task mastery. *Child Development, 48*, 217–224.

Mathewson, S. B. (1931). *Restriction of output among unorganized workers.* New York: Viking Press.

Matsui, T., Kakuyama, T., & Onglatco, M. L. (1987). Effects of goals and feedback on performance in groups. *Journal of Applied Psychology, 72*, 407–415.

Matsui, T., Okada, A., & Inoshita, O. (1983). Mechanism of feedback affecting task performance. *Organizational Behavior and Human Performance, 31*, 114–122.

Matsui, T., Okada, A., & Kakuyama, T. (1982). Influence of achievement need on goal setting, performance, and feedback effectiveness. *Journal of Applied Psychology, 67*, 645–648.

Matsui, T., Okada, A., & Mizuguchi, R. (1981). Expectancy theory prediction of the goal theory postulate, "the harder the goals, the higher the performance." *Journal of Applied Psychology, 66*, 54–58.

McClelland, D. C. (1961). *The achieving society.* Princeton, NJ: Van Nostrand.

Mento, A. J., Cartledge, N. D., & Locke, E. A. (1980). Maryland vs. Michigan vs. Minnesota: Another look at the relationship of expectancy and goal difficulty to task performance. *Organizational Behavior and Human Performance, 25*, 419–440.

24   LOCKE AND LATHAM

Mento, A. J., Steel, R. P.., & Karren, R. J. (1987). A meta-analytic study of the effects of goal setting on task performance: 1966-1984. *Organizational Behavior and Human Decision Processes, 39,* 52-83.

Milgram, S. (1974). *Obedience to authority.* New York. Harper & Row.

Mills, P. K. (1983). Self-management. *Academy of Management Review, 8,* 445-453.

Miner, J. B. (1973). The real crunch in managerial manpower. *Harvard Business Review, 51* (6), 146-158.

Miner, J. B. (1980). *Theories of organizational behavior.* Hinsdale, IL: Dryden.

Mobley, W. H. (1982). *Employee turnover: Causes, consequences and control.* Reading, MA: Addison-Wesley.

Mobley, W. H., & Locke, E. A. (1970). The relationship of value importance to satisfaction. *Organizational Behavior and Human Performance, 5,* 463-483.

Mowday, R. T., Porter, L. W., & Steers, R. M. (1982). *Employee-organization linkages.* New York: Academic Press.

Mowen, J. C., Middlemist, R. D., & Luther, D. (1981). Joint effects of assigned goal level and incentive structure on task performance: A laboratory study. *Journal of Applied Psychology, 66,* 598-603.

Oldham, G. R. (1975). The impact of supervisory characteristics on goal acceptance. *Academy of Management Journal, 18,* 461-475.

O'Reilly, C., & Chatman, J. (1986). Organizational commitment and psychological attachment: The effects of compliance, identification, and internalization on prosocial behavior. *Journal of Applied Psychology, 71,* 492-499.

Orne, M. T. (1962). On the social psychology of the psychological experiment with particular reference to demand characteristics. *American Psychologist, 17,* 776-783.

Peters, T. J., & Waterman, R. H. (1982). *In search of excellence.* New York: Harper & Row.

Pinder, C. C. (1984). *Work motivation,* Glenview, IL: Scott Foresman.

Podsakoff, P. M., & Williams, L. J. (1986). The relationship between job performance and job satisfaction. In E. A. Locke (Ed.), *Generalizing from laboratory to field settings* (pp. 202-253). Lexington, MA: Lexington.

Porter, L. W., & Lawler, E. E. (1968). *Managerial attitudes and performance.* Homewood, IL: Dorsey.

Punnett, B. J. (1986). Goal setting: An extension of the research. *Journal of Applied Psychology, 71,* 171-172.

Rakestraw, T. L., & Weiss, H. (1981). The interaction of social influence and task experience on goals, performance and performance satisfaction. *Organizational Behavior and Human Performance, 27,* 326-344.

Reber, R. A., & Wallin, J. A. (1984). The effects of training, goal-setting, and knowledge of results on safe behavior: A component analysis. *Academy of Management Journal, 27,* 544-560.

Roberson-Bennett, P. (1983). *The relation between need for achievement and goal setting and their joint effect on task performance.* Unpublished doctoral dissertation, University of Maryland.

Roethlisberger, F. J., & Dickson, W. J. (1939). *Management and the worker.* Cambridge, MA: Harvard University Press (1956 edition).

Rothkopf, E. A., & Kaplan, R. (1972). Exploration of the effect of density and specificity of instructional objectives on learning from text. *Journal of Educational Psychology, 63,* 295-302.

Ryan, T. A. (1970). *Intentional behavior.* New York: Ronald.

Schmidt, K. H., Kleinbeck, U., & Brockmann, W. (1984). Motivational control of motor performance by goal setting in a dual-task situation. *Psychological Research, 46,* 129-141.

Schweiger, D. M., & Leana, C. R. (1986). Participation in decision making. In E. A. Locke

(Ed.), *Generalizing from laboratory to field settings* (pp. 147–166). Lexington, MA: Lexington.

Seashore, S. E. (1954). *Group cohesiveness in the industrial work group*. Ann Arbor: Survey Research Center, Institute for Social Research, University of Michigan.

Shaw, K. N. (1984). *A laboratory investigation of the relationship among goals, strategies, and task performance*. Unpublished doctoral dissertation, University of Maryland.

Smith, K. G., Locke, E. A., & Barry, D. (in press). Goal setting, planning effectiveness and organizational performance: An experimental simulation. *Organizational Behavior and Human Decision Processes*.

Stedry, A. C. (1960). *Budget control and cost behavior*. Englewood Cliffs, NJ: Prentice-Hall.

Steers, R. M. (1975). Task-goal attributes, n achievement and supervisory performance. *Organizational Behavior & Human Performance, 13*, 392–403.

Stone, E. F. (1986). Job scope–job satisfaction and job scope–job performance relationships. In E. A. Locke (Ed.), *Generalizing from laboratory to field settings* (pp. 189–206). Lexington, MA: Lexington.

Taylor, F. W. (1967). *Principles of scientific management*. New York: Norton.

Taylor, M. S., Locke, E. A., Lee, C., & Gist, M. (1984). Type A behavior and faculty research productivity: What are the mechanisms? *Organizational Behavior and Human Performance, 34*, 402–418.

Terborg, J. R. (1976). The motivational components of goal setting. *Journal of Applied Psychology, 61*, 613–621.

Tubbs, M. E. (1986). Goal-setting: A meta-analytic examination of the empirical evidence. *Journal of Applied Psychology, 71*, 474–483.

Vroom, V. (1964). *Work and motivation*, New York: Wiley.

Wagner, J. A., & Gooding, R. Z. (1987). Shared influence and organizational behavior: A meta-analysis of situational variables expected to moderate participation–outcome relationships. *Academy of Management Journal, 30*, 524–541.

Weiner, B. (1986). *An attributional theory of motivation and emotion*. New York: Springer-Verlag.

White, F. M., & Locke, E. A. (1981). Perceived determinants of high and low productivity in three occupational groups: A critical incident study. *Journal of Management Studies, 18*, 375–387.

Williams, L. J., & Hazer, J. T. (1986). Antecedents and consequences of satisfaction and commitment in turnover models: A reanalysis using latent variable structural equation methods. *Journal of Applied Psychology, 71*, 219–231.

Wood, R. E. (1986). Task complexity: Definition of the construct. *Organizational Behavior and Human Decision Processes, 37*, 60–62.

Wood, R. E. & Locke, E. A. (1986). Goal setting and strategy effects on complex tasks. To appear in B. Staw & L. Cummings (Eds.), *Research in organizational behavior* Vol. 12, Greenwich, CT: JAI Press. Australian Graduate School of Management, Sydney.

Wood, R. E., Mento, A. J., & Locke, E. A. (1987). Task complexity as a moderator of goal effects: A meta-analysis. *Journal of Applied Psychology, 72*, 416–425.

Yukl, G. A., & Latham, G. P. (1978). Interrelationships among employee participation, individual differences, goal difficulty, goal acceptance, goal instrumentality, and performance. *Personnel Psychology, 31*, 305–323.

2

The Translation
of Work Motivation
into Performance

Uwe Kleinbeck
Bergische Universität-Gesamthochschule Wuppertal

Klaus-Helmut Schmidt
Institut für Arbeitsphysiologie an der Universität Dortmund

GOALS—A KEY VARIABLE IN MOTIVATION
AND PERFORMANCE

It is a well-known fact that organizations have to put a great deal of effort into the task of motivating their members to accept organizational goals, because this is a powerful determinant of effective work.

The picture, however, is not one sided: Individual members or organizations also have goals developing through the interaction of personal motives, expectancies, and the Motivating Potential of the work situation.

In both cases organizational members either develop goals selecting one or more of them for action or they accept—more or less—an assigned goal. The selection or acceptance of goals is traditionally described and explained by expectancy models of work motivation (Locke & Henne, 1986; Vroom, 1964; see Fig. 2.1), which function well for getting an understanding about the way goals come into being but which do not help to understand the way goals effect performance.

Depending on the interactions among personal motives, the motivating potential of work, expectancies, and assigned goals, behavioral intentions develop many of which include one or more specific goals aiming at more or less concrete action outcomes (see Fig. 2.1). The difference between an intention and a goal can be characterized on two dimensions: An intention is less concrete than a goal; a goal is more action oriented than an intention.

For the action-oriented function of goals—effecting performance—we need a different theoretical framework and we start this chapter by discussing some variables that turn out to be candidates for a role in such a theoretical framework. We assume that the translation of selected or accepted

27

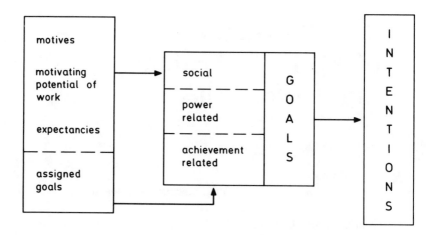

FIG. 2.1.   The motivational process.

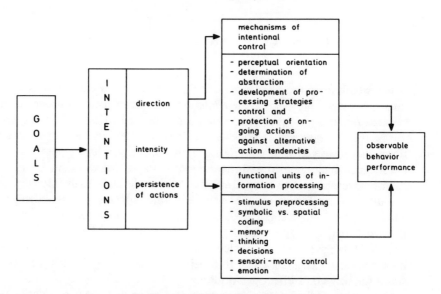

FIG. 2.2.   The volitional process.

goals into performance can be described as a *volitional* process (Fig. 2.2), a psychologically relevant process that has been neglected since the times of Ach (1910) and Lindworski (1923).

This *volitional* process is based on some mechanisms of intentional control interacting with functional units of information processing. It describes the way goals are translated into performance, whereas the *motivational* process—in the reduced meaning of the term motivation as we use it here— only describes the conditions of goal development.

**Control of Performance—a Function of Goals Neglected
in Theories of Motivation**

Stimulated by the work of Locke and his coworkers, Klaus-Helmut Schmidt
and I started a research program to find out some of the variables responsible for the effects of goals on performance. Looking through the relevant
literature (e.g., Ach, 1935; Hacker, 1983; Locke, Latham, & Erez, 1988), we
could put together the following list of goal characteristics:

—Goals determine perceptual processes (selective attention).
—Goals direct and focus attention according to task requirements.
—Goals organize sequences and/or hierarchies of subgoals.
—Goals help to develop new processing strategies.
—Goals are used as memory patterns to be compared with feedback
 action results.
—Goals protect ongoing activities against alternative action tendencies.

Our research planning was based on the assumption that these goal-
oriented mechanisms of intentional action control are no doubt necessary
components for explaining ongoing behavior, but they do not suffice. Behavior at work also depends on other psychic functions well known from
the information-processing metaphor, giving us concepts like stimulus pre-
processing, symbolic versus spatial coding, memory, and others (Fig. 2.2).

At this point we defined our task to find a theoretical approach combining factors like goals—as endpoints of motivational and at the same time as
starting points of volitional processes—and cognitive factors as they are described in models of information processing.

The main questions arising at the beginning of our research program
grew out of the difficulties to measure goal effects on information processing. We saw three problem areas for classical single-task paradigms designed to reveal the relations between goals and performance: (1) We do not
know the function relating volitional resources set free by goals to performance; (2) we do not know the functional units involved in task performance; (3) we do not know anything about the status of alternative action
tendencies arising during performance.

Along the path of finding solutions for these problems we "rediscov-
ered" the dual-task technique that was used earlier in cognitive psychology
(Binet, 1890) and in European work psychology to measure mental strain
(Bornemann, 1943).

**The Translation of Goals into Task-Specific Action:
Methodological and Conceptual Considerations**

To acquire knowledge about the process of translating motivation into
actions, one has to find answers to questions like the following: If goal-

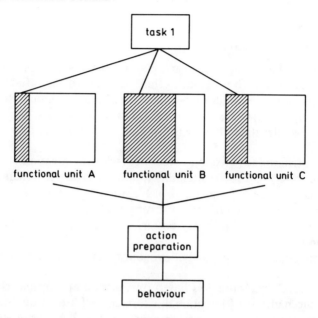

FIG. 2.3. Schematic representation of a task requiring the use of three functional units and the degree of involvement of these functional units.

specific volitional resources effect information processing specifically, how can operating functional units be identified? Are goal effects specific for different functional units of information processing? How can we observe the development of alternative-action tendencies that might interfere with the ongoing activity?

To answer these questions a researcher has to cope with a multiple task searching for information on three levels: What psychic functional units are involved in the preparation and execution of actions? Do goals effect performance in a task-specific way? Are there competing alternative-action tendencies interfering with ongoing behavior?

The easiest way to perform this multiple task successfully is to conduct dual-task experiments. The dual-task paradigm gets information about the structure of functional units involved in information processing while performing a task (Wickens, 1984). This can be illustrated by the following series of figures, representing a vigilance task (task 1) and two different secondary tasks.

Figure 2.3 presents three functional units, A, B, and C, involved in information processing controlling ongoing behavior. The hypothesized amount of involvement of each functional unit and their limits of capacity is also shown. Functional unit A is used only to a small degree for the preparation of action. Similar demands are placed on functional unit C. For performing the hypothetical task in Fig. 2.3, it is necessary to invest a large portion of the capacity of functional unit B. To find out if these assumptions about the involvement of these functional units for action preparation are correct,

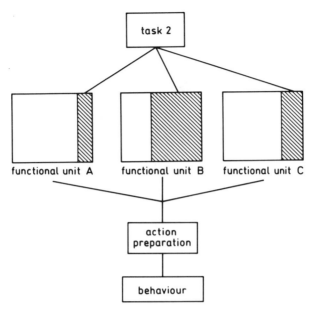

FIG. 2.4. Schematic representation of a task requiring the use of three functional units and the degree of involvement of these functional units.

one has to find a second task for which the involved functional units are known and also the degree of their involvement. Let us assume that we know a task like that in Fig. 2.4. Combining these two tasks leads to the prediction that there will be interference between them because of a clear overdemand on functional unit B, the capacity of which is not large enough to satisfy the demands of each single task. This should be seen in the data most clearly by plotting them as a Performance Operating Characteristic (POC) (Fig. 2.5). In our example the POC should look like the one in Fig. 2.5, showing a decrease in performance at one task every time performance at the other task increases. A task combination without overlapping demands from both tasks involved will show no interference effect and will produce a quite different POC (Fig. 2.6).

The experimental paradigm of the dual-task technique can best be illustrated by describing the combination of a tracking task and a simple auditory reaction task. The tracking task was performed continuously, whereas the reaction task required the investment of mental resources only at discrete points in time. This can be seen in Fig. 2.7. The upper row of the figure illustrates auditory reaction performance elicited by an acoustic signal (1,000 Hz) lasting for 100 ms. The signal is then repeated after 4 s, so that there are 15 signals per minute (Schmidt, Kleinbeck, & Brockmann, 1984).

The second row of Fig. 2.7 illustrates tracking performance over a time period of 6 seconds. There are phases of tracking performance influenced directly by the reaction task and others not directly influenced by a simulta-

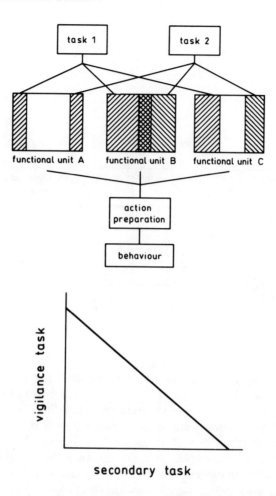

FIG. 2.5.   Schematic representation of two tasks performed simultaneously with interference at functional unit B; performance data can be plotted as a Performance Operating Characteristic (POC).

neously performed reaction. The direct double-load phase was defined empirically as the reaction time plus an additional time of 1.5 s.

The Detection of Task-Specific Functional Units

Changing the goals for the tracking task—demanding a 20 or 40% increase in performance over the individual average performance standard—caused a decrease in tracking errors and a simultaneous increase in reaction time. Similarly, when instructions demand improvement in reaction time, the reaction times get shorter whereas tracking errors increase (Fig. 2.8). The

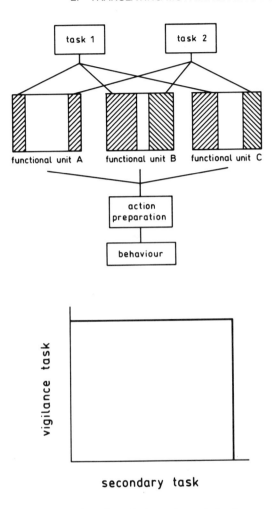

FIG. 2.6. Schematic representation of two tasks performed simultaneously without inter-ference; the POC shows a rectangular form.

trade-off function using the indirect double-load measure is flatter than the one using direct double-load phases.

This performance-operating characteristic demonstrates that the infor-mation-processing operations required by both tasks are controlled by simi-lar functional units with a limited capacity (for more details see Schmidt, 1987). By using systematic, model-based variations of secondary tasks, the dual-task technique can be used to detect and identify all the functional units required for the main task. These can then be seen as components of a taxonomy of psychic functional units involved in the course of carrying out work activities (Wickens, 1984).

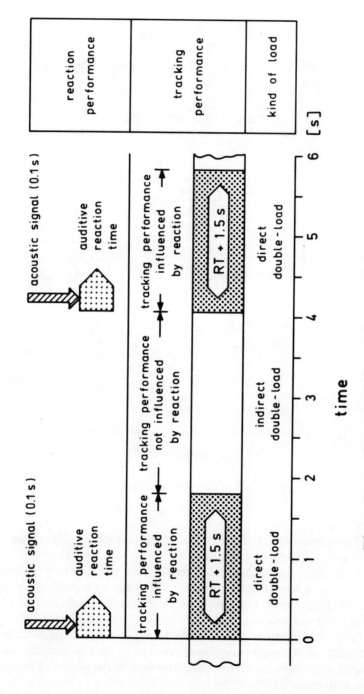

FIG. 2.7 Direct and indirect double load in a manual tracking task and an auditive reaction (from Kleinbeck, 1985).

34

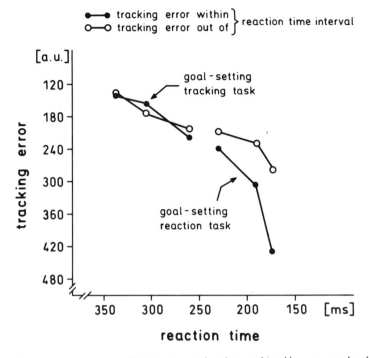

FIG. 2.8.   Performance trade off between reaction time and tracking error under different goal-setting conditions for the tracking task and the reaction task (from Schmidt, 1987).

ARE THERE DIFFERENT GOAL EFFECTS
IN DIFFERENT DUAL-TASK COMBINATIONS?

In a second set of experiments we used a vigilance task (Detection of Repeated Numbers, DORN) in combination with some further tasks of which I present two, namely a simple auditory reaction task and a more complex auditory arithmetic task (Adding).

In the detection task observers have to look at three-digit numbers presented repeatedly. If the same numbers occur in two sequential presentations, subjects have to react as quickly as possible by pressing a key.

The simple auditory reaction task is the same as explained before whereas the auditory arithmetic task requires the subject to listen to a series of one-digit numbers presented by a computer-controlled speech system. If one number and the following one add up to nine, subjects have to react by pressing a key.

Looking directly into the data one can observe that the interference patterns between these tasks differ according to the two task combinations. Figure 2.9 shows an increase in performance in the vigilance task when goals demand an improvement. At the same time one can observe performance decreases for the vigilance task (see left half of Fig. 2.9). With harder goals for the adding task (see right half of Fig. 2.9), subjects improve in adding performance whereas at the same time performance decreases for the vigilance task.

A quite different interference pattern shows up for the task combination with a vigilance and a simple auditory reaction task. Notice in Fig. 2.10 that there is no clear tradeoff between performances in both tasks.

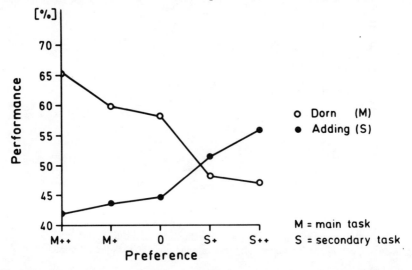

FIG. 2.9. Performance tradeoff between a vigilance task (DORN) and an arithmetic task (ADDING) with different preference instructions for either one or the other task.

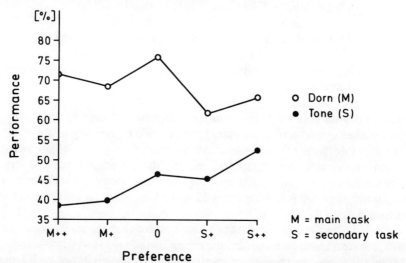

FIG. 2.10. Performance tradeoff between a vigilance task (DORN) and a simple auditory reaction task (TONE) with different preference instructions for either one or the other task.

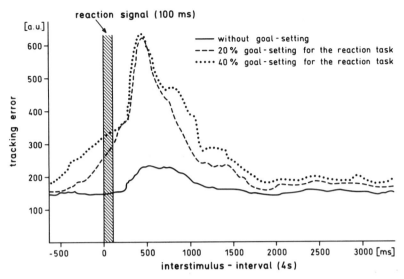

FIG. 2.11. Differences of tracking errors within a fix interstimulus interval of 4s under different conditions of goal setting for the reaction task; tracking errors were averaged over all available interstimulus intervals.

These results indicate the fact that the same goals have different effects dependent on the specific characteristics of the task. In a situation with interference between two tasks, goals can be translated into action for one task, but at the same time performance in the second task cannot be kept in line with the set standard. Because structural capacity is lacking performance in this case decreases. In task combinations without interferences, goals can be translated into actions more easily.

The Detection of "Hidden" Effects of Motivation

A microanalysis of data from the dual-task paradigm reveals a further characteristic of the technique, related to the method's distinctiveness. The method can be used to expose a psychological-process variable usually concealed in other experimental paradigms. To demonstrate this we arranged the data of the tracking/auditory reaction experiment described earlier in a new way. We took all the 4-second interstimulus intervals and put them one over the other. The averaged tracking for each measurement point (50 Hz; that means one measure every 40 ms) is presented in Fig. 2.11 for three goal-setting conditions. The figure shows a decrease in tracking performance when a reaction is made. With harder goals for the reaction task the decrements in tracking performance get larger. This is not surprising and is in fact to be expected on the basis of results from other studies. Much more interesting is the fact that tracking performance starts worsening even before the reaction-triggering signal occurs.

At this point subjects are expecting the signal; this expectation, coupled perhaps with reaction preparation, demands such a high investment of resources that it interferes with tracking performance even before action because the limits of structure specific capacity are transgressed. The dual-task technique, therefore, is able to reveal the hidden effects of a subjective expectancy that develops in the process of preparing an action (Schmidt, 1987).

DISCUSSION OF THE RESULTS

The dual-task technique has been shown to be an effective method for analyzing the effects of goal setting on action (Austin & Bobko, 1985). Results from this paradigm can be applied to the behavior of people in organizations and can be considered a basic situation for a series of organizational situations in which goal setting and goal commitment are important for work quality and quantity.

During work on two simultaneous tasks, two goals have to be translated into action at the same time. When two tasks that structurally interfere with each other are combined, subjects have to relax their goal commitment for one task in order to realize their goals for the other. The dual-task technique has been used to analyze the strategies used for this, revealing the conditions under which goal commitment is weakened and permitting models to be constructed that include factors having positive and negative effects on goal commitment.

This kind of experimentation stimulates ideas proposing the dual-task paradigm as a useful metaphor for understanding the effects of goal conflict. This conflict will create problems especially in situations characterized by structural interference; that means when two tasks place demands on the same or similar functional units of information processing that have only a limited capacity. One way of handling the conflict could be trading off one task against the other. This is accompanied in most cases by a change in commitment for one of the goals. Dual-task experiments could be used to study such coping styles for goal conflicts, and they could be regarded as tools to explore other possibilities of handling conflicts of this kind.

Dual-task analysis not only informs about the effects of the Motivating Potential of task characteristics; it also provides insights into the functioning of information processing responsible for coping with special tasks. So it is possible to identify the places where changes in motivation are transformed into action preparation.

Last but not least, the dual-task technique offers its services as a method of revealing some effects of motivation being "hidden" in single-task performance. In one example we could present data showing the "psychic costs" of expectancies indicated by decreasing performance in a second task performed during the time passing while waiting for the signal to start the first task.

Because of these possibilities offered by the technique, we hope that the dual-task paradigm will be used more and more in the psychology of work motivation, especially when it is concerned with the translation of motivation into performance.

REFERENCES

Ach, N. (1910). *Über den Willensakt und das Temperament* [Volitional act and temperament]. Leipzig: Quelle & Meier.

Ach, N. (1935). Analyse des Willens [Analysis of volition]. In E. Abderhalden (Ed.). *Handbuch der biologischen Arbeitsmethoden* (Bd. VI). Berlin: Urban & Schwarzenberg.

Austin, J. R., & Bobko, P. (1985). Goal-setting theory: Unexplored areas and future research needs. *Journal of Occupational Psychology, 58*, 289–308.

Binet, A. (1890). La concurrence des etats psychologiques [The concurrence of psychological states]. *Revue Philosophique de la France et de l'Etranger, 24*, 138–155.

Bornemann, E. (1943). Untersuchungen über den Grad der geistigen Beanspruchung [Studies on the degree of mental load]. *Arbeitsphysiologie, 12*, 142–191.

Hacker, W. (1983). Ziele—eine vergessene psychologische Schlüsselvariable? Zur antriebsregulatorischen Potenz von Tätigkeitsinhalten [Goals-a forgotten psychological key variable?]. *Psychologie für die Praxis, 2*, 5–26.

Kleinbeck, U. (1985). *Arbeitspsychologische Beiträge zur motivationalen Beeinflussung von Bewegungsleistungen* [Motivational influences on motor performance—a contribution of work and organizational-psychology]. Düsseldorf: VDI-Verlag.

Lindworski, J. (1923). *Der Wille* [Volition]. Leipzig: Barth.

Locke, E. A., & Henne, D. (1986). Work motivation theories. In C. L. Cooper & I. Robertson (Eds.), *International review of industrial and organizational psychology* (pp. 1–35). Chichester, England: Wiley.

Locke, E. A., Latham, G. P., & Erez, M. (1988). The determinants of goal commitment. *Academy of Management Review, 13*, 23–39.

Schmidt, K.-H. (1987). *Motivation, Handlungskontrolle und Leistung in einer Doppelaufgabensituation* [Motivation, action control and performance in a dual task situation]. VDI-Düsseldorf: VDI-Verlag.

Schmidt, K.-H., Kleinbeck, U., & Brockmann, W. (1984). Motivational control of motor performance by goal-setting in a dual task situation. *Psychological Research, 46*, 129–141.

Vroom, V. H. (1964). *Work and motivation*. New York: Wiley.

Wickens, C. D. (1984). *Engineering psychology and human performance*. Columbus, OH: Charles E. Merril.

3

An Action Control Conceptualization of Goal-Setting and Feedback Effects

Conny H. Antoni
University of Mannheim

Jürgen Beckmann
Max-Planck-Institute für Psychologische Forschung

AN ACTION CONTROL CONCEPTUALIZATION
OF GOAL SETTING AND FEEDBACK EFFECTS

Many jobs in organizations are characterized by sometimes monotonously recurring demands. This applies not only to the classic example of assembly-line jobs or monitoring tasks but also to the majority of administrative jobs. Even those people who are highly committed to their monotonous jobs find it difficult to constantly devote sufficient attention to their tasks to perform adequately. This means that they can be motivated to do well but given job characteristics prevent the transformation of their motivation into the respective performance.

Locke (1964, Locke & Latham, 1984) has proposed a motivational technique that seems to work in increasing unsatisfactory task performance: goal setting. This approach presumes that, given sufficient ability, goal acceptance, and task-relevant feedback, individuals who are confronted with specific hard goals outperform those who are given easy, nonspecific, "do best," or no goals (Locke, Shaw, Saari, & Latham, 1981). Although a number of studies furnished evidence that this technique works in fact (see Locke et al., 1981 and Tubbs, 1986, for an overview), there are just a few studies trying to explain *how* it works.

Steers and Porter (1974) have pointed out that merely knowing which task–goal attributes are associated with performance is not sufficient. From a psychological standpoint it is more important to analyze the dynamics behind the effects of goal setting, that is, to explain the process whereby task–goal attributes affect performance. The few attempts to explain the underlying psychological processes propose various mechanisms but do not seem to give a comprehensive psychological model. For example, there have been some studies discussing effort and strategy as mechanisms by which goals affect performance (Earley, Wojnaroski, & Prest, 1987, Terborg, 1976). Campion and Lord (1982) suggest a control-systems model to explain why both goal and feedback are needed for behavioral adjustment and regulation. However, their model does not address the crucial question of what determines whether or not an individual will persist in pursuing a difficult goal despite arising difficulties. This criticism also applies to a number of other models that have been proposed (cf. Campbell & Pritchard, 1976; Dachler & Mobley, 1973; Locke, Cartledge, & Knerr, 1970; Locke & Latham, 1984; Mento, Cartledge, & Locke, 1980; Steers & Porter, 1974).

Neither control-systems theories nor expectancy–valence theories adequately explain the process focusing information processing on the task at hand. Both assume that human behavior is rather static and free of conflicts: Once individuals have chosen the action alternative with the highest expected subjective utility, they will stick to it as long as no better alternative is available; furthermore, they will constantly monitor task performance and will adjust behavior in response to encountered feedback/goal discrepancies to reach the chosen goal (cf. Campbell, Dunnette, Lawler, & Weick, 1970; Mitchell, 1979, 1982; Powers, 1973).

This is no realistic view of human behavior. In contrast, Atkinson and Birch (1970) have pointed out that while working on tasks requiring persistence concurrent stimuli will divert one's attention and thereby impair task performance. This may be called a problem of action control. Such problems of action control are documented in the results of a recent study which provides evidence that individuals quite often do not actually do what they intend to do despite sufficient ability (e.g., Kuhl & Eisenbeiser, 1987). This is especially true for tasks with recurring demands, where task completion takes a long time during which a number of competing action tendencies can be instigated. However, usually even such tasks can be completed satisfactorily. Thus it can be concluded that individuals have a number of action-control strategies at their disposal to solve the action-control problems.

THE THEORY OF ACTION CONTROL

Recently Kuhl (1984, 1985) has formulated a theory of action control. In this theory Kuhl assumes that to maintain action control an individual can employ several strategies to strengthen a current intention and to protect it against interference until it is performed. Such strategies include *selective attention* to various components of an intention, *encoding control* (e.g., to encode primarily information-promoting action realization), *emotion control* (e.g., to arouse activating emotions based on metacognitive knowledge), and *motivation control* (to strengthen selectively the motivation basic to the current intention).

The efficiency of action-control processes should be determined by two different control modes: action orientation versus state orientation. Action orientation occurs when an individual seeks to implement an action plan and simultaneously focuses on his or her present state, the intended future state, the discrepancy between the present and the future state, and action alternatives that may transform the present state into the desired future state. State orientation occurs when an individual excessively focuses on his or her past, present, or future state without attending to any action plan that may bring about a change in the present situation.

Action-control processes (e.g., protecting the current intention) require a considerable amount of processing capacity. State orientation (e.g., ruminating about past failures) consumes a lot of the individual's processing capacity. Therefore, state orientation interferes with the efficient use of action-control processes and, hence, the realization of an intention may be severely impaired (cf. Kuhl, 1981).

This assumption is supported by a number of studies showing that state orientation interferes with action-control processes like selective attention (Kuhl, 1983a), emotion control (Kuhl, 1983b), parsimonious information processing (Kuhl & Beckmann, 1983), and motivation control (Beckmann, 1986; Beckmann & Kuhl, 1984). Whether an individual is state oriented or action oriented in a given situation depends on the interaction of situational and dispositional factors.

A questionnaire has been developed to assess the disposition toward action or state orientation (see Kuhl, 1985, 1989). A very powerful situational determinant of state orientation is the prolonged exposure to uncontrollable aversive events, e.g., a series of unexpected and uncontrollable failure (Kuhl, 1981). Furthermore, confronting individuals with a task without specifying the requirements (e.g., not telling them where and when they shall perform the task) seems to increase state orientation (Kuhl & Helle, 1984). In contrast, providing individuals with a clear action structure (Kuhl, 1983a) and focusing their attention on the task, e.g., by instructing them to verbalize their hypotheses while working on a concept-formation problem (Kuhl, 1981), seems to increase action orientation.

Setting hard, specific goals and providing individuals working on a task with feedback about their performance should focus their attention on the task in a similar way. We suggest that setting hard, specific goals and giving task-relevant feedback is another way of increasing action orientation by situational manipulation.

Increasing action orientation by goal setting will be particularly useful for rather monotonous tasks requiring constant attention. Action orientation is required to effectively screen the attention from distracting stimuli (competing action tendencies) in order to maintain high performance on such tasks. Therefore, without explicit goal setting instructions action-oriented individuals should outperform state-oriented individuals on these tasks.

However, the performance of state-oriented persons should increase when their attention is focused on the task by providing external goals and task-relevant feedback. Such a situational induction of an action-control strategy should minimize the differences in performance between action-oriented individuals who should do well without explicit external goal setting, and state-oriented individuals.

This leads to the suggestion that action-control processes moderate the effects of goal setting. According to our conceptualization action-control processes, and hence goal attainment, should be more efficient whenever an action-oriented mode of information processing is induced. Furthermore we propose that hard, specific goals with task-relevant feedback will increase action orientation. With these considerations in mind, the following two hypotheses were formulated for the present study: (1) When no specific hard goals are set and no feedback is given, individuals who are action oriented should outperform individuals who are state oriented; (2) when specific, hard goals and feedback are given, state-oriented individuals should perform as well as action-oriented individuals.

Method

Subjects.   Participants were 76 male blue-collar workers employed at various production departments of a multinational chemical company. Almost all (92%) the participants had completed 9th grade and 73% had served an apprenticeship. The average age was 45, the youngest being 24, the oldest, 58. Tenure was very high, with an average of 22 years (minimum 3 years, maximum 37 years). The experiment was conducted at the beginning of four 2-day safety-training courses. The four training groups were almost equal in size and randomly assigned to the experimental conditions.

Design.   Two of these groups were given specific, hard, external goals plus feedback. The other two groups did not receive specific external goals or feedback. Subjects' action versus state orientation was assessed through the action-control scale (Kuhl, 1985). Based on a median split of this scale, participants in both conditions were divided in action- and state-oriented individuals. Thus a 2 (action- vs. state-orientation) by 2 (specific, hard goal plus feedback vs. unspecific goal without feedback) experimental design resulted.

Procedure.   On their arrival at the training center participants were asked to take part in a study to test their speed and accuracy in detecting safety hazards at work. All subjects agreed. Next, they filled out two ques-

TABLE 3.1
Internal Consistency (Cronbach's Alpha) and Discriminant Validity of the
Performance-(AOP), Failure-(AOF), and Decision-related (AOD) Subscale
of the Action-Control Scale (cf. Kuhl, 1984).

	AOP	AOF	AOD
Cronbach's alpha	.71	.74	.82
Achievement motivation	.20**	.11	.22*
Test anxiety	− .33**	− .01	− .36**
Extraversion	− .07	− .21*	− .07
Self-consciousness	− .22*	.15	− .24*
Future orientation	.20*	− .08	.21*
Cognitive complexity	.03	− .14	09

*$p < .05$
**$p < .01$

tionnaires, the action-control scale (Kuhl, 1985) and an achievement–
motive scale (Gjesme & Nygard, 1970). The achievement–motive scale was
used to control achievement motivation to rule out possible alternative explanations based on this construct. The achievement–motive scale consists
of two subscales, with 15 items each measuring fear of failure (Cronbach's
Alpha = .88) and hope for success (Cronbach's Alpha = .81).

The action-control questionnaire (Kuhl, 1985) consists of three scales
with 20 binary items, each measuring three types of action versus state orientation. One scale measures the extent to which attention is diverted from
or focused on the personal state following experiences of failure (action vs.
state orientation following failure, AOF). A second scale measures the extent to which disregard or attention is focused on state-related information
prior to forming an intention, which may result in indecisiveness and an inability to terminate the decision-making process (decision-related action vs.
state orientation, AOD). The third scale measures the extent to which attention is focused on a desired goal state instead of being focused on the performance of the behavior (goal-centered action vs. state orientation, AOP).
Such a desired goal state is not equivalent to the performance goals in goal-
setting theory. Desired goal states referred to in the AOP scale should
rather be considered as positive states resulting from the achievement of a
performance goal. Psychometric analyses have yielded favorable results: internal consistency coefficients ranging between 0.71 and 0.82 (Cronbach's
alpha) and discriminant validity ranging between 0.01 and 0.36 (cf. Table
3.1; more information about the reliability and validity of action-control
scale is given in Kuhl, 1984, 1985, 1989).

As we have elaborated, we assume that hard, specific goals with task-
relevant feedback should focus the information processing on the enactment of action-related aspects of the intention and away from perseverating
thoughts about the desired goal. Because the performance-oriented scale of

the action-control questionnaire measures the extent to which people are able to focus their attention on the performance of an act, we chose this scale for our analysis. A sample item from the AOP scale says: "When I'm reading something interesting, I sometimes busy myself with other things for a change" (state-oriented answer); I often stick with it for a long time" (action-oriented answer).

After the questionnaires were completed the experimental task was explained. Participants were then shown slides depicting hazardous work situations. Each slide was projected for 1 second, followed by an answer slide listing five violations of safety regulations in a multiple choice format that was presented for 2 minutes. The participants were asked to mark the correct violation that they thought was depicted on the preceding slide on an answer sheet while the answer slide was projected. They were allowed 2 minutes to respond, because this provided sufficient time for reflection as a pretest had shown. Each group was shown 10 practice slides prior to the actual test to acquaint them with the task and to develop a standard of excellence. After the practice session, all subjects were given feedback about their performance and asked to score their individual training result.

The test itself consisted of 30 pairs of slides. In the experimental condition, "specific, hard, external goal plus feedback," the participants were told to score at least 24 out of 30 possible correct solutions. After each trial they were told whether they had been right or wrong. To keep their goals and goal discrepancies salient, the participants were asked to keep score on their answer sheets. In the experimental condition, "unspecific external goal without feedback," participants were simply told to do their best and get as many correct answers as possible. In this condition participants were not informed about their performance until after the 30th trial. After the 30th trial subjects in all conditions were told how many correct answers they had attained.

Because subjects might develop some kind of personal goal for the task based on their training experience irrespective of external goal setting, we tried to assess whether they accepted the externally set goals. Therefore, *after* specifying the experimental instructions (i.e., after we set the external goal) and before starting the test, we asked all subjects to set their personal goal on a 4-point scale (ranging from at least 10 to at least 25 out of 30 possible points) as a manipulation check. Furthermore, we asked for an estimate of the subjective probability of attaining this goal, its subjective importance and difficulty, as well as the extent of the willingness to expend efforts to reach it on 4-point, verbally anchored Likert scales.

Results

As Table 3.2 shows, the findings of the present study concerning the effects of goal setting are consistent with findings of past goal-setting research. A

TABLE 3.2
T-Test of Groups' Means Between Unspecific, External Goal Group
Without Feedback (UG) and the Specific, Hard External Goal with
Feedback (SHG)

Variable	UG	SHG	t	df	p
Test score	19.65	22.03	− 2.22	74	.029
Training score	6.68	7.05	− .71	74	.479
Subjective goal	2.91	3.36	− 2.21	74	.030
Goal expectancy	3.92	3.85	.50	74	.619
Goal importance	3.84	4.13	− 1.69	74	.095
Goal difficulty	3.51	3.54	− .11	74	.909
Intended effort	4.35	4.36	− .04	74	.965

significant main effect indicates that the hard, specific, external goal group
with feedback outperformed ($M = 22.03$) the unspecific external goal group
without feedback ($M = 19.65$; $t(74) = -2.2$; $p < .05$).

The externally set goal seems to have affected subjective goal setting because the group with the external, specific, hard goal set a higher personal goal ($M = 3.36$) than the group without the external, specific goal
($M = 2.91$; $t(74) = -2.2$; $p < .05$). This can be interpreted as a check indicating a successful experimental manipulation. Alternative explanations
such as pretest differences in task proficiency influencing subjective goal
setting can be discarded. Indeed, as expected training performance did influence subjective goal setting significantly ($r = .66$, $p < .005$). However,
both groups had similar scores on the training trials (hard, specific goal
condition $M = 7.05$; do best condition $M = 6.68$; $t(74) = -.71$; n.s.). Furthermore subjective goal setting was not influenced by action-control processes. It did not correlate with the AOP scale ($r = .03$, n.s.).

Despite differing external and subjective goals, Table 3.2 shows that the
two groups did not differ significantly with respect to the subjective expectancy for reaching them, nor to the subjective importance, subjective difficulty, and intended effort to reach them.

So far, these results simply replicate former findings concerning the goal-
setting effect. Our hypotheses, however, do not question this effect but
rather address the underlying process of goal setting. Next our hypotheses
concerning this process were examined.

Hard, specific goals with task-relevant feedback should focus the information processing on the enactment of action-related aspects of the intention and away from perseverating thoughts about the desired goal. Because
the performance-oriented scale of the action-control questionnaire (AOP)
measures the extent to which people are able to focus their attention on the
performance of an act, we chose this scale for our analysis.

The median split ($Md = 8.23$) for the 76 participants on the goal-oriented
scale (AOP) of the action-control questionnaire resulted in two groups with

TABLE 3.3
Test Scores (Means Adjusted for Covariates) Obtaining State-Oriented and
Action-Oriented Subjects in the Unspecific External Goal Without
Feedback Condition and the Specific, Hard External Goal
with Feedback Condition.

	Unspecific External Goal without Feedback		Specific, Hard External Goal with Feedback
State orientation	17.91	22.89	20.40
Action orientation	20.99	21.77	21.37
	19.44	22.33	

41 action-oriented and 35 state-oriented participants, respectively. A 2 (action vs. state orientation) by 2 (specific, hard goal plus feedback vs. unspecific goal without feedback) analysis of covariance was completed on subjects' test scores as the dependent variable. Because it was found that subjects' achievement motive score and age were significantly correlated with performance, these variables were used as covariates after the prerequisites of the analyses of covariance were tested (fear of failure, beta = .33; $t(64) = 2.7$; $p < .05$; and age beta = .29; $t(64) = 2.43$; $p < .05$). We did not employ performance scores on the practice trials as a covariate, as is suggested by Mento, Cartledge, and Locke (1980), because relevant action-control variables affecting both training and test performance would be eliminated. This could be expected, because the first 10 training trials can be regarded as tasks without specific goal and without feedback. Hence the influence of a state- versus action-oriented mode of information processing should already be found in the training trials. Using performance scores on the practice trials would therefore eliminate the influence of the key variables that we are interested in. Due to missing data only 34 state-oriented subjects could be used for the 2 by 2 analyses of covariance. Because of the unequal cell frequencies, the method of unweighted means for the analysis of covariance in the ANOVA model (Winer, 1971) was used.

A significant main effect emerged for the specific, hard goal factor versus the unspecific goal factor, $F(1, 64) = 13.5$; $p < .05$. This effect is due to higher scores of the specific, hard-goal group with feedback ($M = 22.33$) as compared to the group with unspecific goals without feedback ($M = 19.44$). This main effect was significant ($F(1, 64) = 13.5$ $p < .05$).

However, Table 3.3 shows that this effect is due to the state-oriented individuals increase in performance when specific, hard goals are given as compared to the unspecific goal condition. Action-oriented subjects are almost not affected by goal setting. Hence, a significant interaction effect of the goal-setting factor and action versus state orientation results: $F(1, 64) = 6.3$, $p < .05$. Planned comparisons reveal that for state-oriented participants the difference in test scores between the hard, specific goal condition ($M = 22.89$) and the unspecific goal condition ($M = 17.91$) is significant ($t(64) = 4.1$; $< .01$). In contrast, there was no significant difference in performance of action-oriented subjects in the unspecific goal condition ($M = 20.99$) when compared to the specific, hard goal condition ($M = 21.77$; $t(64) = -.6$; n.s.).

Further comparisons reveal that action-oriented participants outperformed state-oriented participants in the unspecific goal condition without feedback, $t(64) = 2.7$; $p < .01$. The difference between action- and state-oriented participants in the specific, hard goal plus feedback condition is not significant ($t(64) = 1.0$, n.s.).

As expected, the influence of a state- versus action-oriented mode of information processing on task performance could already be found in the training trials. These first 10 trials can be regarded as tasks without specific goals and without feedback. Similarly, as on the test trials action-oriented participants scored significantly higher ($M = 7.36$) in the training trials than state-oriented participants ($M = 6.23$, $F(1, 64) = 5.03$, $p < .05$).

DISCUSSION

This study clearly replicates the goal-setting effect. The groups with hard, specific external goals and feedback outperformed the groups with unspecific external goals without feedback. However, in search for the cognitive processes underlying the goal-setting effect, we intended to go beyond a simple replication. Based on Kuhl's theory of action control, we proposed a theoretical model for the cognitive processes underlying goal-setting effects. According to our model, goal setting can be considered a means to focus an individual's attention persistently on repetitive tasks despite distracting stimuli or competing action techniques that may be instigated. Accordingly, goal setting is assumed to induce action orientation in individuals who are state oriented. Action orientation is a control mode that facilitates action control.

The study conducted to test these assumptions concentrated on the interaction between the disposition towards action or state orientation and external goal setting and feedback. Our basic assumption was that goal setting is an action-control strategy ensuring high performance level especially on repetitive tasks. Action-oriented individuals should be able to employ this strategy without external inducement. Therefore, external goal setting should not further increase their performance. In contrast, state-oriented individuals should require external assistance to efficiently employ this strategy. Hence, goal setting should be a motivational technique that works in the case of state orientation but is unnecessary in the case of action orientation. The results of the present study support this assumption.

Only the initially state-oriented participants improved their performance in the specific goal and feedback condition, whereas action-oriented subjects showed no goal-setting effect. Action-oriented subjects who are less dependent on external, task-oriented guidance for their attention and information processing than state-oriented subjects scored significantly higher than the latter, when no goals were set and no feedback was given. When specific goals and feedback were provided the difference in performance between the two groups disappeared, presumably because the attention and information processing of the initially state-oriented subjects were centered on the task at hand.

Based on these results we conclude that goal-setting effects are moderated by action-control processes. In the absence of specific goals and feedback a state-oriented mode of information processing is reinforced, whereas specific goals and feedback focus attention and information processing on the task and hence augment an action-oriented control mode.

Nevertheless, there are still some questions left to be answered. State-oriented individuals even outperformed action-oriented individuals when hard goals were set and feedback was given, although this effect was not significant. This might be a hint that action- and state-oriented individuals process external goals and feedback differently. Subjects in the mode of state orientation might try to reach extremely hard goals, when their information processing is centered on the task at hand by external guidance. In contrast, action-oriented individuals who are less dependent on external guidance and able to set their own goals might reject external ones, when they realize that they cannot reach these goals. It might be that they would just ignore them and follow their own goals. If this is the case goal setting would simply have no effect on the performance of action-oriented individuals. It could also be possible that for action-oriented individuals goal setting can produce a reactance effect (Brehm, 1966), when the discrepancy between external and self-set goals becomes too big. This should result in a reduction of effort spent on the task. This assumption corresponds to the effect reported by Locke (1968), that individuals tend to reject hard external goals if they have already set their own personal goals and perform quite poorly on the task. If the preceding reasoning is correct, one could say that individuals tend to reject hard external goals if they consider them to be unrealistically hard and if they are able to set their own goals. Hence, especially for action-oriented subjects, setting hard external goals might have potentially detrimental effects on the performance. Further research with varying levels of hard goals and within-subjects designs to assess goal acceptance is clearly needed to answer these questions.

REFERENCES

Atkinson, J. W., & Birch, D. (1970). *A dynamic theory of action*. New York: Wiley.

Beckmann, J. (1986). *When dissonance reduction fails: Increased performance in a case of deficient action control*. Unpublished manuscript, Max–Planck-Institut für psychologische Forschung, München, F.R.G.

Beckmann, J, & Kuhl, J. (1984). Altering information to gain action control: Functional aspects of human information processing in decision making. *Journal of Research in Personality, 18*, 223-237.

Brehm, J. W. (1966). *A theory of psychological reactance.* New York: Academic Press.

Campbell, J. P., Dunnette, M. D., Lawler, E. E., & Weick, K. E. (1970). *Managerial behavior, performance, and effectiveness.* New York: McGraw-Hill.

Campbell, J. P., & Pritchard, R. D. (1976). Motivation theory in industrial and organizational psychology. In M.D. Dunnette (Ed.), *Handbook of industrial and organizational psychology* (pp. 63-130). Chicago: Rand McNally.

Campion, M. A., & Lord, R. G. (1982). A control systems conceptualization of the goal setting and changing process. *Organizational Behavior and Human Performance, 30*, 265-287.

Dachler, H. P., & Mobley, W. H. (1973). Construct validation of an instrumentality-expectancy-task-goal model of work motivation: Some theoretical boundary conditions. *Journal of Applied Psychology Monograph, 58*, 397-418.

Earley, P. C., Wojnaroski, P., & Prest, W. (1987). Task planning and energy expended: Exploration of how goals influence performance. *Journal of Applied Psychology, 72*, 107-114.

Gjesme, T., & Nygard, R. (1970). *Achievement-related motives: Theoretical considerations and construction of a measuring instrument.* Unpublished manuscript, University of Oslo.

Kuhl, J. (1981). Motivational and functional helplessness: The moderating effect of state versus action orientation. *Journal of Personality and Social Psychology, 40*, 155-170.

Kuhl, J. (1983a). Aufmerksamkeitslenkung und Handlungskontrolle [Attention focusing and action control]. In J. Kuhl, *Motivation, Konflikt und Handlungskontrolle* (pp. 268-269). Heidelberg: Springer Verlag.

Kuhl, J. (1983b). Motivationstheoretische aspekte der depressionsgenese: Der Einfluβ von lageorientierung auf Schmerzempfinden, Medikamentenkonsum und Handlungskontrolle. [Motivational aspects of the development of depression: The influence of state orientation on pain perception, analgesics consumption, and action control]. In M. Wolferdorf, R. Straub, & G. Hole (Eds.), *Der depressive Kranke in der psychiatrischen Klinik: Theorie und Praxis der Diagnostik und Therapie* (pp. 411-424). Regensburg: Roderer.

Kuhl, J. (1984). Volitional aspects of achievement motivation and learned helplessness: Toward a comprehensive theory of action control. In B. A. Maher (Ed.), *Progress in experimental personality research* (Vol. 13, pp. 99-171). New York: Academic Press.

Kuhl, J. (1985). Volitional mediators of cognition-behavior consistency: Self-regulatory processes and action versus state orientation. In J. Kuhl & J. Beckmann (Eds.), *Action control: From cognition to behavior* (pp. 101-128). New York: Springer Verlag.

Kuhl, J. (1989). Development of the action/state orientation scale: psychometric analyses. In J. Kuhl & J. Beckmann (Eds.), *Volition and personality: Action- versus state-oriented modes of control.* Toronto, Göttingen: Hogrefe-Verlag.

Kuhl, J., & Beckmann, J. (1983). Handlungskontrolle und Umfang der Informationsverarbeitung: Wahl einer vereinfachten (nicht optimalen) Entscheidungsregel zugunsten rascher Handlungsbereitschaft [Action control and extent of information processing: Choice of a simplified (non optimal) decision rule in favor of rapid action readiness]. *Zeitschrift für Sozialpsychologie, 14*, 241-250.

Kuhl, J., & Eisenbeiser, T. (1987). Mediating versus meditating cognitions in human motivation: Action control, inertial motivation, and the alienation effect. In J. Kuhl & J. W. Atkinson (Eds.), *Motivation, thought, and action* (pp. 288-306). New York: Praeger.

Kuhl, J., & Helle, P. (1984). Motivational and volitional determinants of depression. The degenerated intention hypothesis. *Journal of Abnormal Psychology, 95*, 247-251.

Locke, E. A. (1964). *The relationship of intentions to motivation and affect.* Doctoral dissertation, Cornell University, 1964. Dissertation Abstracts International, 25, 6081 (University Microfilms No. 65-3729).

Locke, E. A., Cartledge, N., & Knerr, C. S. (1970). Studies of the relationship between satisfaction, goal setting and performance. *Organizational Behavior and Human Performance, 5*, 484–500.

Locke, E. A., & Latham, G. P. (1984). *Goal setting: A motivational technique that works!* Englewood Cliffs, NJ: Prentice-Hall.

Locke, E. A. (1968). Toward a theory of task motivation and incentives. *Organizational Behavior and Human Performance, 3*, 157–189.

Locke, E. A., Shaw, K. M., Saari, L. M., & Latham, G. P. (1981). Goal setting and task performance: 1969–1980. *Psychological Bulletin, 90*, 125–152.

Mento, A. J., Cartledge, N., & Locke, E. A. (1980). Maryland versus Michigan versus Minnesota: Another look at the relationship of expectancy and goal difficulty to task performance. *Organizational Behavior and Human Performance, 25*, 419–440.

Mitchell, T. R. (1979). Organizational behavior. *Annual Review of Psychology, 30*, 234–281.

Mitchell, T. R. (1982). Expectancy-value models in organizational psychology. In N. T. Feather (Ed.), *Expectations and actions: Expectancy value models in psychology* (pp. 125–160). Hillsdale, NJ: Lawrence Earlbaum Associates.

Powers, W. T. (1973). *Behavior: The control of perception*. Chicago: Aldine.

Steers, R. M., & Porter, L. W. (1974). The role of task–goal attributes in employee performance. *Psychological Bulletin, 81*, 434–452.

Terborg, J. R. (1976). The motivational components of goal setting. *Journal of Applied Psychology, 61*, 613–621.

Tubbs, M. E. (1986). Goal setting: A meta-analytic examination of the empirical evidence. *Journal of Applied Psychology, 71*, 474–483.

Winer, B. J. (1971). *Statistical principles in experimental design*. New York: McGraw-Hill.

4
Performance Quality and Work Motivation

Miriam Erez
Israel Institute of Technology

INTRODUCTION

Performance quality is becoming a crucial determinant of organizational competitiveness, and there is a growing interest on how to motivate employees to improve quality of products and services (Feigenbaum, 1983; Garvin, 1986; Peters & Waterman, 1982).

Quality refers to a degree of excellence of what is produced, and it can be clearly distinguished from quantity, which refers to the total amount of what is produced. Performance quality is commonly measured by the rate of correct responses that is the total number of responses minus the number of errors divided by the total number of responses. Such a ratio is useful in industry for comparative purposes, because one cannot measure different products in units of quality and compare them on an absolute scale (Feigenbaum, 1983; Jamieson, 1982).

Yet, motivational studies have focused mainly on performance quantity rather than quality. Goal-setting studies, specifically, have rarely set quality goals or dual goals of both quantity and quality (Latham & Lee, 1986; Locke, Shaw, Saari, & Latham, 1981).

The few goal-setting studies that have collected quality data have been summarized by Austin and Bobko (1985) and Latham and Lee (1986). These studies, however, have not assigned simultaneous goals of both quantity and quality. For example, Terborg and Miller (1978) specifically assigned three different types of goals—do best, quantity goals, and quality goals, to three groups of subjects who were required to assemble tinkertoy models. Results indicated that the highest level of performance quantity was obtained by subjects in the quantity goal condition, whereas subjects

53

in the quality goal condition obtained the highest level of performance quality.

Garland (1982) measured both performance quantity and quality, but he did not set specific quality goals. The task required subjects to list objects that could be described by a given adjective. Results indicated a significant effect of goal difficulty on performance quantity, but only a marginally significant effect on the number of errors.

Bavelas and Lee (1978) assigned quantity goals on two different tasks, and they measured both performance quantity and quality. Results indicated a quantity–quality tradeoff on both tasks; quality significantly decreased with level of goal difficulty.

The finding of Bavelas and Lee fits with the research in cognitive psychology that demonstrated a speed–accuracy tradeoff, where accuracy significantly decreases as speed increases.

The Speed-Accuracy Tradeoff and Motivation

The speed–accuracy tradeoff exemplifies the basic premise of cognitive psychology, that the human information processing is a system of limited resources (Navon & Gopher, 1979). According to Navon (1984), a resource is defined as "any internal input, essential for processing, that is available in quantities that are limited at any point in time." (p. 217). The process of encoding the stimulus and executing the response is time consuming. Therefore, time scarcity results in errors.

Reaction time and error rate represent two dimensions of the efficiency of processing information. The speed–accuracy operating characteristic demonstrates that maximum efficiency, which is the minimum cost in speed for increasing accuracy, has commonly been found in intermediate levels of speed–accuracy sets (Fitts, 1966; Hick, 1952; Howell & Kreidler, 1963, 1964; Pachella, 1974; Wickens, 1984).

Research on the speed–accuracy tradeoff is based on the assumption that subjects perform at their maximum capacity. However, two recent studies (Erez, Gopher, & Arzi, in press; Schmidt, Kleinbeck, & Brockman, 1984) proposed that motivational factors affect the total allocation of cognitive resources to two simultaneously performed tasks. Erez et al. (in press) found that self-set goals without monetary rewards had the greatest contribution to the dual-task performance (letter typing in right hand and digit classification in left hand). The lowest level of dual-task performance was obtained by subjects who were assigned goals without monetary rewards. Thus, motivational conditions had differential effects on the dual-task performance.

Schmidt et al. (1987) showed that goal specificity and difficulty had a significant effect on the allocation of cognitive resources. When two tasks were performed simultaneously, more resources were allocated to the task with a specific and difficult goal than to the one with no specific goal. The dual-task paradigm is similar to the speed–accuracy or quantity–quality paradigm, because in all these cases limited cognitive resources must be shared for the concurrent attainment of the goals.

Erez and Arad (1986) demonstrated that the trade-off relationship between performance quantity and quality can be affected by cognitive-motivational factors. For example, subjects who had more information on how to perform the task were less likely to reduce quality for an increase in quantity than the less informed subjects.

Expectancy of success is an additional factor that may affect the amount of resources to be allocated for the attainment of multiple goals such as both performance quantity and quality. According to expectancy theory (Vroom, 1964), action–outcome associations determine the force to perform an act. A person can be attracted to certain behavioral outcomes, but he/she would not take an action to obtain the outcomes unless the person has high expectations for action–outcome contingencies. Numerous studies have supported the effect of expectancies on behavioral choice, learning, and performance (e.g., Eden & Ravid, 1982; Erez, 1979; Heneman & Schwab, 1972; Mitchell & Beach, 1976)

The concept of self-efficacy (Bandura, 1982), which is related to expectancy, proposed that the behavior is affected by the belief of "how well one can execute courses of action required to deal with prospective situations" (p. 122). Individuals with high perceptions of self-efficacy set higher goals for themselves (Bandura & Cervone, 1986), exert more effort, show more persistence in task performance, and obtain higher levels of performance than individuals with low perceptions of self-efficacy (Bandura & Cervone, 1983; Cervone & Peake, 1986; Locke, Frederick, Lee, & Bobko, 1984).

Perhaps an increase in the motivational force to exert effort in performance activates the cognitive resources to be allocated for reaching the goal. Thus, in the quantity–quality paradigm, it is not necessary to attenuate quantity for improving quality when more resources are activated by high expectations. The quantity–quality trade-off is attenuated by the motivational factor of expectancy.

This study examines the motivational effects of goal setting and of expectancy of success on performance quantity, performance quality, and on the quantity–quality tradeoff. The effect of four goal-setting conditions was examined; do best, moderate, difficult, and self-set goals.

The following hypotheses were postulated:

1. General goals of "do your best" lead to lower performance than specific and difficult goals.

2. Goal difficulty will have a positive effect on performance quantity.

3. Quality will be negatively related to quantity for difficult but not for moderate goals.

4. High expectations to attain the goal (number of *correct* responses) attenuate the quantity–quality tradeoff. Namely, performance quantity increases with goal difficulty without any decrease in quality for the high-expectancy subjects. An increase in quantity is accompanied by a decrease in quality for the low-expectancy group.

5. Subjects with high expectations will set higher goals for themselves than others.

Method

Subjects. The sample consisted of 96 undergraduate engineering students from the Technion–Israel Institute of Technology. Seventy-three percent of the subjects were men and 27% were women. Ages ranged from 20 to 33 with an average of 24. Subjects were assigned at random to one of two experimental conditions. Each subject performed four experimental stages.

Design. The experiment was a 2 by 4 within-subject factorial design, consisting of two levels of the between factor, expectancy of success (high/normative), and four levels of the within factor, goal conditions in the following order: do best, moderate, difficult, and self-set goals.

Task. The task consisted of arithmetic problems, subtraction of two-figure numbers. The tens digit of the subtrahend was smaller than the tens digit of the minuend, and the units digit of the subtrahend was greater than the units digit of the minuend, for example, $73 - 58 = 15$. Each problem was used once only.

The experimental task was computerized so that all operations, instructions, exercise display, feedback, time control, experimental manipulation, and data collection were accomplished by computer.

Procedure. Subjects were randomly assigned to one of the two expectancy conditions (high and normative expectancy of success). Subjects were separated from each other by partitions and performed the task individually and interactively with the computer. All the experimental instructions appeared on the screen at the beginning of each experimental stage. Then, the arithmetic problems appeared on the screen one at a time. A problem disappeared as soon as the subject answered it by hitting the keyboard, and the following problem immediately appeared. Subjects were given three 90-second practice trials. The second trial served as an ability measure and the third trial as the do best goal condition. Following the do best condition the expectancy manipulation was introduced. There were three stages as follows: moderate goals, difficult goals, and self-set goals, consisting of three 90-second trials each. Instructions for setting the goals were given at the beginning of each stage (moderate, difficult, and self-set). Goal level and the expectancy condition continually appeared on the top left side of the screen. At the end of each trial, feedback was given on the top of the screen, indicating the number of total answers and the number of correct answers. At the beginning of each performance trial, subjects were questioned about their expectancy of success, perceived level of goal difficulty, and their goal commitment. The questions appeared on the screen one at a time and disappeared only after the subject answered it. At the end of the experiment subjects were debriefed.

Manipulation

Expectancy of Success. This was manipulated by assigning the subjects at random to one of two groups: high expectancy and normative expectancy. Subjects assigned to the high-expectancy group were given the following message on the display: "Your achievement in the practice trial has been compared to other groups' achievement and was found to be in the highest quarter (the top 25%). You can expect high achievement in the following stages as well. Therefore, you are classified in the category of high expectancy of success." Subjects assigned to the normative-expectancy group were given the following message on the display: "Your achievement in the practice trial has been compared to other groups' achievement and was found to be around average. You can expect a moderate level of achievement in the following stages as well. Therefore, you are classified in the category of moderate (normative) expectancy of success."

Goal Conditions. There were four stages. Each stage involved three 90-second trials. The stages were: (1) Practice trials—the third trial served as the do best condition; (2) assigned moderate goal of 17 correct answers in 90 seconds; (3) assigned difficult goal of 25 correct answers in 90 seconds; and (4) self-set goal, i.e., a goal selected by the subject.

Measures

Manipulation Check Questionnaire. Expectancy of success was measured by two items: "Relative to others, what level of performance do you expect to achieve?" and "What is your chance to accomplish the present goal?" The correlation between the two items was $r = .53$ (alpha $= .77$).

Perceived goal difficulty was measured by two items: "How difficult is the present goal for you?" and "If you could choose the time limit for the present goal yourself, how many seconds do you need to reach it?" Responses ranged on 9 points from 1 (50 seconds) to 9 (130 seconds). The Pearson correlation between the two items was $r = .34$ (alpha $= .42$).

Goal Commitment.   This was measured by two items: "Commitment to a goal means acceptance of it as your own personal goal and your determination to attain it. How committed were you to attaining the goal that was set?" and "To what extent did you strive to attain the goal that was set?" The Pearson correlation between the two items was $r = .70$ (alpha = .86). Responses for all items (except one) were measured on a 7-point Likert-type scale.

Ability.   Ability was measured by the performance in the second practice trial that lasted 90 seconds.

Performance.   Performance *quantity* for each stage was calculated by the average total number of answers in the three trials of the stage. Performance *quality* was measured by the ratio between the number of correct answers and the total number of answers. Thus,

$$\text{quality} = \frac{\text{number of correct answers} \times 100}{\text{total number of answers}}$$

Each step of the experiment lasted 90 seconds. Some subjects reached their goal in less than 90 seconds. Therefore, the *time left* from the moment the subjects reached their goal and the official termination time was measured. Thus, time left equaled 90 seconds minus—the actual duration of performing the goal.

The intercorrelations among the three performance measures were as follows: Performance quantity with quality $r = -.09$; with time left $r = .18$; Performance quality with time left $r = -.15$.

RESULTS

Manipulation Checks

Expectancy of Success and Goal Difficulty.   The expectancy, as measured by the manipulation check items, was significantly higher in the high- rather than the normative-expectancy group: ($\overline{X}$ Hi = 4.9 SD = 0.84, $\overline{X}$ Norm. = 4.48, SD = .76; $t = -2.37, p < .01$).

The perceived level of goal difficulty was significantly higher for the condition of objectively difficult than of moderate goals ($\overline{X}$ Diff. = 5.03, SD = 1.4, $\overline{X}$ Mod. = 3.9, SD = 1.26; $t = -9.39, p = .00$). In the moderate goal condition 57% of the subjects attained 17 answers, and 23% attained the goal of 17 correct answers. In the difficult goal condition 6.6% gave 25 answers and only 3% were able to attain 25 correct answers (thus, goals were challenging and very challenging).

Goal Commitment.   Goal commitment was significantly higher for the high-rather than the normative-expectancy groups ($\overline{X}$ Hi = 5.36, SD = 1.98,

$\overline{X}$ Norm. = 5.03, SD = 1.97, t = 1.96, p < .05), and for the moderate rather than difficult goals ($\overline{X}$ Mod. = 5.39, SD = 1.11, $\overline{X}$ Hi = 5.00, SD − 1.28, t = 2.27, p < .05). Goal commitment significantly correlated with subjects' expectancy of success, r = .45.

Goal commitment did not affect performance measures for moderate goals (p > .05). In the difficult goal condition, however, goal commitment was positively and significantly (p < .01) correlated with performance quantity (r = .29). The most significant correlations between goal commitment and performance measures were found for the self-set goals (quantity, r = .39; quality, r = .31; time left, r = − .36, < .002).

Goal Difficulty for Self-Set Goals. The absolute level of goal difficulty set by the high-expectancy subjects was not significantly different from the level of difficulty set by subjects in the normative-expectancy group ($\overline{X}$ Hi = 20.08, SD = 4.9; $\overline{X}$ Norm. = 18.96, SD = 6.3, t = − .97, p > .05). However, there was a significant effect of relative goal difficulty. This was measured by the discrepancy between the level of the self-set goal and performance level in the difficult goal condition. Results showed that the relative goals set by the high-expectancy subjects were significantly higher than the relative goals set by the normative expectancy group (relative goals: $\overline{X}$ Hi = 2.11, SD = 0.30; $\overline{X}$ Norm. = 0.05, SD = 0.36; t = 2.35, p < .05).

Performance in the Practice Trials. There was a significant difference between the first and second trials in mean performance scores, but there was no significant difference between the second and third trials ($\overline{X}_1$ = 13.55, SD = 4.88, $\overline{X}_2$ = 15.24, SD = 5.34, $\overline{X}_3$ = 15.57, SD = 4.19, $t(1\text{-}2)$ = 2.29, p < .05, $t(3\text{-}2)$ = 0.47, p < .52). The lack of a significant difference in performance between the second and third trials indicates that there was no improvement due to learning effect. Thus, performance in the following stages can be attributed to the manipulations.

Performance. The effects of expectancy and goal-setting condition on each of the performance measures were analyzed by repeated measures analysis of covariance (ANCOVA) using goal-setting conditions as the repeated factor and ability as the covariate. The homogeneity of the beta coefficients for the covariate (ability) was tested, and no significant differences were found among the groups.

The mean performance scores are summarized in Table 4.1, and the analyses of covariance are presented in Table 4.2.

Performance Quantity. The analysis of covariance (see Table 4.2a) demonstrated a significant effect of goal-setting conditions and no significant effect of expectancy. Using the Schefé test to compare the subgroups, there were significant differences between the do best and the difficult and self-set

TABLE 4.1
Means (SD in Parentheses) and Adjusted Means of Performance Criteria

Measures	Expectancy	Do Best Means	Adj. Means	Moderate Goal (= 17) Means	Adj. Means	Difficult Goal (= 25) Means	Adj. Means	Self-Set Goal Means	Adj. Means
Perf	Norm.	15.79	15.39	15.73	15.33	18.08	17.68	16.78	16.38
		(4.74)		(1.66)		(3.68)		(5.17)	
Quantity									
	High	15.02	15.42	15.38	15.78	17.29	17.69	17.31	17.71
		(3.80)		(2.32)		(3.63)		(4.04)	
Perf.	Norm.	84.37	84.50	90.14	90.27	87.62	87.75	86.19	86.33
		(17.00)		(7.00)		(11.00)		(16.00)	
Quality									
%	High	89.47	89.34	90.45	90.32	89.24	89.11	90.50	90.37
		(10.00)		(9.00)		(8.00)		(7.00)	
Time Left	Norm.	0.17	0.17	9.05	9.05	1.62	1.62	12.03	12.03
		(0.59)		(10.93)		(6.41)		(20.68)	
(secs.)									
	High	0.11	0.11	8.17	8.17	0.58	0.58	3.85	3.85
		(0.17)		(9.57)		(2.52)		(10.24)	

Perf. = Performance.
Norm = Normative.
Adj. = Adjusted.

goal conditions. In addition, there was significant difference between moderate and difficult goal conditions.

Performance Quality.   There was a significant main effect of expectancy of success on performance quality (Table 4.2b). Performance quality was significantly higher for subjects in the high-expectancy than the normative-expectancy group.

Time Left.   Results in Table 4.2d demonstrated two main effects of expectancy and goal-setting conditions. Time left by subjects in the high-expectancy group was significantly shorter than in the normative-expectancy group. The post-hoc contrasts showed that the time left in the moderate and self-set goal conditions was significantly longer than that in the do best and the difficult goal conditions. In addition, there was a significant interaction effect of expectancy and goal-setting treatments. Post-hoc contrasts analyses were conducted to further explain the interaction effect. Results showed that the largest difference between the two expectancy groups was in the self-set goal condition ($p < .001$). The next largest difference was in the difficult goal condition ($p < .07$). No significant differences were found in the moderate and do best conditions.

TABLE 4.2
Two-Way Analyses of Covariance of Performance by Expectancy of
Success and Goal-Setting Treatments

Measure	Source	DF	MS	F
a) Performance Quantity	Expectancy	1	19.51	1.96
	Goals	3	120.58	12.10***
	Expectancy X Goals	3	9.14	0.92
	Ability	1	1659.89	166.51***
	Error	375	9.97	
$R^2 = 0.36$				
b) Performance Quality	Expectancy	1	0.063	5.33*
	Goals	3	0.002	1.55
	Expectancy X Goals	3	0.012	1.02
	Ability	1	0.23	19.48***
	Error	375	1.00	
$R^2 = 0.08$				
c) Time Left	Expectancy	1	619.20	6.26**
	Goals	3	1895.67	19.16***
	Expectancy X Goal	3	343.67	3.48***
	Error	376	98.83	
$R^2 = 0.16$				

*$p < .05$.
**$p < .01$.
***$p < .001$.

The Quantity–Quality Tradeoff.   The Pearson correlations between performance quantity and quality are summarized in Table 4.3.

The overall correlation between performance quantity and quality was significantly negative ($r = -.43$). Additional analysis revealed differences be-

TABLE 4.3
Pearson Correlation Coefficients between Quantity and Quality

	Do Best Goals	Moderate Goals	Difficult Goals	Self-set Correlation	Overall
Normative expectancy	−.48*	.09	−.62**	−.79**	−.54**
High expectancy	.00	.15	−.07	.27	.09
Overall correlation	−.33*	.04	−.44**	−.71**	−.43**

*$p < .001$.
**$p < .0001$.

tween the experimental conditions in this correlation. A significant negative correlation was found for the normative-expectancy group ($r - .54$), but no significant correlation was found for the high-expectancy group ($r = .09$). The difference between the two correlations was significant ($z = 2.96, p < .001$).

A highly significant negative correlation between quantity and quality was found in the self-set condition ($r = -.71$), followed by the difficult goal ($r = -.44$) and the do best condition ($r = -.33$). No significant correlation was found for the moderate goal condition. These highest negative correlations were due entirely to the normative-expectancy group.

DISCUSSION

The findings of this study lead to three important conclusions: First, the motivational factor of expectancy of success positively and significantly affects performance quality; second, the trade-off relationship between quantity and quality is affected by motivational factors; high expectations attenuate the trade-off relationship, whereas lower levels of expectations increase the tradeoff between performance quantity and quality; third, the effect of expectancy is amplified when subjects self-set their goals.

The significant effect of expectancy can be explained by several factors: The high-expectancy subjects were more confident that they could reach their goal, which was set in terms of the number of correct responses and involved both quantity and quality criteria. Their expectancy score, as measured in the manipulation check, was higher than that of the normative-expectancy group; second, the high-expectancy subjects were more committed to their goals and, by implication, were more willing to exert effort in performance than the other group. Commitment was significantly related to the subjects' expectancy scores; third, they had a different time strategy compared to the normative group. The high-expectancy subjects have more fully used the time allotted to them for performing the task. The time left from the moment they reached their goal until the end of the 90 second trial was significantly less than the time left for the normative-expectancy group.

The superiority of the high-expectancy group in performance quality when goals were specifically set is consistent with Bandura's (1986) theory of self-efficacy. The individuals who are confident in their ability to obtain the goal expend more energy, as indicated by their commitment level, and develop better strategy planning than individuals who are less confident. The results support the author's argument that high expectations activate more cognitive resources that were required for obtaining the goal.

In addition to the expectancy effect, the goal-setting treatments were found to have differential effects on the quantity–quality tradeoff. The most significant tradeoff was in the self-set goal condition ($r = -.71$), followed by the difficult goal ($r = -.44$) and the do best ($r = -.33$) conditions. However, there was no quantity–quality tradeoff for moderate goals. The latter finding supports previous results (Pachella, 1974; Wickens, 1984).

Self-set rather than assigned goals facilitated the display of individual differences in the quantity–quality tradeoff. It seems that the cognitive judgments that individuals make of their success probability affect the goal they set for themselves, their time strategy, and their actual performance.

The level of goal difficulty chosen by subjects in the self-set condition was affected by their expectancy level. High-expectancy subjects set higher goals for themselves relative to their previous performance than normative-expectancy subjects. Thus, relative to their previous performance the high-expectancy subjects were more willing to exert effort than the other group. Similar results were found by Bandura and Cervone (1983, 1986).

Note that the sequence of goals might have affected the results of the self-set goals. Our main interest, however, was in the differences in the self-set goals between the high- and normative-expectancy groups.

Subjects in the "do best" condition showed a relatively low level of performance quantity but, at the same time, utilized nearly the whole time frame available for carrying out the task. In contrast, subjects in the moderate goal condition performed at a similar level but within a shorter time frame. One possible explanation suggests that the setting of goals activates the notion of time constraints. The awareness of time constraints resulted in a higher ratio of performance units per second in the moderate rather than in the general goal condition. Hence, subjects were more efficient in the moderate than the general goal condition.

Time and effort were considered to be the two resources that individuals can control to improve their performance. The two resources are better utilized when subjects have specific goals and high expectancy. The effect is most observable when subjects display their individual-difference characteristics in the self-set goal condition.

This study has interesting implications for the work setting. First, it indicates the importance of measuring performance quality independent of performance quantity. Second, it demonstrates the contribution of motivational factors to the improvement of productivity on both performance criteria. Third, it seems that the time strategy developed by subjects contributed to their effective performance on both criteria. Therefore, it is recommended that employees be trained in developing better strategies for using their time. Fourth, it seems that employees' attention on performance quantity and quality is affected by the nature of the instructions for setting the goals, and the nature of feedback on performance. When the two are defined in mixed terms of quantity and quality, such as the number of correct responses, subjects focus mainly on one criterion of performance quantity. Therefore, we suggest defining goals and feedback in terms of quantity and quality independently, in order to focus attention on both criteria. The latter recommendation should be examined further in future research.

ACKNOWLEDGMENTS

I would like to thank Mrs. Hanna Gavish for the data collection and analysis, and Mrs. Dalia Harel for the programming of the computerized task.

REFERENCES

Austin, J. R., & Bobko, P. (1985). Goal-setting theory: Unexplained areas and future research needs. *Journal of Occupational Psychology, 58*, 289–308.
Bandura, A. (1982). Self-efficacy mechanisms in human agency. *American Psychologist, 37*, 122–147.
Bandura, A. (1986). *Social foundation of thought and action: A social cognitive theory*. Englewood Cliffs, NJ: Prentice–Hall.
Bandura, A., & Cervone, D. (1983). Self-evaluative and self-efficacy mechanisms governing the motivational effects of goal system. *Journal of Personality and Social Psychology, 45*, 1017–1028.
Bandura, A., & Cervone, D. (1986). Differential engagement of self-reactive influences in cognitive motivation. *Organizational Behavior and Human Performance Processes, 38*, 92–113.
Bavelas, J., & Lee, E. S. (1978). Effects of goal level on performance: A trade-off of quantity and quality. *Canadian Journal of Psychology, 32*, 219–240.
Cervone, D., & Peake, P. K. (1986). Anchoring, efficacy and action: The influence of judgmental heuristics in self-efficacy judgments and behavior. *Journal of Personality and Social Psychology, 50*, 492–501.
Eden, D., & Ravid, G. (1982). Pygmalion versus self-expectancy: Effects of instructor and self-expectancy on trainee performance. *Organizational Behavior and Human Performance, 30*, 351–364.
Erez, M. (1979). Expectancy theory prediction of willingness to be retrained: The case of ratings advancement in the Israeli Merchant Navy. *Journal of Occupational Psychology, 52*, 35–40.
Erez, M., & Arad, R. (1986). Participative goal-setting: Social, motivational and cognitive factors. *Journal of Applied Psychology, 71*, 591–597.
Erez, M. Gopher, D., & Arzi, N. (in press). *Effects of self-set goals and monetary rewards on dual task performance. Organization Behavior and Human Decision Processes.*
Feigenbaum, A. V. (1983). *Total quality control*. New York: McGraw-Hill.
Fitts, P. M. (1966). Cognitive aspects of information processing III: Set for Speed versus Accuracy. *Journal of Experimental Psychology, 71*, 849–857.
Garland, H. (1982). Goal levels and task performance: A compelling replication of some compelling results. *Journal of Applied Psychology, 64*, 245–248.
Garvin, D. A. (1986). Quality problems, policies and attitudes in the United States and Japan: An exploratory study. *Academy of Management Journal, 29*, 653–673.
Heneman, H. G., & Schwab, D. P. (1972). An evaluation of research on expectancy theory: Prediction of employee performance. *Psychologycal Bulletin, 78*, 1–9.
Hick, V. E. (1952). On the rate of gain of information. *Quarterly Journal of Experimental Psychology, 4*, 11–26.
Howell, W. C., & Kreidler, D. L. (1963). Information processing under contradictory instructions set. *Journal of Experimental Psychology, 65*, 39–46.

Howell, W. C., & Kreidler, D. L. (1964). Instructional sets and subjective criterion levels in a cognitive information-processing task. *Journal of Experimental Psychology, 68*, 612–614.

Jamieson, A. (1982). *Introduction to quality circles*. Reston, VA: Reston.

Latham, G. P., & Lee, T. W. (1986). Goal setting. In E. A. Locke (Ed.), *Generalizing from laboratory to field settings* (pp. 101–118). Lexington, MA: Lexington Books.

Locke, E. A., Frederick, E., Lee, C., & Bobko, P. (1984). Effect of self-efficacy, goals and task strategies on task performance, *Journal of Applied Psychology, 69*, 694–699.

Locke, E. A., Shaw, K. N., Saari, L. M., & Latham, G. P. (1981). Goal setting and task performance: 1969–1980. *Psychological Bulletin, 90*, 125–152.

Mitchell, T. R., & Beach, L. R. (1976). A review of occupational preference and choice research using expectancy theory and decision theory. *Journal of Occupational Psychology, 49*, 231–248.

Navon, D. (1984). Resources—a theoretical soup stone? *Psychological Review, 91*, 216–234.

Navon, D., & Gopher, D. (1979). On the economy of the human processing system. *Psychological Review, 86*, 214–253.

Pachella, R. G. (1974). The interpretation of reaction time in information-processing research. In B. H. Kantowitz (Ed.), *Human information-processing* (pp. 41–82). Hillsdale, NJ: Lawrence Erlbaum Associates.

Peters, J. J., & Waterman, R. H. (1982). *In search of excellence*. New York: Harper & Row.

Schmidt, K. H., Kleinbeck, U., & Brockman, W. (1984). Motivational control of motor performance by goal-setting in a dual-task situation. *Psychological Research, 46*, 129–141.

Terborg, J. R., & Miller, H. E. (1978). Motivation behavior and performance: A closer examination of goal-setting and monetary incentives. *Journal of Applied Psychology, 63*, 29–39.

Vroom, V. (1964). *Work and motivation*. New York: Wiley.

Wickens, C. D. (1984). *Engineering psychology and human performance*. Columbus, OH: Charles E. Merril.

5
Intrinsic Motivation Reconsidered

Henk Thierry
University of Amsterdam
The Netherlands

INTRODUCTION

The concept of intrinsic motivation has gradually been accepted in our language. Although references in the literature date back to the 1920s, this concept became widely known among behavioral scientists through the work of Herzberg, Mausner, and Snyderman (1959) and Deci (1975). Today, intrinsic motivation also occurs in daily language, e.g., when somebody tries to explain the basic cause of a curious, not very common, leisure-time pursuit.

Yet, one may question whether this concept is as clear, unambiguous, and well founded as its frequent use suggests. Herzberg defined it quite differently from Deci. When various other theories use intrinsic or internal motivation, it appears that definitions given vary considerably and are usually very loose if not utterly vague. These qualifications also characterize the way in which this concept is used in practice, in particular in the areas of work and education.

But it is not the lack of clarity and unequivocality that concerns us primarily. The state of various other theories in the behavioral sciences is not basically different. Our main point is that intrinsic motivation as a concept is *scientifically untenable.* The very distinction between intrinsic and extrinsic motivation has blurred our understanding of human motivation, both in theory and in practice. It has caused many to conceive motivation as originating either "from within" the person or "from without." Actually, this implies that the well-known person–situation dilemma is considered in terms of a contrast, thus hampering further theorizing on the complex *in-*

teractions between personal and situational characteristics as they jointly determine human motivation. In practice it has led to the erroneous assumption that "external controls"—such as when deadlines are set, money is paid contingent on performance, and so forth—generally result in lower levels of (intrinsic) motivation.

In this chapter we first explore the colloquial use of intrinsic motivation. Then various definitions are given, based on a review of the literature. Subsequent to an appraisal of Deci's cognitive evaluation theory, some conclusions are made. Our main conclusion is that the differentiation between intrinsic and extrinsic motivation originates in a delusion.

INTRINSIC MOTIVATION: A FIRST EXPLORATION

When groups of people, like students, are asked to indicate what intrinsic motivation stands for, replies often show the following core element: "something from within, from the inner part of the person is causing some specific behavior to occur." Usually, this is equated to "internal" motivation. Opposite to this is extrinsic or "external" motivation. Now the cause for some specific behavior to occur is to be found "in something in the environment, external to the person." Thus, we recognize here the well-known "person–situation" subject area, but phrased in terms of a *contrast*: Behavior is caused either from within or from without.

This first, still rather global, qualification coincides rather well with the way in which these concepts are often used in practice. Intrinsic motivation would imply that a student at school or an employee in a company works *on his/her own force*. A teacher or a manager does not need to occupy her or himself with this. Actually, she or he would not be able to exert any influence, because one is or is not intrinsically motivated: It originates "within" the person. Extrinsic motivation would relate in particular with setting deadlines and with getting material and immaterial rewards. Both the student and the employee manifest a certain behavior, because they may get or avoid other outcomes in their "environment" that come within reach as an effect of the results of their behavior.

Thus, a second qualification should be mentioned: Extrinsic motivation implies an *instrumental* relationship between behavioral results and desired outcomes. The person is not vitally interested in his/her very behavior, but in particular in the outcome that results from it. Whoever wants to get a compliment from a specific somebody, in return for which some work has to be done (like completing schoolwork at home), is not focused on those tasks, but on the recognition she or he expects to receive from performing well.

Does this second qualification also bear on intrinsic motivation? Now problems occur. As we see in the next section, various definitions of intrinsic motivation stress that outcomes or rewards for a person are embedded *in* certain behaviors (e.g., Naylor, Pritchard, & Ilgen, 1980). Whoever performs well each time, in the example just given, without getting any compliment (or any other reward from "without"), considers performing well apparently to be motivating. A first problem is that this statement is tautological in nature: It holds that intrinsic motivation would reside in those behaviors that *are* apparently motivating; that is, of course, not acceptable. Another problem is that an activity—considered in itself—can never be an outcome, logically speaking. The activity must provide the person with something she or he needs or desires. The activity, whatever its nature, always *results* in some outcome. Yet, this very statement closely resembles the definition given previously of an instrumental ("extrinsic") relationship.

The last problem—an activity can never be its own outcome—has been recognized, taking several other definitions of intrinsic motivation into account. Intrinsic motivation would, according to another approach, consist of the *feelings* attached to or resulting from performing specified activities. Thus, intrinsically motivated people would be satisfied, happy, enjoy themselves, favor the things they do, and so forth. Again a problem crops up: Is satisfaction now conceptually similar to intrinsic motivation? If that is the case, how should extrinsic motivation be defined? There is no definition of the latter concept implying people to be dissatisfied, unhappy, and so on. But each definition of motivation—whether or not a distinction is being made between intrinsic and extrinsic types—does indeed state that a person strives for something that has not yet been reached or realized (e.g., Orlebeke, 1981; Petri, 1981; Thierry & Koopman-Iwema, 1984).

Still another qualification should be signaled: Often there is a *normative* component involved. Intrinsic motivation is frequently considered as being positive, good, constructive, "as it should be." Extrinsic motivation, on the contrary, has negative connotations: It is "allowed" as inevitable in the case of absence of intrinsic motivation, but in essence it is not constructive and of secondary importance. Extrinsic motivation shows that something is lacking or runs short: It is essentially a surrogate. Thus it is clear that intrinsic and extrinsic motivation are viewed as being opposite to one another. It seems moreover that a zero-sum notion is used. Both types of motivation are not occurring next to each other—let alone that the one may reinforce the other—but are embedded in a mutually compensatory relationship: More of one necessarily implies less of the other.

This initial discussion of ways in which the two concepts are frequently used in practice shows that the distinction between them is equivocal at best. This bears in particular on definitions of the concept of intrinsic motivation. In the next section the main literature on this topic is briefly reviewed.

INTRINSIC MOTIVATION: VARIOUS DEFINITIONS

Woodworth (1918) was among the first to advocate a line of thought that is akin to what is now called intrinsic motivation. He posited sensory, motor, and cognitive abilities as being energized by drives like curiosity and self-preservation, which activities may be *rewarding in themselves*. This latter theme returned 20 years later in Allport's (1937) concept of "functional autonomy": An activity or drive being instrumental in nature may acquire autonomous properties and act on its own behalf.

In the early 1950s various researchers emphasized, according to Heckhausen (1980), the concept of "self-reinforcement." Against the point of view (held by, e.g., Hull and Skinner) that behavior is exclusively determined by "external" reinforcement, they stated to have observed repeatedly that rats and monkeys perform all kinds of activities that are not drive reducing (Hull) in nature. Such behaviors tend to have a self-reinforcing effect, caused, for example, by a drive to explore. Koch (1956) thus expressed the hope that an "intrinsic grammar" might be developed, based on facts and models that would explain under which conditions animals as well as human beings continue to be involved with solving problems.

The preceding references to intrinsic motivation do embody several problems, but they at least show considerable convergence. Herzberg, Mausner, and Snyderman chose quite another avenue: They published (1959) the very well-known, and at once very controversial, "Two Factor Theory" on job motivation. Work satisfaction would be caused by factors quite different from those leading to job dissatisfaction. Satisfaction results, according to the theory, when a person performs well, carries some responsibility, earns promotion, and receives recognition. Consequently, she or he will experience opportunities for growth. These aspects of the work content are called *motivators* or intrinsic factors. A neutral or indifferent attitude occurs when one or more intrinsic factors are not more than partly fulfilled or even absent. Dissatisfaction on the other hand is caused by aspects of the work context, such as physical work conditions, social relations, and company policies. When these are not fulfilled, the person gets the experience of being blocked in his/her growth opportunities. These aspects are called extrinsic of *hygienic* factors: Again a neutral or indifferent attitude develops when these factors are adequately present.

This theory has inspired a great many researchers to test its hypotheses. The research results have caused the so-called "Herzberg controversy" to occur (cf. Thierry, 1969; Thierry & Drenth, 1971). Briefly summarized, the issue is at stake to which extent Herzberg's theory is method bound. Herzberg used a critical incident technique with an internal criterion (that is, chosen by each of his respondents). Data collected by means of less vulnerable methods show each time, however, that the theory is not sustained. For example, aspects of work content appear to strongly affect both satisfaction

TABLE 5.1
Definitions of Intrinsic Outcomes (Dyer & Parker, 1975)

	%
Derived directly from or inherent in the task of job itself—associated with the content of the task or job	35
Administered or mediated by the individual himself—internally mediated or self-reinforcing	24
Subjective or intangible—in the form of "feelings"	14
Satisfies higher order needs (Maslow)	8

and dissatisfaction. Yet, many practitioners (and some scientists) continue to believe in and support the theory, primarily because it encompassed a strong plea for job enrichment. It is obvious that a meaning quite different from those mentioned earlier has now been given to the concept of intrinsic motivation. It relates to features of the content of work, although it actually lumps together quite distinct issues: one's behavior (performance), behavior of others (recognition), and one's feelings (growth). Outcomes of factor analyses show, moreover, that work content variables load on different factors and not on one common "content" factor; analogous results apply to work context variables.

In the same year White (1959) defined the core component of (intrinsic) motivation in a way slightly similar to approaches mentioned in the beginning of this section. According to him, the "sense of competence" is vital: the feeling to cope effectively with one's environment. Ten years later De-Charms (1968) stated that human beings strive for "personal causation": They themselves want to be the cause of their behavior.

Against this background the results of Dyer and Parker's research (1975) should be interpreted. They administered a questionnaire to a random sample, specifically of members of the Society of Industrial and Organizational Psychology (Division 14) within the American Psychological Association. Their first question focused on how intrinsic and extrinsic outcomes ought to be defined. A content analysis with high interrater reliability showed the results on Tables 5.1 and 5.2.

Next the respondents were asked to classify 21 outcomes as either intrinsic or extrinsic. Examples included recognition, salary, and pride in work.

TABLE 5.2
Definitions of Extrinsic Outcomes (Dyer & Parker, 1975)

	%
Derived from the environment surrounding the task or work—associated with the context of the task or job	45
Administered or mediated by the organization or their agents—externally mediated	24
Objective or tangible—in the form of concrete objects or events	5

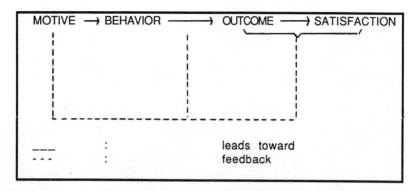

FIG. 5.1   Cycle of motivation (briefly summarized).

The results revealed very little agreement. Curiously enough, the highest levels of agreement occurred for two outcomes that were preceded by the term *feelings*, i.e., feelings of worthwhile accomplishment, and feelings of self-fulfillment. Both feelings were considered as intrinsic by the vast majority. Quite embarrassing for those who advocate a distinction between intrinsic and extrinsic motivation is that the respondents giving a similar reply to the first question varied as much in their responses to the second as did the others.

Considering the results in Tables 5.1 and 5.2, there is indeed some confusion of tongues. Respondents giving the first definition in both tables probably had Herzberg's theory in mind (work-content versus work-context aspects). The third definition in both tables—"subjective" versus "objective"—relates to the confusion signaled in the preceding section. Intrinsic outcomes would be identical to the feelings somebody has.

But not only intrinsic *outcomes* are equated with feelings. In the next section we see that intrinsic *motivation* also has been operationalized various times in terms of feelings. This view is untenable: This argument is based on the main components of the motivation cycle, which is very briefly summarized in Fig. 5.1. In this figure, only core components of the motivation cycle are included; conditioning and intervening variables have been left out of consideration. Human beings strive to satisfy various *motives* (needs and goals). Thus, they attempt to get specified outcomes that represent for them the motives pursued: for each motive separately a category of potential outcomes can be defined. To get actually one or more of these outcomes they manifest a certain *behavior*. *Outcomes* actually received provide them with more or less *satisfaction*, depending among other things on the effort they had to exert and the extent to which outcomes received coincide with what they aspired. This result—the relation between outcomes received and the degree of satisfaction—is fed back to both motive and behavior. Consequently, the cycle of motivation is repeated, or changes occur regarding prevailing motives and/or behaviors manifested.

If intrinsic motivation would be defined merely as a feeling, then only the last component in Fig. 5.1 is at stake. This means that intrinsic motivation would be identical to the *result* of the motivation cycle. Obviously, this cannot explain the very occurrence of the cycle; that is, how behavior gets motivated at all (see also Pritchard, Campbell, & Campbell, 1977).

The second definition in Tables 5.1 and 5.2—mediation of an outcome by the person him or herself or by anybody else—seems to offer a slightly better approach. If a woman conceives herself to be able to provide an outcome for certain behaviors—such as when she perceives, according to White, that she copes effectively with her environment—then such an *outcome* might be called intrinsic. Yet, this offers no definition or explanation of intrinsic *motivation*. Has the individual the impression that the outcome for certain behaviors is provided by somebody else, then this outcome might be called extrinsic.

This *formal* definition is in itself acceptable. It implies that the determining factor for categorizing an *outcome* as intrinsic (or extrinsic) would merely be the source that is providing the outcome *according to the person's view*. Nonetheless, it is questionable whether we have gained more insight into the content of the intrinsic–extrinsic distinction, the more because it is hardly possible to determine beforehand which outcomes belong to which category (cf. Dyer & Parker, 1975). And again, there is still no basis to define unequivocally the concept of intrinsic *motivation*.

In conclusion, Heckhausen's (1980) classification is presented. It is easy to recognize several approaches touched on earlier. According to him, there are at least six different conceptualizations of intrinsic motivation:

1. It relates to a *drive*. Resulting activities are not aimed at drive reduction or at achieving homeostasis.

2. It refers to all activities having *no goal*, like playing. It relates to behavioral actions per se, to the activities involved in coping effectively with one's environment (cf. White), and so forth. When a goal is being pursued, then extrinsic motivation is at stake.

3. It concerns behavior that aims at achieving the maintenance or the reinstallment of an *optimal operation level*, such as arousal (Hebb, 1955), incongruence of informational input (Berlyne, 1960), or adaptation (Helson, 1964).

4. It is the feeling of *personal causation* (DeCharms, 1968), separately or in combination—as Deci (1975) states—with the feeling of competence (White, 1959).

5. It is the *enjoyment* in an action, being fully involved, the feeling of being embedded in a stream (Czikszentmihalyi, 1975).

6. It refers to a *common denominator* between the means (behavior) and the goal (Heckhausen, 1980), such as when goals of performance relate to the very performance or to one's level of competence.

In this overview, the most important descriptions and definitions of intrinsic outcomes and of intrinsic motivation have been described. However, several approaches were not mentioned at all, such as when authors define the meaning of "intrinsic" in terms of what it is *not*. An example would be: There is no apparent external cause for somebody's behavior discernible, as an effect of which that behavior is intrinsically motivated. We meet this kind of reasoning in the next section. Yet we have to conclude that an unambiguous definition of intrinsic *motivation* has still to be found, although it is possible to define intrinsic *outcomes* in a strictly formal manner. But before recommendations are given, we highlight major issues of one of the very well-known motivation theories developed during the past 15 years, namely Deci's cognitive evaluation theory.

COGNITIVE EVALUATION THEORY

Deci (1975, Deci & Porac, 1978) took his point of departure in the link Lepper construed between DeCharms' concept of personal causation and Bem's self-perception theory (1972). When somebody likes to perform an activity and is moreover being rewarded for that, overjustification can occur. The person questions whether she or he was performing at his/her own "free will"; thus the level of (intrinsic) motivation decreases. But if a reward that was announced or received earlier is not provided, the level of (intrinsic) motivation can increase. Underjustification is now the result; dissonance reduction may explain why motivation will become stronger.

According to Deci, human beings have two basic, survival-oriented needs: the need for Competence and the need for Self-Determination. Each person looks for situations that challenge him/her to a certain extent, which challenge she or he tries to meet. Intrinsically motivated behavior may be defined as *the behavior a person chooses to feel competent and self-determining*. Every now and then primary drives—like those associated with hunger and thirst—will interrupt these behavioral cycles. If a contingent financial reward is tied to intrinsically motivated behavior, then the locus of causality, according to Deci, will change. The person does not ascribe the cause of his/her behavior any more to him or herself, but to the external source. Consequently, the level of intrinsic motivation will decrease. Why is this so? Each outcome has two components, as Deci indicated: a *controlling* and an *informational* component. The first one is involved with respect to a contingent financial reward: A source external to the person indicates what is and what is not wanted and thus "controls" behavior. The second component prevails in the case of a contingent verbal reward, at least with males: Feedback provided relates to the extent of competence and self-determination. This causes an increase in intrinsic motivation. With females words of praise lead to some dependence of the "speaker," and thus to less intrinsic motivation. Deci did not offer any explanation for this phenomenon.

This theory received much attention, in particular because of the hypothesis—in addition to what was stated earlier concerning over-justification—that a contingent financial reward *reduces* the level of in-trinsic motivation. Expectancy theory (Vroom, 1964) would predict that ex-trinsic and intrinsic outcomes operate next to each other and relate mutu-ally *additive*. Operant conditioning theory (Skinner) predicts a *positive interaction* effect to occur: both outcomes may reinforce one another. It is obvious that if Deci's theory gets support and is tenable various forms of payment by results systems—in particular those in which performance is re-warded frequently—should not be applied to tasks with a high quality of work (which "stimulate" intrinsically motivated behavior to occur). Setting deadlines and administering regular tests of school performance might also have a negative impact on the level of intrinsic motivation.

Parts of cognitive evaluation theory were tested meanwhile in laboratory settings (overviews in Boal & Cummings, 1981; Deci & Ryan, 1985; Lepper & Greene, 1978: Thierry & Koopman-Iwema, 1981; Vinke, 1985). Typically, each subject gets a series of puzzles to be solved in the first session. Having acquired some experience, an intermission is announced. The experimenter leaves the room and observes the subject by means of a monitor, a one-way screen, etc. During intermission the subject may do what she or he prefers to do: read a newspaper or journal, smoke a cigarette, solve more puzzles, and so forth. Behavior during intermission is vital, according to Deci: If the subject opts for solving more puzzles, then she or he is intrinsically mo-tivated. If she or he engages in any other behavior during intermission, then the level of intrinsic motivation is interpreted as low and that of extrin-sic motivation as high. In the second session subjects in the experimental condition are instructed that they will get money for each puzzle solved (contingent financial), or they will be told how well they did (contingent verbal), or that they will receive a certain amount of money after having solved all tasks (noncontingent financial), and so forth. After some time again an intermission takes place: The results show, according to Deci, that subjects work on the puzzles less during the second intermission if contin-gent financial rewards had been supplied before.

However, Koopman-Iwema (1982) found that in Deci's first experiments the provision of contingent financial rewards resulted in more motivation, contrary to what Deci has stated, than in the control condition. When a distinction is made between interesting and uninteresting tasks (e.g., Ham-ner & Foster, 1975), remarkable results occur. Subjects working on an inter-esting task increased their performance under the condition of contingent pay, whereas the degree of interest for their task did not change. First, both outcomes are not in agreement with Deci's theory. Second, both measures of intrinsic motivation (an objective and a subjective one) apparently do not capture the same thing.

When we summarize the main research outcomes gained during the past 13 years, the following conclusions result (e.g., Boal & Cummings, 1981):

1. The theory as a whole has not been tested in any experiment; only parts of the theory have been subjected to tests.
2. Giving a noncontingent financial reward causes different results to occur. In the case of interesting tasks, the level of intrinsic motivation decreases in various cases, which is in opposition to the prediction based on Deci's theory.
3. Some reservation should be taken into account with respect to the (exclusively for male respondents) positive relationship between verbal rewards and intrinsic motivation.
4. The withdrawal of extrinsic rewards may lead, as Deci predicts, to more intrinsic motivation.

Consequently, there is not so much support for Deci's theory (see also Bandura, 1977). The fourth point is indeed in agreement with the theory, but it may be equally well explained in terms of cognitive dissonance reduction. More seriously, the theory as a whole has never been subject to test. Locke and Henne (1986) express some severe shortcomings: Not a single study provides direct evidence for the full Deci model or even substantial parts of it. Almost the entire theory is based on weak inference and indirect evidence; the claim that money—when controlling—undermines intrinsic motivation is a seriously misleading description of the studies; the theory does not distinguish intrinsic motivation—i.e., the desire for competence and self-determination—from motivation based on the pleasure of the activity itself.

Vinke (1985) conducted two laboratory experiments, confronting hypotheses originating from Deci's theory with those based on reinforcement processes. He gave his respondents—among others students of the Royal Military Academy—"mind benders" as tasks to solve. Mind benders are puzzles in small plastic boxes within which, for instance, a marble has to be put, by moving the box appropriately, in a specified position. Per puzzle a maximum of 1 minute was allowed. On the basis of the results of an extensive pilot study, three categories of mind benders could be distinguished: interesting, neutral, and dull tasks. Next to the control condition various experimental conditions were imposed: contingent financial reward (after each task); noncontingent financial reward (after each session); contingent verbal reward; noncontingent verbal reward; withdrawal of each experimental condition for half the respondents during the last session. Many variables have been measured repeatedly. Unfortunately, results indicate "mixed evidence": Neither of the two theories received unambiguous support. A second experiment is now running.

Many researchers have criticized the way intrinsic motivation has been *operationalized* by Deci and by others. Measures include: task interest (the subject's response to one or more questionnaire items); satisfaction, e.g., with the task (one or more questionnaire items); performance during puzzle sessions (an objective measure); a free choice to continue with the task after the very experiment is over: the intention to continue (as indicated on a questionnaire) and/or actual performance behavior (an objective measure); performance behavior during an intermission (an objective measure).

Results of various studies show that correlations between these measures are often very low. For instance, Vinke (1985) found high correlations among three successive measures of task interest and among successive measures of performance during intermission, but hardly between both types of measure (cf. Shing & Lorenzi, 1983). Also low correlations occurred between satisfaction, performance during puzzle sessions, and the intention to continue puzzling after the experiment.

Here we meet again the problem signaled in previous sections: How should we define and operationalize intrinsic motivation? Earlier we voiced objections against criteria such as satisfaction and task attitudes; these may be taken as components of a cycle of (intrinsic) motivation, but they cannot represent the very concept. At least it is necessary to have behavioral indices. This leads us to the criterion used by Deci and by several other researchers: performance (on puzzles) during an intermission.

Locke and Henne (1986) wonder how this behavior may provide for a valid indication of the need for competence, which need is, as Deci states, fundamental. Various other authors hold that criterion behavior ought to be measured *during* work on tasks when one is supposed to be intrinsically motivated, and not during a free time period. In our view, there is still another tricky problem. Essentially, an *inverse argument* is being given. Whoever, in Deci's terms, makes a free choice among various activities and opts for solving puzzles without the existence of any (observable) external cause to do so "must" be intrinsically motivated. The conclusion is made that a specific reason causes the behavior concerned—the person wants to feel her or himself competent and self-determining—because another reason is not monitored. Of course, the researcher observes a certain behavior, but she or he appears not to be able to locate an external source impacting on that behavior. Thus, intrinsic motivation is being defined in terms of what it is not. How valid is this interpretation?

EVALUATION

One may argue that researchers who ascribe the causes of a specific behavior of their subjects to processes occurring "within" each person *because* external stimuli cannot be monitored are jumping to a conclusion. At least, it is needed to specify under which terms one may conclude that external stimuli are absent. Otherwise, a major counterargument would be that the situational characteristics pertaining to motivated—indeed puzzling, curious, challenged—subjects have not been analyzed at all. Thus, the plausibility of the researchers' argument would considerably increase when the conditions on the basis of which they conclude intrinsic motivation to be operative would be clearly different from those leading them to conclude that extrinsic motivation is at stake. Now Lawler's extensive review (1976) shows that *similar* conditions facilitate the occurrence of intrinsic and extrinsic motivation. These are: fast feedback about the quality of task performance, both during the performing and about the end result; increasing the amount of self-control; structuring the task in terms of adequate individual autonomy with norms set rather high, as an effect of which the task is perceived as challenging.

Taking these conditions, a (work)situation may thus in principle be made *more or less fit* to the occurrence of intrinsic and extrinsic motivation. In other words, by means of "external" interventions more or less (intrinsic) motivation will result. Such a "situational engineering" is quite an essential point of view in various theories focusing on increasing levels of (intrinsic) motivation, such as Hackman and Oldham's Job Characteristics Model (1980). According to this model, redesigning jobs along the lines of five core job characteristics will result among other things in higher "internal" work motivation by means of affecting some critical psychological states (see also Algera's chapter, this book).

We now want to draw a few conclusions. First, there is no good argument to infer from a specific behavior occurring during experimentally induced intermissions, that (more or less) intrinsic motivation exists. Second, it is logically contradictory that extrinsic interventions may affect—increase or decrease—the level of intrinsic motivation (that implies at least that there are no external causes). Consequently, is the distinction between extrinsic and intrinsic motivation still defendable?

To clarify this issue, we return once more to Deci's thesis: Tying a contingent financial reward to intrinsically motivated behavior causes the locus of causality to change from "within" to "without," because something or somebody else is controlling that behavior. How exactly does this process take place? Deci and Lepper and Greene indicate that this is still not quite clear. Unfortunately, recent changes made in cognitive evaluation theory (cf. Deci and Ryan, 1985) have made the theory untestable. Pritchard et al. (1977) emphasize that external events do not affect the level of intrinsic motivation directly, but in an indirect manner, that is, by means of effecting change in one or more determinants of intrinsic motivation. Collar and Barrett (1987) found that the cognitive labels associated with a task, i.e., scripts like "work" or "play," may impact on intrinsic motivation.

Let us assume, as an example, that a female employee is absorbed in performing certain activities for a long time, also in her free time, and that her behavior may be called intrinsically motivated. Somebody contacts her and makes the offer that after having accomplished the task she is currently engaged with, one of the chairs in her room will get a better cover. Successful accomplishment of the next task will get her a second chair nicely covered, and so forth, subsequent to which the carpet will be replaced, etc. How will our intrinsically motivated worker react? Possibly she will like the offer, but more likely she will refuse it, perhaps being slightly irritated. Covers of chairs are quite uninteresting to her, or she takes the stand that such benefits are to be considered as general provisions that should not be related to the quality of her performance. In other words, although this outcome is quite convertable in terms of money, not each extrinsic outcome is affecting behavior (cf. Phillips & Freedman, 1985). At least it is necessary that the employee *values* the outcome and that the outcome is to some extent *meaningful* in the context within which the task is being performed (cf. Kruglanski et al., 1975). Assume that later on a specified amount of money is offered to her for each task performed. Let us suppose that our employee now gets interested, because a slightly higher income has various meanings to her. What will happen? Will she stop working in her free time, or will she work differently? That is not very likely, assuming that the employee expects that a specified performance will result in a specific bonus. Our employee values the bonus, although the very standards for successful performance have not been changed. Consequently, the researcher needs to have two independent measures: one for the level of intrinsic motivation, the other for the level of extrinsic motivation.

When the "locus," as Deci states, shifts toward the bonus—or better, towards the person or office that provides the reward—then extrinsic motivation will be stronger and intrinsic motivation will be weaker. In the case the person thinks it attractive to be also financially rewarded for absorbing work, both types of motivation will be strong. As it is assumed that the bonus is attractive to the person and that accomplishment of the task will lead to more pay, it is very unlikely to expect that extrinsic motivation will be low.

What may be learned from Deci's empirical data in this respect? Actually nothing: It is remarkable that there is *no research* whatsoever known to us, in which an independent measure of extrinsic motivation has been included. Effects have been analyzed of providing (or withdrawing) an extrinsic outcome on the level of intrinsic motivation. It is assumed in this respect that a decrease of intrinsic motivation would coincide with a comparable increase of extrinsic motivation. That leads to impossible consequences. Would it be possible to measure extrinsic motivation at all in the experiments reviewed and in our example just mentioned? The answer is, only in terms of the *same* behavior that is at stake concerning intrinsic motivation: performing tasks (e.g., making puzzles), whether or not during an intermission. Thus, the distinction extrinsic–intrinsic has become meaningless.

This leads, as we see it, to an unavoidable conclusion: There is neither intrinsic nor extrinsic motivation. The very distinction resides in a delusion. Psychologists should try to analyze, explain, and predict determinants of individual behavior. When subjects ascribe the causes of some behavior to something within or without themselves, that event may be psychologically interesting. But it can never offer an adequate answer to the issue of behavioral determinants. The intrinsic–extrinsic motivation distinction resides in a *naive* psychology.

We plead therefore for skipping both motivational concepts and, consequently, this terminology. Research on motivation (e.g., in work settings) is still very much needed. But motivation should be considered as affected by both personal and situational characteristics, which relate *interactively* to one another and not as simple opposites. As indicated earlier, a formal use of the words intrinsic and extrinsic *outcomes* may be justifiable as far as the subject's perception is meant whether causes of his/her behavior reside in him/herself or in the environment. We question however whether this distinction is theoretically worthwhile.

SUMMARY

Concepts like intrinsic and extrinsic motivation have gained a certain popularity, both in the literature and in practice. A closer analysis of the latter usage indicates that the well-known person–situation dilemma is at stake. Definitions of intrinsic motivation in the literature reveal various contradictory points of view as well as a lot of ambiguity. Then, Deci's cognitive evaluation theory is scrutinized as well as relevant major research findings. The main statement of this contribution holds that the intrinsic–extrinsic motivation distinction is based on a delusion and ought to be skipped accordingly.

ACKNOWLEDGMENTS

The author gratefully acknowledges the critical comments made by Robert D. Pritchard, Joan L. Meyer, and an unknown reviewer on an earlier draft.

REFERENCES

Allport, G. W. (1937). *Personality: A psychological interpretation*. New York: Holt.
Bandura, A. (1977). *Social learning theory*. Englewood Cliffs, NJ: Prentice-Hall.
Berlyne, D. E. (1960). *Conflict, arousal and curiosity*. New York: McGraw-Hill.
Boal, K. B., & Cummings, L. L. (1981). Cognitive evaluation theory: An experimental test of processes and outcomes. *Organizational Behavior and Human Performance, 28*, 289–310.
Collar, D. F., & Barrett, G. V. (1987). Script processing and intrinsic motivation: The cognitive

sets underlying cognitive labels. *Organizational Behavior and Human Decision Processes, 40*, 115-135.

Czikszentmihalyi, M. (1975). *Beyond boredom and anxiety*. San Francisco: Jossey-Bass.

DeCharms, R. (1968). *Personal causation*. New York: Academic Press.

Deci, E. L. (1975). *Intrinsic motivation*. New York: Plenum Press.

Deci, E. L., & Porac, J. (1978). Cognitive evaluation theory and the study of human motivation. In M. R. Lepper & D. Greene (Eds.), *The hidden costs of rewards*. New York: Wiley.

Deci, E. L., & Ryan, R. M. (1985). *Intrinsic motivation and self-determination in human behavior*. New York: Plenum Press.

Dyer, L., & Parker, D. F. (1975). Classifying outcomes in work motivation research: An examination of the intrinsic–extrinsic dichotomy. *Journal of Applied Psychology, 60*, 455-458.

Hackman, J. R., & Oldham, G. (1980). *Work redesign*. Reading, MA: Addison-Wesley.

Hamner, W. C., & Foster, L. W. (1975). Are intrinsic and extrinsic rewards additive: A test of Deci's cognitive evaluation theory of task motivation. *Organizational Behavior and Human Performance, 14*, 398-415.

Hebb, D. O. (1955). Drives and the C.N.S. *Psychological Review, 62*, 243-254.

Heckhausen, H. (1980). *Motivation und handeln*. Heidelberg: Springer-Verlag.

Helson, H. (1964). *Adaptation-level theory*. New York: Harper & Row.

Herzberg, F., Mausner, B., & Snyderman, B. B. (1959). *The motivation to work*. New York: Wiley.

Koch, S. (1956). Behavior as "intrinsically" regulated: Work notes toward a pretheory of phenomena called "motivational." In M. R. Jones, (Ed.), *Nebraska Symposium on Motivation 1956*. Lincoln: University of Nebraska Press.

Koopman-Iwema, A. M. (1982, June). De puzzel van het prestatieloon: Arbeidsgedrag en motivatie [The puzzle of incentive payment: Motivation and behavior at work]. *Psychologie*, 15-21.

Kruglanski, A. W., Riter, A., Amitai, A., Margolin, B., Shabtai, L., & Zaksh, A. D. (1975). Can money enhance intrinsic motivation? *Journal of Personality and Social Psychology, 31*, 744-750.

Lawler, E. E. (1976). Control systems in organizations. In M.D. Dunnette (Ed.), *Handbook of industrial and organizational psychology*. Chicago: Rand McNally.

Lepper, M. R., & Greene, D. (Eds.) (1978). *The hidden costs of rewards*. New York: Wiley.

Locke, E. A., & Henne, D. (1986). Work motivation theories. In C. L. Cooper & I. Robertson, *International review of industrial and organizational psychology 1986*. New York: Wiley.

Naylor, J. C., Pritchard, R. D., & Ilgen, D. R. (1980). *A theory of behavior in organizations*. London: Academic Press.

Orlebeke, J. F. (1981). Motivatie [Motivation]. In J. F. Orlebeke, P. J. D. Drenth, R. H. C. Janssen, & C. Sanders (Eds.), *Compendium van de psychologie, deel IV*. Muiderberg: Coutinho.

Petri, H. L. (1981). *Motivation: Theory and research*. Belmont: Wadsworth.

Phillips, J. S., & Freedman, S. M. (1985). Contingent pay and intrinsic task interests: Moderating effects of work values. *Journal of Applied Psychology, 70*, 306-313.

Pritchard, R. D., Campbell, K. M., & Campbell, D. J. (1977). Effects of extrinsic financial rewards on intrinsic motivation. *Journal of Applied Psychology, 62*, 9-15.

Shing-Yung Chang, G., & Lorenzi, P. (1983). The effects of participative versus assigned goal setting on intrinsic motivation. *Journal of Management, 9*, 55-64.

Thierry, Hk. (1969). *Arbeidsinstelling en prestatiebeloning* [Job attitudes and incentive payment]. Utrecht: Het Spectrum.

Thierry, Hk., & Drenth, P. J. D. (1971). De toetsing van Herzbergs "two-factor"-theorie. [Testing Herzberg's "two factor" theory]. In P. J. D. Drenth, P. J. Willems, & Ch.J. de Wolff (Eds.)., *Bedrijfspsychologie: Onderzoek en evaluatie* [Industrial psychology: Research and evaluation]. Deventer: Van Loghum Slaterus.

Thierry, Hk., & Koopman-Iwema, A. M. (1981). *De rol van intrinsieke en extrinsieke motiva-*

tie in het arbeidsgedrag [The role of intrinsic and extrinsic motivation in behavior at work]. Universiteit van Amsterdam: Arbeids- en Organisatiepsychologie.

Thierry, Hk., & Koopman-Iwema, A. M. (1984). Motivation and satisfaction. In P. J. D. Drenth, Hk. Thierry, P. J. Willems, & Ch.J. de Wolff (Eds.), *Handbook of work and organizational psychology*. Chichester, England: Wiley.

Vinke, R. H. W. (1985). *Intrinsieke en extrinsieke motivatie in het arbeidsgedrag* [Intrinsic and extrinsic motivation in work behavior]. Eindverslag ZWO-onderzoek. Universiteit van Amsterdam: Arbeids- en Organisatiepsychologie.

Vroom, V. H. (1964). *Work and motivation*. New York: Wiley.

White, R. W. (1959). Motivation reconsidered: The concept of competence. *Psychological Review, 66*, 297-333.

Woodworth, R. S. (1918). *Dynamic psychology*. New York: Columbia University Press.

Part II
Design Principles
for Improving
Work Motivation

In the area of work motivation there are numerous empirical findings in support of theoretical and methodological advances in applied research. Moreover, substantial technological developments have been made in the last years. Today we know much more about the effectiveness of motivation techniques, for example, how to change the motivating potential in organizations in order to make work more interesting and effective. Hackman and Oldham have contributed substantially to this knowledge and progress through their Job Characteristics Model. J. Algera has reviewed important studies on this model and has summarized their findings. He explains which parts of the model are valid and supported by empirical evidence and where further investments are needed. In sum, this chapter shows possible practical applications of the model when designing motivation principles in organizations.

Further motivation techniques can be derived from looking at the goal setting model in the context of achievement behavior. The field study of Kleinbeck and Schmidt done in a manufacturing department of an electronics company demonstrates that employees are much better in organizing the working hours when they can use a computer system that provides them with a feedback on their actual performance level with reference to the production goals. Beyond the evidence of an improved work situation the study shows a decrease in psychological stress and strain as a consequence of motivation techniques.

Pritchard also uses the concepts of goal-setting and feedback as a basis for his approach. He shows that the measurement of production indices with regard to concrete goals and specific kinds of financial incentives goes along with a substantial increase in effectiveness as well as an increase in productivity.

The development and application of motivation techniques needs good managers. Graen has pointed this out in his contribution. He has developed a dyadic role concept of management getting support from findings in social psychology. This model of planning productive management systems outlines how such a system can be developed and how it can be used to increase productivity.

The last two chapters of Part II deal with absenteeism. Quast, Kleinbeck, and Stachelhaus provide evidence for a clear relationship between such variables as motivating potential, instrumentality of absence behavior, and times of absence. Latham and Frayne have developed techniques to reduce absenteeism. They present an intervention program to increase the self management of employees with regard to their own attendance behavior. The results of the intervention program shows that attendance in a company is determined by motivational factors and that this training is effective in changing work motivation.

6

The Job Characteristics Model of Work Motivation Revisited

Jen A. Algera
Eindhoven University of Technology, Eindhoven, The Netherlands
and
Hoogovens Steel Works, IJmuiden, The Netherlands

INTRODUCTION

About 20 years ago Turner and Lawrence (1965) published their book, *Industrial jobs and the worker: An investigation of response to task attributes*. This study focused on characteristics of the job content as the determinant of behavior and attitudes of the work performer. Although the researchers were aware of the many possible intervening variables between task attributes and worker responses, they tried to make the "risky leap" between these two classes of variables. The definitions of the variables in this study, in particular regarding the task attributes, can be considered as the origins of the variables in the Job Characteristics Model (JCM). This model proposed by Hackman and Oldham (1975, 1976, 1980) has led to much empirical research. A set of measuring instruments, the Job Diagnostic Survey (JDS), is available to measure the variables in the model. The model states that motivation, satisfaction, and work performance are achieved when three "critical psychological states" (i.e., experienced meaningfulness of the work, experienced responsibility for outcomes of the work, and knowledge of the results) are present in the individual. Five "core job dimensions" (skill variety, task identity, task significance, autonomy, and job feedback) are supposed to influence these critical psychological states. Various individual-difference variables (e.g., growth need strength) are conceived as moderator variables of the relationships between job dimensions—critical psychological states and critical psychological states—personal and work outcomes. In addition, the five core job dimensions can also be combined by means of a multiplicative formula to a single score, called motivating potential score (MPS), which is an indication of

85

job complexity. The JDS and the model are for the explicit purpose of task redesign.

The Job Characteristics Model can be viewed as belonging to the "task characteristics approach" (see Fleishman & Quaintance, 1984). In this approach tasks are considered as a set of conditions that are imposed on the task performer. This viewpoint indicates that tasks are described in terms of their objective, intrinsic properties. Task characteristics are seen as the independent variables that influence the work behaviors and attitudes we wish to predict. Fleishman and Quintance (1984) review a number of taxonomies based on the task characteristics approach. The studies of Farina and Wheaton (1973) are probably the most representative for this approach. They considered five intrinsic task components: an explicit goal, procedures, input stimuli, responses, and stimulus–response relationships. Each component contains certain salient characteristics, e.g., degree of operator control (component stimulus–response relationship). In the area of predicting work behavior and work attitudes from task characteristics, the Job Characteristics Model has generated by far the most research and discussion. In this chapter we present this model and evaluate its worth as a guide for job redesign in practice.

REVIEW OF THE EMPIRICAL RESEARCH

As stated before the JCM has stimulated much empirical research. In the early 1980s two reviews appeared (Aldag, Barr, & Brief, 1981; Roberts & Glick, 1981) and more recently four meta-analysis studies have been published (Fried & Ferris, 1987; Loher, Noe, Moeller, & Fitzgerald, 1985; Spector, 1985; Stone, 1986). However, these reviews and meta-analyses often focus more or less on specific issues associated with the model, such as the psychometric properties of the measuring instruments (Aldag et al., 1981) or the moderating effects of some variables as suggested by the model (Spector, 1985). In this chapter we limit ourselves to the major issues of the earlier reviews. Intervention strategies on the basis of the model are also discussed. From that point of view the question is rather what can bring about a change in job characteristics. Stated otherwise, job characteristics are considered as dependent variables in that case.

Objective or Perceived Job Characteristics

Probably the most critical discussions concerning the JCM have centered around the issue of objectivity of the job characteristics. In the original study by Turner and Lawrence (1965), task attributes were considered as primarily determined by technology: "By task attributes, we meant such characteristics of the job as the amount of variety, autonomy, responsibility and interaction with others built into its design" (p. vi). Although they also measured task perceptions by job incumbents as an additional variable, in their design task attributes were seen as objective properties of tasks and measured by judgments of the researchers on the basis of observations and interviews with the supervisor. In more recent studies, however, job characteristics are measured mostly by the perceptions of the job incumbents. This is consonant with statements by Hackman and Lawler (1971) and Hackman and Oldham (1975, 1976, 1980). In their view the perceptions of job characteristics are the major determinants of behavior and attitude of job incumbents. But, on the other hand, job perceptions are seen as reflections of objective characteristics of jobs that can be changed in job redesign. This dilemma is nicely illustrated by Hackman and Oldham (1980): "Yet the job characteristics model in its present form does not differentiate between objective and perceived properties of tasks, and it is not known whether the motivational benefits of enriched work derive primarily from objective task characteristics [even if those characteristics are not perceived by the performer] or from employee perceptions of task characteristics [even if those perceptions are influenced by nonjob factors]" (p. 97).

The issue of objectivity of job characteristics has been most confusing. In a very critical review of the model Roberts and Glick (1981) state that task design research has not moved beyond an exploratory stage. A major objection against much research in this area is that researchers do not make a clear distinction between *within-person* relations, *person–situation* relations, and *situational* relations. In fact, in many studies in this area a research design is used that can, strictly speaking, only lead to results pertaining to within-person relations. The methodological Achilles heel is that both the observations on the independent variables (task characteristics) and on the dependent variables (behavior and attitudes of job incumbents) derive from the same source of information. This creates the danger of *common method variance* in independent and dependent variables. A possible alternative explanation for the (high) correlations found with such a design cannot be excluded, namely cognitive consistency within the individual. For that reason, Aldag et al. (1981) recommend the use of indices of task characteristics that are not dependent on reports from focal job incumbents.

In the late 1970s, Salancik and Pfeffer (1978) provided another model, contrary to the basic assumptions of the JCM, to explain the relationships between attitudes and task perceptions. In their Social Information Processing (SIP) approach it was suggested that, at least partially, social and informative cues in the workplace influence task perceptions. The social environment of the individual provides cues and information that shape both task perceptions and attitudes. In other words, they suggest that job perceptions and attitudes are largely socially constructed realities. This view thus questions the relation between objective and perceived task characteristics.

A review of 10 studies addressing the controversy between the JCM and the SIP approach is provided by Thomas and Griffin (1983). Both experimental and field research was included. Results indicate that some elements of the perceived task environment are predominantly influenced by the objective task, other elements are primarily influenced by social information cues, and some elements are influenced by both types of determinants. They conclude that the task attributes approach has not been refuted by these studies, but in fact there is support for an overlapping model, rather than one or the other of the two models. This discussion on the effects of objective task changes and social information cues on task perceptions has been continued (Caldwell & O'Reilly, 1982; Salancik, 1984; Stone, 1984; Stone & Gueutal, 1984).

The linkage between objective and perceived task characteristics has in fact been explored by two types of analyses (Fried & Ferris, 1987). *First*, by means of objective manipulation of jobs and by means of quasi-experimental studies. The question is whether objective changes in job characteristics result in changes of job perception in the expected direction. In general in these studies, mainly related to the evaluation of the SIP approach, it turns out that objective manipulations of jobs result in changes in the job perceptions in the direction of the objective change. *Second*, correlations between incumbents' ratings and ratings of other sources (e.g., supervisors, peers, or researchers) can be viewed as an indication of the link between objective and incumbents' perceived task characteristics. Fried and Ferris (1987) provide data from 15 studies of this type. The median of simple correlations is .63, whereas the median of median correlations, in studies with more than one task characteristic, turns out to be .56. For studies using the JDS this last value is .54. Thus, it can be concluded that there exists a certain amount of overlap between perceptions of task characteristics by job incumbents and others. The results of these two types of analyses indicate that objective and perceived task characteristics are related, but that relationship is not perfect and room is left for other determinants of task perceptions, such as social information cues.

Attempts to Construct Objective Indices.   In addition to improving the objectivity by having nontask performers such as superiors and/or researchers assess jobs on certain task characteristics, sporadic attempts have been made to construct truly objective indices (not using an assessment procedure). Globerson and Crossman (1976), for instance, attempted to find an objective indicator that would correspond to the subjective reaction of "variety." They developed a measure, nonrepetitive time (NRT), as an indicator of variety, which is based on the summation of the time duration of *different* task elements within the cycle time. This means that the score is higher the more frequently different task elements occur within the cycle time of the task and the longer the duration of each of the elements. Globerson and Crossman (1976) found a positive relation between NRT and the subjectively registered reactions of complexity, variety, and interest. However, it is entirely the question if the cycle time can be established in an objective fashion in all cases.

It is not at all easy to find objective indicators that might serve as valid measures. In experiments in psychophysics it is probably evident what physical stimulus external to the individual is responsible for a particular psychological sensation. But this is much more difficult to identify in the more complex concrete work situation. Hill (1969), for example, pointed out that there is no clearly defined physical correlate of perceived variety. In other words, it is not possible to specify the nature of the physical stimulus that gives rise to the perception of variety, except perhaps that one can say it has to do with the structure of the work. Based on a series of experiments, Hill (1969) came to the conclusion that the entropy (a measure for the differentiation within a system) of the total set of tasks would be a useful objective measure. Wood (1986) recently presented a very interesting general theoretical model for task description that attempts to combine the "behavior requirements" and the "task qua task" approaches. This model postulates three essential components relevant to every task: *products, (required) acts*, and *information cues*. Wood (1986) defines the first component, products, as a result of behavior that may be observed and described independent of the behavior or act. In other words, this component should be described without taking into consideration the goals and expectations of the task performer. The second component, (required) acts, is primarily determined by the *direction* of an act, that is, the specific activity or process that is performed during the act, and which can be described independent of the individual who performs it and the context in which the act takes place. The third component, information cues, is defined as information on attributes of stimulus objects on which the individual bases the assessments that he or she must make during task performance. In this approach, task description means that first the *product* is identified, and then the required inputs at the level of specific acts and information cues that are important in the performance of these acts.

Based on this general framework, Wood subsequently defines the concept of "task complexity." He distinguishes three types of task complexity: *component, coordinative*, and *dynamic*. The first type, component complexity, is defined as a function of the number of distinct acts required for task performance and the number of distinct information cues that must be "processed" in performing the task. The second type, coordinative complexity, refers to the nature of the relations between tasks inputs (acts and information cues) and task products. This measure is expressed in terms of the number and the nature of the relations (e.g., the chronological order) of the acts within the task. The third type, dynamic complexity, has to do with changes in the relations between task inputs and task products during the performance time. This concept is expressed in terms of changes over time in the two previous measures, component and coordinative complexity, and the degree of predictability of these changes. A linear combination of the three types of complexity just described provides a measure of total task complexity. No data are yet available on the construct validity of these concepts. For this, it would need to be investigated whether they can differentiate between tasks of differing complexity, and data would be needed on their ability to predict such matters as achievement level, attitude, and behavior variables at an individual level.

Wood (1986) remarks that it is not always possible to calculate complexity scores with the formulas he presented, certainly not in field settings. This once again illustrates our earlier statement that it is extremely difficult to develop and validate truly objective measures in this area. And Wood's approach leaves us with the question to what extent the identification of acts and the information cues linked to them can be established in an objective fashion in all cases. A second remark from the point of view of task characteristics relevant to motivation and satisfaction is important here. It involves the level at which a task characteristic is defined. The previously cited attempts to develop an objective measure involved indices at the level of the task or task elements. But if we look at the dependent variables (e.g., work satisfaction, quality and quantity of work performance, psychological complaints, absenteeism, etc.), it would be more realistic to define the independent variables at the level of the job. This would probably be possible with an approach such as the one by Wood, by using some form of summation over the separate tasks that make up a job.

The Dimensionality of Job Characteristics

The issue of dimensionality has also given impetus to much empirical research. In the original study by Turner and Lawrence (1965) one single index, the Requisite Task Attributes-index (RTA-index), was used. This index consisted of a weighted sum of the six requisite task attributes that were moderately correlated (responsibility, autonomy, required interactions, optional interactions, variety, knowledge and skill). However, no information on internal consistency is available concerning the items that belong to the same requisite attribute. As mentioned before, five a priori job dimensions are considered in the JCM. But at the same time one index (MPS) is provided, based on a multiplicative model, used as an indication of job complexity. There had been many studies testing the a priori structure of the JDS and similar instruments, e.g., the JCI (Job Characteristics Inventory; Sims, Szilagyi, & Keller, 1976). For example, Dunham, Aldag, and Brief (1977) studied the factor structure of the JDS in 20 different samples of respondents. The results of this study indicate that the underlying dimensionality of the JDS is inconsistent across samples.

The five-factor structure was found in only two of the 20 samples. Usually a smaller number of dimensions (four, three, or even two) was found. In a recent study by Fried and Ferris (1986), in which a reanalysis of the original JDS database was performed, a three-factor structure was found to provide the best solution. Task identity and job feedback were retained as legitimate job dimensions, but skill variety, task significance, and autonomy were found to collapse into a single factor. In addition, it was found that age, education, and position level moderated the underlying factor structure. High-position level and high-education subgroup analyses revealed support for a five-dimensional structure, where as low-position level and low-education subgroups reflected four-, three-, or two-factor dimensionality. In another recent study, Idaszak and Drasgow (1987) point at a measurement artifact, caused by reverse-scored items, as a major source of inconsistencies found in studies that have attempted to obtain empirical support for the five-factor structure.

There are two main problems in comparing research results. First, the instruments used in the various studies are not identical. Second, and far more important, there is quite a difference in the range of jobs that provide the basis for the studies. This has severe implications for the resulting structures. At one extreme, correlations among job characteristics are computed on the basis of perceptions of job incumbents of a variety of jobs from different branches of industry and at different organizational levels. At the other extreme, there are studies where the sample of job incumbents is much more homogeneous and is limited to one department of a factory (Wall, Clegg, & Jackson, 1978). Another point in this issue is whether the basic data refer to the level of jobs or to both the level of jobs and individual perceptions. In most studies the database consists of individual job perceptions across different jobs. For examples, in the Fried and Ferris (1986) study the database contained nearly 7,000 respondents working in nearly 700 different jobs. In such a situation the variance between scores partly reflects objective differences between jobs and partly differences between perceptions of the same job. That means, in the terminology of Roberts and Glick (1981), that we cannot speak of *situational* relations that involve only characteristics of objective jobs or situations that are invariant across people.

The Role of the Critical Psychological States

The supposed mediating role of the critical psychological states has not been tested too often. Also, quite different methods have been used, such as partial correlations (Hackman & Oldham, 1976), path analysis (Wall et al., 1978), and the analysis of linear structural relations (Algera, van der Flier, & van der Kamp, 1986). The results of these analyses are not positive for the model. One finding is that the specified relations between the core job dimensions and the critical psychological states do not behave, looking at the correlation patterns, as predicted by the model. Research on testing the supposed causal relationships in the model by means of sophisticated statistical techniques is quite scarce.

Wall et al. (1978) tested the model by means of path analysis. Much of the data, especially on the role of "critical psychological states," did not conform to the model. When the JCM was tested against an alternative model, the alternative model accounted for a significantly greater portion of the variance than the JCM. An important difference between the two models was that the alternative model did postulate direct causal relationships between job characteristics and outcome variables. Because direct relationships between core job dimensions and outcome variables would have the same implications for job design, as would be the case if the critical psychological states had behaved in accordance with the model, Wall et al. (1978) did not reject the model entirely. They do suggest some reformulations, such as ascribing an intermediate role to "internal work motivation" as a "critical psychological state."

In the path analysis by Wall et al. (1978), path coefficients were estimated by performing a series of regression analysis. That means that the relations in the model are not tested simultaneously. However, Algera et al. (1986) provide a simultaneous test of the causal relations among the variables in the model by means of the LISREL model (Jöreskog & Sörbom, 1978). This model was used for "causal modeling," i.e., for hypothesis testing in the context of an entire system of nonexperimental data. The word "modeling" refers to the fact that the data analysis will have to be guided by theoretical specification, and the word "causal" refers to the fact that such a specification is typically intended to explain, rather than to describe, the data. In their study, Algera et al. (1986) tested the JCM and some modifications of the JCM in two different samples. The results indicate a bad fit between the JCM and modifications of JCM and the data. The conclusion is that it is virtually impossible to model the precise causal links between the many variables in this area of research, taking the model as a whole.

Whereas for the attitudinal outcomes (e.g., overall satisfaction, growth satisfaction), the patterns of correlations would probably allow for a mediating role of the critical psychological states, looking at the patterns of correlations with performance (Fried & Ferris, 1978), the correlations between job characteristics and performance are in general higher than between critical psychological states and performance. This precludes a mediating role of the critical psychological states for performance variables. Very recently, Hogan and Martell (1987) also provided another example of the structural equations analysis methodology to test some propositions of the JCM in a sample of 208 white-collar government employees. They found no support for a reversed causality model with performance affecting responses about task characteristics. Further, the basic job characteristic model was compared to the same model without mediating psychological states, i.e., job characteristics directly influencing the latent variable satisfaction. The latter modification turned out to give a relatively better overall fit, but the residual variance of the latent variable "satisfaction" explained decreases. Nevertheless, looking at the correlation patterns with (self-reported) performance, again in this study three out of five job characteristics (task significance, skill variety, autonomy) have higher correlations with performance than with the critical psychological states. A disadvantage of this study is that the variance on the JDS variables reflects both variance between jobs and within jobs.

The Effects of Moderator Variables

In the JCM the variable growth need strength (GNS) has been proposed as a moderator variable, and in a later publication (Hackman & Oldham, 1980) *knowledge and skills* and *context satisfactions* are also considered as moderators between job characteristics—critical psychological states and between critical psychological states—outcomes. Most of the times GNS has been studied as a moderator variable, but also other individual-difference variables have been used. White (1978) reviewed a number of studies and came to the conclusion that the generality of effects of individual differences is limited. Shepard and Houghland (1978) also stress the fact that results of research on this subject are not consistent. Roberts and Glick (1981) heavily questioned GNS as a moderator.

However, recent meta-analysis research gives another picture. Loher et al. (1985) studied the "true" relation between job characteristics and job satisfaction, using meta-analysis methods, and also studied GNS as a possible moderator. They found a correlation between a job characteristics index and job satisfaction of .39. The relation between job satisfaction and separate job characteristics ranged from .32 (task identity) to .46 (autonomy). For the high GNS group, relations between job characteristics and satisfaction were substantially stronger than for the low GNS group. An interesting finding is that the variance in the correlations for the high GNS groups is eliminated after controlling for sampling error and measurement unreliability. But this variance is still large for the low GNS group, even after correcting for these two statistical artifacts. On the basis of this finding, Loher et al. (1985) suggest that factors that do not influence the relation between job characteristics and job satisfaction for high GNS employees do play a role for employees low on GNS. In their view for low GNS employees, the success of enrichment activities may be dependent on factors such as workgroup appreciation of job enrichment or management support for enrichment activities. Spector (1985) presents the results of the moderating effect of higher order need strength, including the GNS measure from the JDS, on the relationship between job scope and employee outcomes in a meta-analysis containing 20 samples. He found higher correlations between job scope and outcomes for employees high on higher order need strength than for employees low on higher order need. This effect was strongest for job satisfaction in comparison with other outcome variables as motivation and performance. He concludes that White's (1978) call for an end to research on the moderator effect to be premature.

Fried and Ferris (1987) provide meta-analysis results on the moderating effect of GNS on the MPS-performance relationship for five studies. They found a stronger relationship of MPS with performance for the high GNS people than for the low GNS people. The 90% credibility value between MPS and performance for the high GNS group was .45 and for the low GNS group, .10.

For the other two moderator variables, context satisfaction and knowledge and skills, Fried and Ferris (1987) state that studies are very scarce for the moderating effects of context satisfaction, and none of the available studies investigates the moderating effect of knowledge and skills.

The Relationship Between Job Characteristics and Outcomes

As stated before, studies testing the JCM as a whole, including the mediating role of the critical psychological states, are rare. In the bulk of the studies direct correlations between job characteristics and outcome variables are presented.

Although most of the studies use perceived job characteristics, measured by the JDS or JCI, to determine the effects of job characteristics on outcomes, there are a small number of studies that address the question of the difference between objective and subjective job characteristics in explaining variance in outcome variables. In those studies both relations between objective, respectively perceived job characteristics, and outcome variables have been studied.

For example, Algera (1983) found similar correlation patterns between 24 job characteristics and 17 dependent variables when job characteristics were rated by job incumbents and when job characteristics were rated by non-job incumbents. Also in other studies (e.g., Oldham, Hackman, & Pearce, 1976; Stone & Porter, 1978), correlations between job characteristics and outcome variables turn out to be similar when job incumbents' ratings and nonjob incumbents' ratings are used as independent variables. The only exception seems to be the study of Brief and Aldag (1978), who found quite different patterns for supervisors and job incumbents. Fried and Ferris (1987) refer to a number of studies (Ganster, 1979; Orpen, 1979; Umstot, Bell, & Mitchell, 1976), where objective manipulation of job characteristics versus perceived job characteristics on attitudinal outcomes are compared.

The results of these studies suggest similar directions for the relationship of objective task manipulation and incumbents' task perceptions to outcomes. However, perceived job characteristics accounted for more variance in satisfaction than objective task manipulation. Fried and Ferris (1987) conclude that the problems with self-rated data are less serious than initially believed.

This conclusion is also sustained by the recent study of Glick, Jenkins, and Gupta (1986). In their study the relative strengths of the effects of method versus substance on relationships between job characteristics and attitudinal outcomes have been compared. In fact, they try to compare the predictions of the job characteristics approach versus the Social Information Processing (SIP) approach. Two analysis strategies were used: multiple regression and structural equations. In the last type of analysis five models were fitted to the observed correlation matrix using LISREL (Jöreskog & Sörbom, 1978). The conclusions from this study are that substantive relationships were observed between job characteristics and effort, which is in favor of the JCM. However, common method effects inflated the correlations between job characteristics and affective outcomes, which is in favor of the Social Information Processing model. Their conclusion based on these findings is that different theories predict different kinds of outcomes. Stated more specifically, the SIP approach provides a better explanation for affective responses, whereas the job characteristics approach is better in predicting more behavior-oriented responses like motivation, effort, and performance. This finding is in accordance with results reported by Griffin (1983).

As far as the relation between job characteristics, as measured by the JDS, and outcomes is concerned, the Fried and Ferris (1987) meta-analysis study seems to be the most comprehensive to date. Their results indicate moderate to strong relationships with attitudinal outcome variables. After corrections for statistical artifacts, job feedback has the strongest relation with overall job satisfaction (90% credibility value .43), autonomy has the strongest relation to growth satisfaction (90% credibility value .71), and skill variety has the strongest relationship with internal work motivation (90% credibility value .52). For the behavioral outcome variables, however, relationships with job characteristics are much lower. With performance the 90% credibility values of task identity and job feedback are .13 and .09, respectively. With absenteeism, relationships are somewhat higher and reach levels for the 90% credibility values for autonomy and job feedback of $-.29$ and $-.19$, respectively.

Another old question addressed by Fried and Ferris (1987) concerns the comparison between the multiplicative MPS and a simple additive index as a better single index. The last index turns out to be superior, both for the attitudinal outcomes and for performance. The differences in 90% credibility values however is not dramatic (.74 vs. .63, .88 vs. .77, .66 vs. .53, and

.27 vs. .23, respectively, for overall job satisfaction, growth satisfaction, internal work motivation, and performance).

The Dependent Variables

In the original JCM (Hackman & Oldham, 1975, 1976) a number of personal and work outcomes have been stated: internal work motivation, satisfaction, quality of work performance, absenteeism, and turnover. In the latest publication by Hackman and Oldham (1980, p. 90), however, absenteeism and turnover have disappeared, whereas quality of work performance has been reformulated in the term work effectiveness. In the research on the JCM some outcome variables have been used more often than others. In general, there are more studies on the personal outcomes (satisfaction, internal work motivation) than on work outcomes (performance, absenteeism, turnover).

In addition to the original outcome variables, several authors have extended the number of outcome variables (e.g., Algera, 1983; Broadbent, 1985). This extension is particularly in the area of mental health variables, such as psychic and psychosomatic complaints (Algera, 1983), or anxiety and depression (Broadbent, 1985). From the viewpoint of causal relations, this category of personal outcome variables has sometimes been proposed as a fourth stage in the process, dependent on satisfaction (Wall et al., 1978). In an article on the "clinical" impact of job design, Broadbent (1985) argues that particular features of jobs are related to particular types of neurotic symptoms. He also stresses the interactive effects of individual characteristics, which influence the vulnerability to stress. As far as the first argument is concerned, Broadbent (1985) provides data from a number of studies that can be interpreted as different job characteristics having different effects. For example, in the studies he mentions, pacing has shown effects predominantly on anxiety rather than depression and no effects on satisfaction. He suggests that satisfaction and anxiety may have different correlates. Further, he states that depression correlates with factors that do no affect anxiety. He concludes that it is a mistake to lump job characteristics together on a single dimension of stress. In his perspective workload and pacing are different from monotony and lack of control. He further emphasizes that individual coping styles may interact with job stress, together with environmental factors such as social support.

An Overall Evaluation of the JCM

Based on the results mentioned in the previous paragraphs, we can come to a more overall evaluation of the main discussion points on the JCM.

The most critical issue probably is the relationship between objective and perceived job characteristics. One can conclude that there exists a relationship between objective and perceived job characteristics. This follows from studies where objective job characteristics have been manipulated and also from studies where the correlations between perceptions by job incumbents and nonincumbents have been determined and their respective correlations with dependent variables have been compared and found to be similar. However, there is also room for other factors than objective job characteristics, such as social cues and common method variance, that can explain a part of the variance in job perceptions. This means that self-reports are not useless as indicators of job characteristics. Glick et al. (1986) suggest that objective data and individual perceptions should be considered as different data sources as differing in their usefulness for answering specific questions.

In the recent studies concerning the competitive situation between the JCM and the SIP approach, some authors advocate an integration of these two approaches. The results of the research provide more support for an integrated viewpoint than for either of the other models (see e.g., Fried & Ferris, 1987; Glick et al., 1986; Thomas & Griffin, 1983; Vance & Biddle, 1985). For example, Vance and Biddle found very interesting results on the interaction of social cues and experience with the "objective" cues by exposure to the task. One interpretation of their results is that the timing of social cues and objective cues might be important. In their study social cues were effective only when they occurred before the subject had a chance to acquire many objective cues. They conclude that job attitudes are formed based on both direct experience with objective characteristics and social information.

In general, one finds rather strong relationships between job characteristics and personal outcomes (e.g., satisfaction), but the correlations between job characteristics and behavioral outcomes (e.g., performance) are much lower. Further, it turns out that specific outcomes are tied to specific job characteristics (Fried & Ferris, 1987; Glick et al., 1986). This would imply that if one has specific organizational outcomes in mind interventions based on specific job characteristics should be considered. Aiming for more general effects, Fried and Ferris (1987) state that job feedback is the job characteristic that is most promising. This is the case, because job feedback is associated with all the personal and behavioral outcome variables investigated in their meta-analysis study (overall job satisfaction, growth satisfaction, internal work motivation, job performance, absenteeism).

A major disadvantage of the JCM is that this model is in fact a static model. It suggests which job characteristics have impact on personal and work outcomes, but it does not say anything on the role of time, for example in the relationship between job characteristics and outcomes. There are very few studies on this issue. Katz (1978a, 1978b) studies the effect of the length of time a job incumbent has been doing the job on the relation between job characteristics and satisfaction. It turned out that the correlation between autonomy and satisfaction was negative for new job incumbents (on the job 0–3 months); it was positive for job incumbents who had been on the job somewhat longer, and it was highest for job incumbents who had been on the job for about 1 year, slowly decreasing to almost zero for job incumbents with over 15 years' service. Recently, Kozlowski and Hults (1986) studied the task complexity–job performance relation as a function of engineering context (R & D vs. Staff) and position tenure. They found a dramatic moderating effect of position tenure on the task complexity–job performance association for the R & D engineers. It is low in the 0–1.5-year period, increases sharply during the 1.6–4.5-year period, and drops off substantially in the $\geq$ 4.6-year period. For staff engineers, however, a slowly declining correlation over position tenure stages was found.

To sum up, the JCM has received support on a number of specific points, in particular on the relationships between perceived job characteristics and attitudinal outcomes. However, the model has also been disconfirmed on other points, such as the causal patterns and the mediating role of the critical psychological states. Nevertheless, the model has not been refuted totally and modifications of the model will probably play a major role in research on job design in the future.

THE JOB CHARACTERISTICS MODEL AS AN INTERVENTION STRATEGY FOR JOB REDESIGN

As stated before, the JCM and its accompanying instrument, the JDS, have been presented for the explicit purpose of job redesign (Hackman, Oldham, Janson, & Purdy, 1975). Reviewing the research on this model, one sees much research on testing (parts of) the model but less studies on the JCM as a guide for interventions. Loher et al. (1985) point at the "disturbing" situation that "few empirical studies of actual job enrichment interventions have been reported in the professional literature" (p. 288). In fact, the emphasis has been much more on the JCM as a help to make a diagnosis of the situation than as a guide for implementation of actual changes in jobs. Five implementing principles (Hackham & Oldham, 1980) have been presented: (1) combining tasks, (2) forming natural work units, (3) establishing client relationships, (4) vertically loading the job, and (5) opening feedback channels. In addition to this, links between these five implementing principles and the five core job characteristics have been suggested. However, this part of the JCM approach has not been worked out thoroughly.

At least a number of questions arise, such as what is the relation between job characteristics on the level of individual jobs and higher levels of the organizational unit or the organization as a whole? Because many jobs do

not stand alone but are an element of a work team or have patterns of con-
nections with other jobs, for intervention one has to look from a much
broader viewpoint than an individual job. Therefore, intervention strategies
based on the JCM approach should be embedded in a broader organization
design viewpoint.

Another question concerns *how* to use the implementation principles, in
other words, how to form "natural" work units in practice. These questions
illustrate that for implementation the focus should be more on job design
as the *dependent* variable than on job design as the *independent* variable.
There have been a number of studies on this issue, but to date very few. For
example, Rousseau (1978) studied the relationship between technological
differentiation at the departmental level, job characteristics at the job level,
and workers' responses. Only recently, researchers begin to change their interest to the organizational context in which jobs are embedded (see e.g.,
Brass, 1985) and try to relate job design to variables as technology, managerial control systems, and organization structure.

Hackman and Oldham (1980) do pose the question: "How hospitable are
organization systems to needed changes?" and notice that rigidities in the
technological, personnel, and control systems can become major constraints for job redesign. For example, they refer to the effects of an increase in job feedback on managerial control systems. Data on job
performance are often supplied to managers for deciding on interventions
to be taken. Changing feedback information flows can have severe impacts
on the functioning of existing managerial control systems.

Recently, Brass (1985) presented some conceptions and research results
on the relationships among technology, interdependence, job characteristics, and their effects on employee satisfaction, performance, and influence
(intraorganizational power). He proposes that technological uncertainties
act as constraints on the structuring of jobs. Technology is viewed as consisting of three phases: input, conversion, and output. Uncertainty, or predictability, can be assessed for each phase. He further stresses the job
interdependence as an essential dimension of technology. For example,
reciprocal interdependence will be correlated with high conversion uncertainty, whereas sequential interdependence will be correlated with low conversion uncertainty. Brass (1985) makes a number of propositions regarding
the relationships between technology and job characteristics, which are
based on the view that organizations desire to reduce uncertainty. This
would imply, for example, that flexibility in the structuring of jobs is required to deal with uncertainty. On the basis of these ideas, Brass (1985)
does predict finding associations between characteristics of technology and
specific job characteristics. He presents empirical data from a study in a
newspaper publishing company. He finds positive and significant correlations of input uncertainty and conversion uncertainty with the job characteristics. For the output dimension he did not find significant positive

correlations. Also zero-order correlations and partial correlations between technological uncertainty, technological interdependence, job characteristics, and satisfaction, performance, and influence are presented.

In general Brass (1985) found support for a number of his hypotheses that technological uncertainty acts as a constraint on the structuring of jobs. He advocates viewing job design from the perspective derived from the notion of requisite variety and the matching of uncertainty and flexibility. He further argues that the concept of uncertainty combined with the notion of requisite variety can be used to integrate micro and macrolevels of organizational studies. Also other authors (e.g., Pierce, 1984) refer to sociotechnical systems notions as a conceptual framework for studying the relation between job design and technology.

A very interesting view on the issue of job characteristics as dependent variables has been presented by Clegg (1984). He provides a theoretical account on the determinants of the objective characteristics of jobs rather than on perceived characteristics. Regarding the conceptualization of technology, he adopts Perrow's (1967) view, labeled as knowledge technology, wherein technology is a variable incorporating more or less uncertainty. Organization structure is seen in the perspective of organizations as information-processing systems that design and structure themselves to cope with prevailing uncertainties. Each functional work group is viewed as an information-processing system that uses certain technostructural arrangements to cope with uncertainties. Clegg further points at the "pattern of local control," a construct that incorporates routinization, target setting, and managerial style, which is influenced by the information-processing requirements. In his conceptualization of objective job complexity, he makes a distinction between *tasks* and *roles*. The former are largely technologically determined, e.g., by level of automation. The latter are largely prescribed by the pattern of local control and refer to job incumbents' opportunities for decision making. These decisions are concerned with daily operations such as setting the work pace, allocating jobs, and rest periods. Managers are supposed to have choices over the technology, structure, and control strategies they adopt.

The distinction between tasks and roles has several implications (Clegg, 1984): (a) Tasks and roles can be designed independently; (b) in the job design literature *tasks* and *roles* are not differentiated, which means that, especially for making comparisons within groups of employees, it is difficult to know what precisely is meant by job complexity; (c) in practice there may be room for redesigning roles without necessarily changing the technological arrangements; (d) most of job redesign interventions in fact are examples of role redesign, where managerial control procedures are changed whereas the task is relatively unaltered; and (e) "joint-optimization is in practice a myth."

There are two main reasons why it is difficult to achieve more complex job designs (Clegg, 1984). The first is that historically and economically more complex designs are seen by engineers and managers as risky. The second is that more complex job designs influence the power relationships in organizations, not only in the direction of management but also in the direction of supporting organizational units, such as maintenance.

To conclude, using the JCM approach as a guide to make interventions in work systems would need much more knowledge on the relationships between variables on the microlevel and the macro (organization) level. We have enough studies now on job characteristics as independent variables. What is needed is more knowledge on the determinants of job characteristics. In other words, research on job characteristics such as in the JCM or the SIP approach should be extended to incorporate organization variables too. In particular, the introduction of new technology and information systems in offices and factories seems to integrate processes in organizations, such as integrated logistic systems. A broader perspective including both organizational variables, such as information and control systems, and job characteristics is needed.

REFERENCES

Aldag, R. J., Barr, S. H., & Brief, A. P. (1981). Measurement of perceived task characteristics. *Psychological Bulletin, 90*, 415–431.

Algera, J. A. (1983). "Objective" and perceived task characteristics as a determinant of reactions by task performers. *Journal of Occupational Psychology, 56*, 95–105.

Algera, J. A., Flier, H. van der, & Kamp, L. J. Th., van der. (1986). Causal modeling of quality of work. In G. Debus & H. W. Schroiff (Eds.) *The psychology of work and organization* (pp. 175–182). Amsterdam: Elsevier.

Brass, D. J. (1985). Technology and the structuring of jobs: Employee satisfaction, performance, and influence. *Organizational Behavior and Human Decision Processes, 35*, 216–240.

Brief, A. P., & Aldag, R. J. (1978). The job characteristics inventory: An examination. *Academy of Management Journal, 21*, 659–670.

Broadbent, D. E. (1985). The clinical impact of job design. *British Journal of Clinical Psychology, 24*, 33–44.

Caldwell, D. F., & O'Reilly, C. A. (1982). Task perceptions and job satisfaction: A question of causality. *Journal of Applied Psychology, 67*, 361–369.

Clegg, C. W. (1984). The derivation of job designs. *Journal of Occupational Behavior, 5*, 131–146.

Dunham, R. B., Aldag, R. J., & Brief, A. P. (1977). Dimensionality of task design as measured by the Job Diagnostic Survey. *Academy of Management Journal, 20*, 209–223.

Farina, A. J., Jr., & Wheaton, G. R. (1973). Development of a taxonomy of human performance: The task characteristics approach to performance prediction. *JSAS Catalog of Selected Documents in Psychology, 3*, 26–27 (Ms. No. 323).

Fleishman, E. A., & Quaintance, M. K. (1984). *Taxonomics of human performance. The description of human tasks*. New York: Academic Press.

Fried, Y., & Ferris, G. R. (1986). The dimensionality of job characteristics: Some neglected issues. *Journal of Applied Psychology, 71*, 419–426.

Fried, Y., & Ferris, G. R. (1987). The validity of the Job Characteristics Model: A review and meta-analysis. *Personnel Psychology, 40*, 287–322.

Ganster, D. C. (1979). The effects of individual differences and objective task scope on task perceptions and satisfaction: A laboratory investigation. *Proceedings of the Academy of Management, 39*, 59–63.

Glick, W. H., Jenkins, G. D., & Gupta, N. (1986). Method versus substance: How strong are underlying relationships between job characteristics and attitudinal outcomes? *Academy of Management Journal, 29*, 441–464.

Globerson, S., & Crossman, E. R. F. W. (1976). Non-repetitive time: An objective index of job variety. *Organizational Behavior and Human Performance, 17*, 231–240.

Griffin, R. W. (1983). Objective and social sources of information in task redesign: A field experiment. *Administrative Science Quarterly, 28*, 184–200.

Hackman, J. R., & Lawler, E. E., III. (1971). Employee reactions to job characteristics. *Journal of Applied Psychology (Monograph), 55*, 259–286.

Hackman, J. R., & Oldham, G. R. (1975). Development of the Job Diagnostic Survey. *Journal of Applied Psychology, 60*, 159–170.

Hackman, J. R., & Oldham, G. R. (1976). Motivation through the design of work: Test of a theory. *Organizational Behavior and Human Performance, 16*, 250–279.

Hackman, J. R., & Oldham, G. R. (1980). *Work redesign*. Reading, MA: Addison–Wesley.

Hackman, J. R., Oldham, G. R., Janson, R., & Purdy, K. (1975). A new strategy for job enrichment. *California Management Review, 17*, 57–71.

Hill, A. B. (1969). The measurement of work variety. *The International Journal of Production Research, 8*, 1, 25–39.

Hogan, E. A., & Martell, D. A. (1987). A confirmatory structural equations analysis of the Job Characteristics Model. *Organizational Behavior and Human Decision Processes, 39*, 242–263.

Idaszak, J. R., & Drasgow, F. (1987). A revision of the Job Diagnostic Survey: Elimination of a measurement artifact. *Journal of Applied Psychology, 72*, 69–74.

Jöreskog, K. G., & Sörbom, D. (1978). *LISREL IV. A general computer program for estimation of linear structural equation systems by maximum likelihood methods*. Uppsala: University of Uppsala.

Katz, R. (1978a). Job longevity as a situational factor in job satisfaction. *Administrative Science Quarterly, 23*, 204–223.

Katz, R. (1978b). The influence of job longevity on employee reactions to task characteristics. *Human Relations, 31*, 703–725.

Kozlowski, S. W., & Hults, B. M. (1986). Joint moderation of the relation between task complexity and job performance for engineers. *Journal of Applied Psychology, 71*, 196–202.

Loher, B. T., Noe, R. A., Moeller, N. L., & Fitzgerald, M. P. (1985). A meta-analysis of the relation of job characteristics to job satisfaction. *Journal of Applied Psychology, 70*, 280–289.

Oldham, G. R., Hackman, J. R., & Pearce, J. L. (1976). Conditions under which employees respond positively to enriched work. *Journal of Applied Psychology, 61*, 395–403.

Orpen, C. (1979). The effects of job enrichment on employee satisfaction, motivation, involvement, and performance: A field experiment. *Human Relations, 32*, 189–217.

Perrow, C. (1967). A framework for the comparative analysis of organization. *American Sociological Review, 32*, 194–208.

Pierce, J. L. (1984). Job design and technology: A sociotechnical systems perspective. *Journal of Occupational Behavior, 5*, 147–154.

Roberts, K. H., & Glick, W. H. (1981). The job characteristics approach to task design: A critical review. *Journal of Applied Psychology, 66*, 193–217.

Rousseau, D. M. (1978). Measures of technology as predictors of employee attitude. *Journal of Applied Psychology, 63*, 213–218.

Salancik, G. R. (1984). On priming, consistency, and order effects in job attitude assessment: With a note on current research. *Journal of Management, 10*, 250–254.

Salancik, G. R., & Pfeffer, J. (1978). A social information processing approach to job attitudes and job design. *Administrative Science Quarterly, 23*, 224–253.

Shepard, J. M., & Hougland, J. C. (1978). Contingency theory: "Complex man" or "complex organization"? *Academy of Management Review, 1*, 2, 23–35.

Sims, H. P., Szilagyi, A. D., & Keller, R. T. (1976). The measurement of job characteristics. *Academy of Management Journal, 19*, 2, 195–212.

Spector, P. E. (1985). Higher order need strength as a moderator of the job scope–employee outcome relationship: A meta-analysis. *Journal of Occupational Psychology, 58*, 119–127.

Stone, E. F. (1984). Misperceiving and/or misrepresenting the facts: A reply to Salancik. *Journal of Management, 10*, 255–258.

Stone, E. F. (1986). Job scope–job satisfaction and job scope–job performance relationships. In E. A. Locke (Ed.), *Generalizing from laboratory to field settings* (pp. 189–206). Lexington, MA: Lexington Books.

Stone, E. F., & Gueutal, H. G. (1984). On the premature death of need satisfaction models: An investigation of Salancik and Pfeffer's views on priming and consistency artifacts. *Journal of Management, 10*, 237–258.

Stone, E. F., & Porter, L. W. (1978). On the use of incumbent-supplied job characteristics data. *Perceptual and Motor Skills, 46*, 751–758.

Thomas, J., & Griffin, R. (1983). The social information-processing model of task design: A review of the literature. *Academy of Management Review, 8*, 672–682.

Turner, A. N., & Lawrence, P. R. (1965). *Industrial jobs and the worker.* Boston: Harvard Graduate School of Business Administration.

Umstot, D. D., Bell, C. H., & Mitchell, T. R. (1976). Effects of job enrichment and task goals on satisfaction and productivity: Implications for job design. *Journal of Applied Psychology, 61*, 379–394.

Vance, R. J., & Biddle, T. F. (1985). Task experience and social cues: Interactive effects on attitudinal reactions. *Organizational Behavior and Human Decision Processes, 35*, 252–265.

Wall, T. D., Clegg, C. W., & Jackson, P. R. (1978). An evaluation of the Job Characteristics Model. *Journal of Occupational Psychology, 51*, 183–196.

White, J. K. (1978). Individual differences and the job quality–worker response relationship: Review, integration, and comments. *Academy of Management Review, 3*, 267–280.

Wood, R. E. (1986). Task Complexity: Definition of the construct. *Organizational Behavior and Human Decision Processes, 37*, 60–82.

7
The Role of Goal Setting and Feedback in Job Design

Klaus-Helmut Schmidt
Institut für Arbeitsphysiologie an der Universität Dortmund

Uwe Kleinbeck
Bergische Universität-Gesamthochschule Wuppertal

INTRODUCTION

To verify the central theoretical assumption that goals or intentions are the most immediate regulators of human behavior (cf. Locke, Shaw, Saari, & Latham, 1981; Ryan, 1970), to date goal-setting research has mainly focused on performance measures as dependent variables, especially on quantity measures. As a consequence, the range of application of the theory to industrial field settings is also nearly exclusively restricted to improvement of productivity (Austin & Bobko, 1985). These restrictions, however, are neither inherently required by the theory nor caused by a lack of other practical problems that the theory may potentially have the power to solve. Quite the opposite, just as in industrial field settings, new, unexplored phenomena can be observed opening goal-setting theory to a broader range of application, and therefore to a broader range of significance as well.

To illustrate this, let us first consider an observation often made in manufacturing plants, and which at first sight has nothing to do with goal setting. This observation refers to the workers' use of the so-called relaxation allowance, that is, the time provided to the workers as an opportunity to recover from the physiological and psychological effects of carrying out the work. In German industry, its total amount ranges from 8% to 12% of the overall working time. It varies, depending on the specific type of work and the conditions under which the work has to be done.

In the case of self-paced work, this time can be taken at the discretion of the individual worker in the form of voluntary rest pauses. In contrast to the additional organized pauses that mainly serve for food intake, the worker can decide when and how often to make use of the relaxation allowance for taking rest breaks of certain lengths.

In many industries, the relaxation allowance was introduced under the assumption that the workers take voluntary breaks when they feel they need them to eliminate or at least to reduce fatigue or other kinds of physiological and psychological strain. Furthermore, it was expected that the time lost by these breaks would be more than compensated by an increase in performance. As many observations and work studies have shown, however, workers do not always behave in accordance with these assumptions. More often, they work continuously without making any break and save up all the permitted rest time until the end of the total work period (cf. Graf, 1944, 1959; Rutenfranz & Stoll, 1966; Schmidt, Kleinbeck, & Knauth, 1988).

The reasons for such a time scheduling of work are still unexplored. Possibly the workers are afraid they may not be able to complete the work assigned to them in the time available and/or they have insufficient information about the progress of work in relation to this final goal. However that may be, this time scheduling can neither be used for leaving work earlier nor is it adequate for reducing work strain. In fact, it may lead to some detrimental effects like self-induced overstress, work rush, and under some circumstances even to a decrease in performance quality due to the increased work pace and the unused opportunities for recovery.

In view of this situation, the question arises in which way the goal-setting approach is able to modify this unfavorable work behavior and thus preclude the aforementioned side-effects associated with it.

Goal setting can help by partitioning the daily amount of work into small, clearly defined subgoals covering the whole working time and by providing the persons with ongoing performance feedback about the progress of work in regard to these goals. Used in this way, the single subgoals do not only serve as check points from which the worker can assess how much work has already been done in relation to the aspired final goal. Beyond that, the distribution of the subgoals throughout the working time should induce the worker to use the total time frame available for carrying out the work, including the rest time permitted. Under the assumption that they actually perform on a level with the subgoals, the workers should be encouraged to take rest breaks whenever they fall short of the time limits of the subgoals assigned.

To illustrate how these ideas can be translated into practice, a practical design approach is presented next.

A COMPUTER-AIDED JOB INFORMATION SYSTEM

The starting point for the development of this approach was given by the management of an electric plant, confronting us with work places in an assembly room where the workers showed just the behavior described previously; that is, they carried out their daily amount of work without taking any breaks and therefore finished it about 1 hour before the official work end. This observation was made after the introduction of a shift from paced work at an assembly line to self-paced work at single work places.

At the same time, the quality control noticed a marked decrease in the quality of the pieces produced. The management expressed the opinion that this decrease in performance quality could be connected with the workers' unfavorable time scheduling, especially with the unused opportunities for taking rest breaks, and asked for support to improve this situation.

At the work places under investigation, the workers had to assemble safety devices applied as elements in electronic control systems. The task consisted of various manual operations that had to be carried out in a fixed sequence. In a first step, different metal and plastic parts had to be fitted into the work pieces that subsequently were secured into fixtures installed in the middle of the work bench. After that, some further parts like clips and metal plates had to be inserted. Because of the very small dimensions of these parts, the operations demanded high manual skill and full concentration. In the next step, little metal springs had to be fitted into small recesses of the pieces. This operation could only be done with the aid of tweezers. The accurate position of these springs within the recesses was the most important requirement for the correct functioning of the entire device. Finally, the pieces completed were delivered into containers arranged at the left and right sides of the fixtures.

In consideration of the complexity and precision of all these operations required, the assumption seemed to be quite plausible that the observed decrease in performance quality could actually be the result of a speed–accuracy tradeoff caused by the increased, self-induced work pace and the unused opportunities for recovery. To give the workers support in improving their time scheduling, a computer-aided job information system was developed. This system was composed of a microcomputer, a keyboard, and a little monitor installed overhead at the left side of the work bench (see Kleinbeck, Schmidt, Schleyer, & Brockmann, 1985, for technical details).

According to the ideas presented at the beginning, at first the microcomputer partitioned the daily amount of work, that is, the number of pieces to be completed, into small subgoals assigned every half hour. The subgoals were displayed on the monitor in the form of a continuous performance graph that covered the whole working time except the organized pauses. In

Fig. 7.1 an example of such an assigned performance graph is presented, in this case one with a straight-lined course. The interruptions of the graph at the times from 9:00 to 9:15 in the morning and from 12:00 to 12:30 at midday indicate the organized breakfast and lunch pauses.

The actual performance output was recorded half-hourly as well and fed back in parallel to the assigned performance graph in the form of black bargraphs. For this the worker had to signal the completion of every work piece by pressing a key on the keyboard. The length of the bargraphs varied in dependence on the number of pieces produced within the half-hour sub-goal periods. In addition, the microcomputer calculated a projection of the number of pieces expected to be completed until the work end under the assumption that the actual performance level achieved up to that time would be maintained in the following time periods. This projection was indicated on a vertical scale arranged at the right side of the monitor picture. The cross symbol represents the current result of this calculation, which could be compared with the assigned daily target, indicated on the scale as a circle (see Fig. 7.1).

To consider individual variations in the readiness to work, the performance graphs could be adjusted individually by calling up a simple subroutine on the keyboard. However, some marginary limitations were set to adjusting the graphs in this way by the fact that in every half-hour period of the working time a fixed minimum of pieces had to be completed. This was to keep the workers from slipping back into their previously described unfavorable time scheduling.

After a practical test of a prototype, all five work places in the assembly room were supplied with such a job information system. Before it was used under normal conditions of production, 15 workers were instructed in the application of its functions. All these persons were highly trained in carrying out the assembly task. They were engaged in it in a job rotation procedure with other comparable assembly tasks.

EVALUATION OF THE SYSTEM

In a follow-up study, it was examined if the information presented by these systems was actually being used in accordance with the expectations. At first, on the basis of the theory of goal setting (Locke et al., 1981; Locke & Latham, 1984), it was expected that the workers perform on a level with the performance graphs assigned to them. Proceeding on this assumption, the distribution of the subgoals throughout the official working time should lead to a lengthening of the effective time frame used for carrying out the work. As a result, this goal-induced lengthening of the effective time frame should slow down the formerly observed unnecessary work pace and, at the same time, should motivate the workers to take rest breaks whenever they

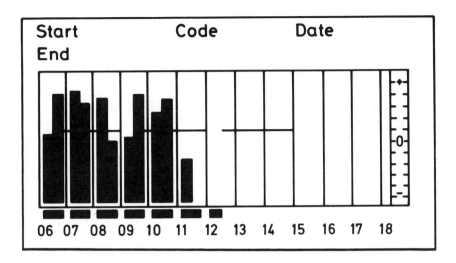

FIG. 7.1.   Arrangement of the information presented on the monitor picture of the job information system.

reach the single subgoals within the half-hour time limits. Finally, on condition that the decrease in performance quality could actually be traced back to a speed–accuracy tradeoff, the expected changes in work scheduling should contribute to an improvement of the quality of the pieces produced.

A further aim of the study was to investigate the strain effects resulting from performing along some assigned performance graphs, which differ in respect to their shape or time course. This was done because, on the basis of the theory of circadian performance rhythms (cf. Folkard & Monk, 1985; Hockey & Colquhoun, 1972), one can expect that it should make a difference for the workers when in the course of the working time they have to perform on a relatively high or low level. This issue, however, is immediately concerned if goal setting—as in this approach—is applied as a means for controlling the performance output over longer periods of time.

As many studies have shown, people's ability or readiness to work is not constant but is subject to temporal variations even over the normal working day. Although the results are far from uniform, the general trend seems to indicate a rapid rise of performance efficiency between 8:00 to 11:00 in the morning, followed by a fall in the midday and early afternoon, a second increase in the late afternoon and, finally, a rapid falloff over the late evening and night period. This circadian performance rhythm parallels to some extent circadian rhythms found in physiological functions, for example, body temperature.

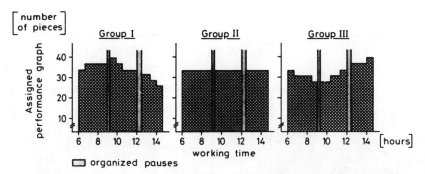

FIG. 7.2.   Shape of the assigned performance graphs.

The integration of these theoretical considerations and findings into the present goal-setting approach leads to the assumption that assigned performance graphs shaped in line with the described circadian variations in performance efficiency should produce weaker strain reactions than graphs deviating more or less from the supposed optimal time course.

Method

To analyze all these issues, the 15 workers trained in the assembly task were randomly split into three groups that were required to perform along one of three different performance graphs (see Fig. 7.2). Group I was assigned a graph that reflected the supposed optimal one; group II had to follow a straight-lined graph, whereas group III had to perform along a curve that resulted from an inversion of the graph assigned to group I. Here the maximum of performance required fell into the periods of decreased efficiency in the early afternoon and the required minimum just in the periods of high-performance efficiency in the midmorning. Under all three goal conditions the total amount of work to be done was constant and corresponded with the previous performance levels; only its distribution was varying over the working time.

The age of the female workers ranged from 18.3 to 29.7 years (with an average of 24.3) and tenure in the organization from 1.8 to 7.2 years (with an average of 4.1). The experimental groups did not significantly differ in regard to these and some other biographical data like education and occupational and family background.

Dependent variables were recorded: quantity and quality of performance, the lengths of rest pauses gained within the half-hour subgoal periods, and, finally, the experienced strain reactions of the workers performing along the different graphs. For each group, all these data were collected on 5 consequent days throughout 1 week.

The quality of the pieces produced was assessed by the internal quality control executed at electronic test stands outside the assembly room. This procedure corresponded with the situation before the installation of the job information systems. The lengths of voluntary rest breaks were measured by conventional work study techniques including the continuous registration of work activities, body posture, work-related communications, and so forth.

For the measurement of the experienced strain reactions (Hacker & Richter, 1984) a standardized questionnaire was applied. This instrument was developed by Plath and Richter (1978, 1984) to assess specifically the psychological strain of workers engaged in assembly and controlling tasks. It consists of three subscales allowing a differentiation of strain with regard to the states of fatigue, monotony, and satiation. These states are usually regarded as being indicative of the effects associated with carrying out repetitive, attention-demanding work activities. Because of its high reliability and discriminant validity (cf. Plath & Richter, 1984), this questionnaire is well established in the German research literature. It was administered every day shortly before the breakfast and lunch pause and at the work end. The two parallel forms of the questionnaire were offered in a permutative sequence matched across the persons, the days, and the daily times of measurement.

Results

The dependent variables were neither influenced significantly by the weekdays alone nor by the interaction of the days with both the other independent factors "performance graph (group)" and "time of measurement." Therefore, the following results relate exclusively to the effects of the performance graphs and the daily times of measurement on the dependent variables.

In Fig. 7.3 the number of pieces actually produced for each group within the half-hour subgoal periods are presented. For the purpose of economy, the data were averaged across days and the indicated time periods that enter as factorial levels (time of measurement) into the ANOVA carried out. The comparison with the assigned performance graphs (see Fig. 7.2) reveals that the performance output of all three groups matches the assigned graphs quite well. The calculated deviations of the actual from the required performance levels are all insignificant and not subject to any group differences. In accordance with the straight-lined graph, group II shows nearly a constant output over time, whereas the performance output of group I and group III takes contrary courses resulting from the contrary curves assigned to them. These divergent goal-induced variations in performance output are reflected in a significant interaction effect of "performance graph" and "time of measurement" ($F(4, 22) = 13.41$, $p < .001$). Apart from these different temporal variations in performance, the average number of pieces produced do not differ significantly among the groups and the indicated time periods.

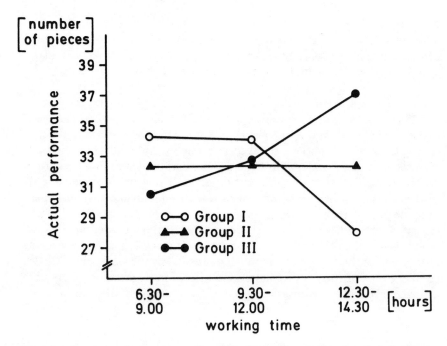

FIG. 7.3. Average performance quantity within the half-hour subgoal periods in dependence on the assigned performance graphs.

The groups do not differ in performance quality as well. In all groups the average quota of pieces produced defectively lay under 1% (group I: .09%; group II: .14%; group III: .19%). In comparison with the situation before the installation of the job information systems, this is a considerable improvement because the former quota had been about 10% and sometimes even more. As the observations of the quality control revealed, this improvement of performance quality was not restricted to the actual experimental period but was maintained in the following months.

Figure 7.4 shows the lengths of rest pauses gained within the half-hour subgoal periods under the different performance graphs. Here, too, the data were averaged across days and the indicated time periods. As expected logically, in each group the lengths of pauses vary in inverse relation to the goal-induced temporal variations in performance output (see Fig. 7.3). Resulting from the reduced performance requirements, in group I the longest breaks are found shortly before the work end. Conversely, the shortest breaks are observed here in group III. In contrast to this, the lengths of pauses gained in group II remain nearly constant over time due to the constant performance goals set by the straight-lined graph. As performance quantity, these different temporal variations in the lengths of rest pauses are the result of a significant interaction effect of "performance graph" and "time of measurement" ($F(4, 22) = 9.45$, $p < .001$). In dependence on the

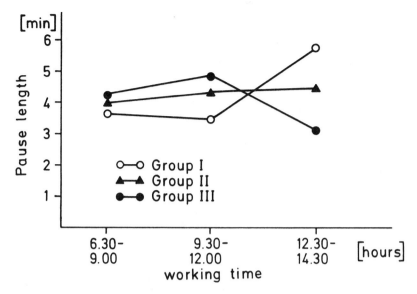

FIG. 7.4.   Average lengths of rest pauses gained within the half-hour subgoal periods in dependence on the assigned performance graphs.

different performance levels required by the graphs, the lengths of rest pauses vary between 3 and 6 minutes within the half-hour subgoal periods.

Apart from these temporal variations, there are no significant group differences in the average amount of time used for taking voluntary breaks. In group I the average length of pauses gained within the half-hour subgoal periods amounts to 4.32 min, in group II to 4.59 min, and in group III to 4.51 min. There is also no significant main effect of "time of measurement" on the average pause lengths.

Although the groups do not differ in the average number of pieces produced and the average amount of rest time used for taking breaks, the assigned performance graphs have some different effects on the experienced strain reactions of the workers. This shows in Fig. 7.5. In line with the calculation instructions prescribed by Plath and Richter (1978, 1984) for their questionnaire, in this figure numerical low values indicate high and negative strain reactions.

At first, the intensity of the strain reactions reflects the temporal variations in performance output induced by the different graphs. This is true for all the measured strain reactions, most clearly, however, for the subjective feelings of fatigue and satiation. Both states are influenced significantly by the interaction effect of "performance graph" and "time of measurement" (fatigue: $F(4, 22) = 5.00$, $p < .01$; satiation: $F(4, 22) = 9.29$, $p < .01$). With respect to the experienced monotony, this interaction effect fails the conventional level of significance ($F(4, 22) = 1.63$, n.s.). Beyond that, all three strain reactions show a significant increase in intensity over

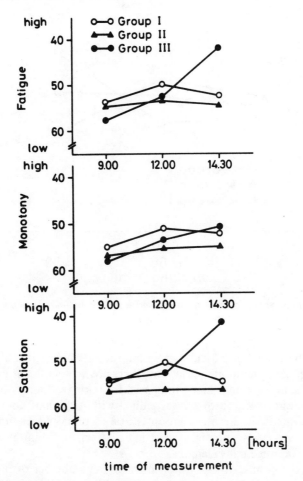

FIG. 7.5. Experienced fatigue, monotony, and satiation in dependence on the times of measurement and the assigned performance graphs.

time (fatigue: $F(2, 22) = 10.32$, $p < .001$; monotony: $F(2, 22) = 7.90$, $p < .01$; satiation: $F(2, 22) = 11.96$; $p < .001$). This effect is caused mainly by the marked increase in group III towards the work end. The feelings of fatigue and satiation are especially subject to these strong temporal changes.

A main effect of the performance graphs is found only on the experienced satiation ($F(2, 11) = 8.23$, $p < .01$). Averaged across the times of measurement, the workers following curve III express a significant higher degree of satiation than the workers following curve I and curve II. Comparable effects of the performance graphs on the experienced fatigue ($F(2, 11) = 0.91$, n.s.) and monotony ($F(2, 11) = 0.97$, n.s.) are not demonstrated.

Discussion

These results are nearly all in line with the expectations about the effectiveness of the information provided by the job information system. They show that the continuous setting of performance goals and the presentation of feedback about the progress of work in relation to these goals are not only effective means for controlling performance output over time. Goals and feedback also prove to be effective means for influencing the time scheduling of work.

Irrespective of the specific time courses of the performance graphs assigned, this effect was produced by inducing the workers to distribute the daily amount of work over all the working time and, thereby, to exhaust the total time frame available for carrying out the work, including the rest time permitted. As a consequence, the workers were encouraged to break the work for taking rest pauses whenever they fell short of the time limits of the single subgoals assigned. This kind of time scheduling answers the initial purposes of the relaxation allowance much better than saving it up entirely until the work end (Rutenfranz & Stoll, 1966).

Under some circumstances like the situation described here, this goal- and feedback-controlled time scheduling of work prove instrumental for improving performance quality. Two mechanisms seem to be responsible for this effect. On the one hand, the goal-induced slowdown of work pace may have reduced the risk of crossing the critical time threshold of a speed–accuracy tradeoff (cf. Pachella & Pew, 1968; Rabbitt, 1981; Schmidt, Sherwood, Zelaznik, & Leikind, 1985). On the other hand, the use of the relaxation allowance for taking many short rest breaks may have removed an accumulation of strain that otherwise is expected to interfere with performing on a high-quality level, especially at tasks demanding full concentration. Whether the one or the other mechanism was involved in the improvement of performance quality cannot be decided definitely on the basis of our data. Likely both contributed to the realization of this consequent effect of the changed time scheduling of work.

The strain reactions of the workers indicate a clear covariation with the performance requirements set by the graphs in the course of time. The higher the levels of performance required, the higher the intensity of the strain reactions experienced by the workers. These performance-dependent temporal variations in strain are most pronounced with respect to the experienced fatigue and satiation. However, this is quite understandable because, on the basis of the theory underlying the questionnaire, the states of fatigue and satiation should be more subject to motivational and emotional reactions to the actual performance requirements of work, in contrast to monotony, which is expected to be more sensitive to the influence of some specific characteristics of work content like variety, complexity, etc. (cf. Plath & Richter, 1984). As the characteristics of work content were not changed under the different performance graphs but only the performance requirements in the course of the working time, the results are well in line with the theoretical assumptions.

In addition to these performance-dependent temporal variations in strain, the workers following curve III appear to be more strained than the workers following curve I and curve II. This effect is mainly due to the marked increase in satiation towards the work end. Although here the performance requirements are on the same high level as the performance requirements in group I at midmorning, in group III the intensity of the experienced satiation is significantly higher than in group I. However, on the basis of the theory of circadian performance rhythms (Folkard & Monk, 1985; Hockey & Colquhoun, 1972), this result is quite reasonable. In group III the workers had to perform their maximum in the periods of decreased efficiency in the early afternoon, whereas the workers in group I had to show their maximum parallel with the increase in performance efficiency at midmorning.

Deviating from our expectations, there were no significant differences in the strain reactions among the workers of group I and group II. Both groups did not differ in postexperimental interviews, in which all groups were asked to evaluate the job information system, especially the performance graph assigned to them. In comparison with the situation before the installation of the systems, both performance graphs were evaluated as uniformly positive, in contrast to performance graph III, which in the opinion of the workers came off badly. Possibly the straight-lined graph did not deviate to such an extent from the supposed optimal graph I to produce marked differences in the strain reactions. However, the strain reactions of the workers following curve III substantiate the general assumption of the theory of circadian performance rhythms, that it really makes a difference for the workers when in the course of the working time they have to perform on high or low levels. This aspect is always to be taken into account if, as in the present approach, goal setting is applied as a means for controlling the performance output over longer time-spans than usually examined in goal-setting studies.

CONCLUSIONS

Based on the present findings, the following conclusions can be drawn. First, goal setting and feedback are not only effective means for determining performance output in general but also are effective means for influencing the manner in which workers distribute their daily amount of work over time. By that, goal setting and feedback have an effect on the time scheduling of work, especially on the workers' use of the relaxation allowance that gives them the opportunity to recover by taking rest breaks of certain lengths. Moreover, this goal- and feedback-controlled time scheduling of work may even by instrumental for improving performance quality. And finally, in view of the theory of circadian performance rhythms, goal setting can help motivate workers to control their performance output in line with the circadian variations in performance efficiency. As a consequence, it may also influence the strain experienced by the workers in the course of carrying out the work.

Of course, our study does not claim to have finally examined all these possible consequent effects of goal setting. These, certainly, deserve further examination. On the contrary, the aim of the study was to direct attention to these often neglected consequent effects and to illustrate how the technique of goal setting can also be applied to optimize them.

REFERENCES

Austin, J. T., & Bobko, P. (1985). Goal-setting theory: Unexplored areas and future research needs. *Journal of Occupational Psychology, 58*, 289–308.

Folkard, S., & Monk, T. H. (1985). Circadian performance rhythms. In S. Folkard & T. H. Monk (Eds.), *Hours of work: Temporal factors in work-scheduling* (pp. 37–52). Chichester, England: Wiley.

Graf, O. (1944). Ein Verfahren zur zwanglosen Steuerung der Arbeitsgeschwindigkeit nach vorgegebenen Arbeitskurven, insbesondere zu physiologisch richtiger Arbeitsablaufregelung [A procedure for controlling work pace by assigned performance curves]. *Arbeitsphysiologie, 13*, 125–139.

Graf, O. (1959). *Arbeitszeit und Produktivität. Bd. 2: Ganztägige Arbeitsablaufuntersuchungen an 200 Arbeitsplätzen* [Working time and productivity]. Berlin: Duncker & Humblot.

Hacker, W., & Richter, P. (1984). *Psychische Fehlbeanspruchung: Psychische Ermüdung, Monotonie, Sättigung und Stress* [Psychic strain reactions: Fatigue, monotony, satiation and stress]. (2nd ed.). Berlin: Springer-Verlag. (Spezielle Arbeits- und Ingenieurpsychologie in Einzeldarstellungen, Bd. 2).

Hockey, G. R. J., & Colquhoun, W. P. (1972). Diurnal variation in human performance: A review. In W. P. Colquhoun (Ed.), *Aspects of human efficiency* (pp. 1–23). London: The English Universities Press.

Kleinbeck, U., Schmidt, K.-H., Schleyer, M., & Brockmann, W. (1985). Ein Arbeitsplatzinformationssystem (AIDA) zur motivationsunterstützenden Selbstkontrolle von industriellen Bewegungsleistungen und zur individuellen Pausenverteilung bei freier Arbeit [A job information system to stimulate self-control of performance and of the distribution of rest pauses]. *Zeitschrift für Arbeitswissenschaft, 39*, 1–5.

Locke, E. A., & Latham, G. P. (1984). *Goal setting: A motivational technique that works.* Englewood Cliffs, NJ: Prentice–Hall.

Locke, E. A., Shaw, K. N., Saari, L. M., & Latham, G. P. (1981). Goal setting and task performance: 1969–1980. *Psychological Bulletin, 90*, 125–152.

Pachella, R. G., & Pew, R. W. (1968). Speed–accuracy tradeoff in reaction time: Effect of discrete criterion times. *Journal of Experimental Psychology, 76*, 19–24.

Plath, H.-E., & Richter, P. (1978). Der BMS(I)—Erfassungsbogen—Ein Verfahren zur skalierten Erfassung erlebter Beanspruchungsfolgen [The BMS(I)-questionnaire: A technique to assess subjective strain reactions at work]. *Probleme und Ergebnisse der Psychologie, 65*, 45–85.

Plath, H.-E., & Richter, P. (1984). *Ermüdung-Monotonie-Sättigung-Stress: BMS-Handanweisung* [Fatigue, monotony, satiation and stress: BMS-manual]. Berlin: Psychodiagnostisches Zentrum.

Rabbitt, P. M. A. (1981). Sequential reactions. In D. H. Holding (Ed.), *Human skills* (pp. 153-175). Chichester, England: Wiley.

Rutenfranz, J., & Stoll, F. (1966). Untersuchungen über die Verteilung von Pausen bei freier Arbeit [The distribution of rest pauses at self-paced work]. *Arbeitswissenschaft, 5,* 132-135.

Ryan, T. A. (1970). *Intentional behavior: An approach to human motivation.* New York: Ronald Press.

Schmidt, K.-H., Kleinbeck, U., & Knauth, P. (1988). *Über die Wirkung von Leistungsvorgaben auf das Pausenverhalten und das Beanspruchungserleben bei freier Arbeit [The effect of performance goals on the distribution of rest periods and subjective strain]. *Zeitschrift für Arbeitswissenschaft, 42,* 96-101.

Schmidt, R. A., Sherwood, D. E., Zelaznik, H. N., & Leikind, B. J. (1985). Speed-accuracy tradeoff in motor behavior: Theories of impulse variability. In H. Heuer, U. Kleinbeck, & K.-H. Schmidt (Eds.), *Motor behavior: Programming, control and acquisition* (pp. 79-123). Berlin: Springer-Verlag.

8

Enhancing Work Motivation Through Productivity Measurement and Feedback

Robert D. Pritchard
Texas A&M University

This chapter deals with enhancing organizational productivity by increasing the motivation of organizational members. What I describe are some of the results of a 4-year project that has dealt with: (a) the development of a new approach to measuring organizational productivity, (b) the implementation and evaluation of this approach in an ongoing organization, (c) the effects of feeding back the productivity data to members of the organizations, and (d) the effects of adding goal setting and incentives to the feedback. In the limited space available, I cannot give a full treatment to any of these aspects of the work. What I do is to present a summary of the productivity measurement system and its application as feedback, focusing particularly on the motivational aspects of the project. More information about the project can be found in Pritchard, Jones, Roth, Stuebing, and Ekeberg (1987, 1988, 1989).

Productivity is an important topic. National economies, industries, individual organizations, and parts of individual organizations are all concerned about productivity. Concern about productivity is not limited to profit-making organizations. Government agencies, educational institutions, nonprofit organizations, and the military are all interested in productivity and its improvement (Pritchard, 1989).

It is easy to understand why productivity, especially productivity improvement, is so important. If market-based economies, industries, or individual organizations become more productive, they provide better products and services at lower cost and thus remain competitive, increase their market share, and in general have more resources to work with.

In fact, the importance of productivity improvement is something that everyone can agree on. This can best be understood by considering the consequences of a lack of productivity improvement. With no productivity growth, there is a fixed pie that all parties continually want a larger slice of. Individuals want to increase their standard of living, unions want more benefits for their members, companies want to make more profits, and different elements of the society want more resources for everything from education to national defense, from roads to recreational facilities. Without productivity growth, one request for resources can only be met at the expense of another. However, with productivity growth, the increase in resources means there is a larger pie to distribute, so all constituencies have a greater chance of being satisfied.

Although productivity is an issue that can be addressed at the level of entire national economies and industries, the focus of the effort I describe has been at the level of the organization and at subunits in the organization. It is at this level where the motivation of individuals has its greatest impact.

To oversimplify a bit, productivity at the level of the organization can be addressed in two ways, either by changing the technology or by changing how well individuals do the work. Our focus is on changing how well the people do the work. I believe that there is a great deal of productivity improvement that can be made by helping individuals and groups use their work resources more effectively. This means increasing motivation in the classic sense (Campbell & Pritchard, 1976) of increasing the amount of effort the individual commits to work behavior, increasing the persistence of that behavior, and making the direction of that behavior much more efficiently directed at the organization's goals.

The basic premise of this work is that if a quality measure of productivity is developed and fed back, it will lead to significant increases in productivity, through increases in motivation.

The basic problem, however, is how to measure productivity. There are a whole host of issues here that could be the subject of an entire book (e.g., Balk, 1975; Felix & Riggs, 1983; Kendrick, 1984; Kopelman, 1986; Mali, 1978; Muckler, 1982; Norman & Bahiri, 1972; Tuttle, 1981). First, there are a variety of complex conceptual issues to be considered. For example, productivity could be considered as an efficiency concept of outputs divided by inputs such as number of units produced divided by labor costs. Or it could be an effectiveness concept dealing with degree of attainment of organizational objectives. There are many other important conceptual questions. Is it possible or even desirable to have a productivity measurement system that can be used at all levels from a subunit of an organization to the level of a national economy? What level of analysis *should* be used? What model of organizations should be assumed? How is productivity different to the economist, the accountant, the industrial engineer, and the behavioral scientist, and how should these differences be integrated?

In addition to these conceptual questions, there are numerous measurement questions. How can an overall index of productivity be generated that includes all aspects of the work? How can the varying importance of different aspect of the work be incorporated into the measurement system? How can productivity be measured so that different units can be directly compared to each other? How can productivity measurement from different units be aggregated to obtain a measure of the entire organization's productivity? How can the measurement be done so that it is molecular enough to be useful to the individuals doing the work, yet be combined so that it gives an accurate picture of the productivity of large organizational units?

One of the things that became clear in dealing with these issues is that there is no one best way to measure productivity. It depends so much on the purpose of measurement. Trying to get an overall index of the financial performance of the organization results in a very different measurement system than one designed to give individuals the information they need to do an optimal job.

One principle, however, is very clear and very powerful; that is, *What you measure is what you get.* The very process of measuring an aspect of productivity identifies it as something that is important, that will be studied, and that people will be accountable for. If this data is formally fed back in addition to being measured, the effect is even stronger. This is a very powerful motivational principle, but it is a two-edged sword. If the measurement and feedback system is a good one, it can result in powerful positive effects for the organization and its members. If the system is incomplete or not entirely consistent with the organization's goals, the system can be counterproductive.

What this research project did was to develop a new approach to measuring organizational productivity that was designed from the start to be a source of feedback to be used to increase productivity. The system attempted to deal with the conceptual and measurement issues raised previously. In the next section the productivity measurement system is described.

THE PRODUCTIVITY MEASUREMENT SYSTEM

The productivity measurement system is termed the ProMES for Productivity Measurement and Enhancement System. Part of its conceptual foundation comes from Naylor, Pritchard, and Ilgen (1980). Developing the productivity measurement system involves four steps. The first is to identify what we call *products*. A product is a type of organizational objective. A unit's products are the things that it is expected to do. A unit that repairs electronic equipment might have as products (a) meeting repair demand, (b) doing high quality repair, and (c) keeping an adequate number of personnel trained to work on the different types of equipment.

These products are listed and reviewed by a group of unit supervisors and incumbents. This group continues to review the list until it is satisfied that all the unit's products are identified and properly phrased. A typical unit would have from three to five products. This list is then reviewed by higher levels of supervision and management for completeness and accuracy. Any disagreements are discussed with the originating group and resolved. At this point, a set of products has been identified and agreed on by multiple levels of the organization.

The second step is to identify *indicators* of the products. An indicator is a measure of the extent to which the unit is accomplishing a product. The group of supervisors and incumbents is asked to think of measures that they could use to show their supervisors how well they are accomplishing their products. For the product of meeting repair demand in the electronic repair unit exemplified before, an indicator might be the percentage of items brought in that were repaired within 1 week. Some products will have multiple indicators to capture all the aspects of the product. Typically, there will be a total of from 8 to 15 indicators for a given unit.

As with the products, the group works on the indicators until the members are satisfied that the list comprehensively covers all the products and represents valid measures of the products. Great care must be exercised at this point to insure that good indicators are generated. It is easy to end up with indicators that are incomplete or that tap the easily measured aspects of the product rather than what is really important but more difficult to measure. It is also important that the indicator be consistent with the product in the sense that generating a large amount of the indicator does in fact achieve the product. This issue needs much more care than it might at first seem. Once the members of the group have finalized the indicators, the process of approval up the organizational hierarchy is done as it was with the products.

Whereas some of the steps used in identifying products and indicators are unique to the ProMES, the basic idea of using something like products and indicators is common to many approaches to productivity (e.g., Felix & Riggs, 1983; Kendrick, 1984; Kopelman, 1986; Tuttle, Wilkinson, & Matthews, 1985). The most unique feature of the system is the next step. Once the products and indicators are identified and approved, this next step is to establish *contingencies*. The term "contingency" should not be confused with the behaviorist's use of the term to mean the relationship between a behavior and a reinforcer. In contrast, we use the term as it is used by Naylor, Pritchard, and Ilgen (1980) to refer to the idea that the level of evaluation of an outcome is contingent on the amount of that outcome. A contingency is the relationship between the amount of the indicator and the effectiveness of that amount of the indicator. Figure 8.1 presents an example of a contingency. The top half of the figure shows the general form of a contingency. The horizontal axis is the amount of the indicator. The value range from the worst feasible level that the indicator could have to the best possible level. On the vertical axis of the figure is the effectiveness

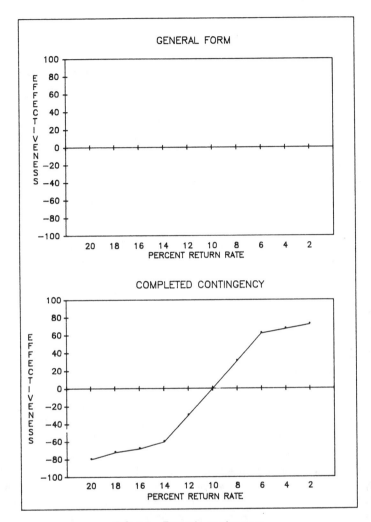

FIG. 8.1 Example contingency.

value of the various levels of the indicator. It ranges from +100, which is maximum effectiveness, to −100, minimum effectiveness. It also has a zero point that is defined as the expected, or neutral, level of effectiveness; that is, the zero point is neither positive nor negative. For this example we have chosen an indicator for the product doing high-quality repairs. The indicator is return rate: the percentage of items that did not function immediately after repair. Assume that the people in the organization indicate that a 2% return rate is the best possible level, and the worst possible return rate would by 20%.

Once the best and worst possible levels of output have been established by the organizational personnel, the next task is to identify the actual function that relates amount of the indicator to effectiveness. We start by determining the zero point; that is, what level of the indicator is the expected level, the level that is neither especially good nor especially bad. Once this is established, a point would be placed on the figure at the intersection of the zero point of the vertical axis and the level of neutral point on the horizontal axis. For example, if the neutral point was identified as a return rate of 10%, it would be so indicated as shown in the bottom half of Fig. 8.1.

Next, the effectiveness levels of the other indicator values are established for this and for the other indicators through a group consensus scaling process described in Pritchard et al. (1987). In essence, the effectiveness levels of the maximum and minimum points of the indicator are established by the group through group discussion and then the effectiveness levels of the remaining points are determined. Steps are taken to insure the accuracy of the indicators relative to each other.

In our example, assume that the personnel in the organization said that to be at the minimum return rate would correspond to an effectiveness value of − 80, and to be at the maximum would be a + 70. After the other points on the function were identified, the contingency might look like the bottom of Fig. 8.1. It indicates that going above the neutral point of a 10% return rate is positive, but this increase is not linear in the sense that once they get to a return rate of 6%, further increases do not represent as great an increase in effectiveness. Likewise, at the low end, once the return rate gets as bad as 14%, they are doing very badly and further decreases are proportionally not as bad.

This process would be followed for each of the indicators, and once they were all scaled and reviewed for accuracy, the contingency set would be complete. There would be one contingency for each of the indicators. These contingencies would then be approved by higher levels of supervision and management, as were the products and indicators.

Two things are particularly noteworthy about the contingencies. The first is that the overall slope of the function expresses the relative importance of the indicator. The steeper the overall slope, the more important the indicator is to overall effectiveness. Thus, the contingencies reflect differential importance.

The second noteworthy aspect of the contingencies is that they can be nonlinear. This is necessary to accurately reflect the realities of an organization's functioning. In many cases, the relationships that actually exist are simply not linear. A linear relationship would mean that to improve a given amount at the low end of the measure is as good as improving that same amount at the high end. It would be very common, for example, for improvements in the middle range of an indicator to result in large improvements in productivity, but at the high end a point of diminishing returns is realized. This frequently occurring nonlinearity is preserved by the system.

Once the contingencies are completed and approved by management, the last step is to put the system together. This would be accomplished by first collecting the indicator data for a given period of time. Assume that the time period selected was a month-long period. The data for the different indicators would be collected at the end of the month. Then, based on the contingencies, effectiveness scores would be determined for each indicator by calculating the effectiveness for that level of the indicator. For example, if the maintenance unit had a return rate of 6% in a given month, examining the contingency in the bottom of Fig. 8.1 indicates that such a return rate is associated with an effectiveness score of +60. Continuing this process would give an effectiveness value for each indicator. Once the effectiveness value for each indicator is determined, they can be summed to get the overall effectiveness of the unit.

This effectiveness score has a distinct meaning in that a score of zero means that organizational personnel are just meeting expectations; their productivity is neither particularly good not bad. As the score becomes positive, they are exceeding expectations. The more positive the score, the more they are exceeding expectations. As the score becomes negative, they are below expectations.

The ability to simply sum effectiveness scores is a major feature of the system. This sum does indeed reflect the overall productivity of the unit because all aspects of the work are combined by the use of the indicators. Furthermore, because the varying importance of the different aspects of the work and the nonlinearities are already included in the contingencies, the sum includes these factors as well.

This information on levels of the indicators, effectiveness for each indicator, and overall effectiveness is then given to the personnel in the form of a written feedback report for each performance period (e.g., each month).

APPLICATION OF THE SYSTEM

This approach to measuring productivity and using these measures as feedback was evaluated by developing the productivity measurement system in five units of an Air Force base in the southwest United States. One unit was similar to the repair group used as the preceding example. The other four units were involved in a large warehouse and had functions to accept incoming property, store and retrieve property when ordered, deliver property around the base, and inspect the property. The number of individuals in each of the five units ranged from 12 to 32.

The design cc isted of developing the system in each of the five units and then instituting a baseline period where productivity data were collected but not fed back to the personnel. After this baseline period of 8–9 months, each of the units received monthly feedback from the system for 5 months. Next, a goal-setting intervention was added to feedback for 5 months. Finally, incentives in the form of time off from work were added to the feedback and goal setting for a final 5 months.

Results during the development of the system indicated that unit personnel were able to develop the components of the system, and data collected on the reliability and validity of the system was supportive.

Effects on productivity are summarized in Fig. 8.2. This figure is the mean overall effectiveness across the five units for each month. The mean increase over baseline was 50% for feedback, 75% for goal setting, and 76% for incentives. The strength and pattern of results were consistent for the five individual units. These results indicate a major increase in productivity. The effects were extremely large, much larger than those found in most research (Guzzo, Jette, & Katzell, 1985).

A number of other findings are pertinent and can be summarized as follows:

1. In addition to the effectiveness data, the raw indicator data showed large increases.

2. The number of personnel in the units stayed the same or decreased slightly from baseline to incentives.

3. Overtime hours decreased from a mean of 1,348 hours per month during baseline to 892 during feedback, 404 during goal setting, and 416 during incentives.

4. Output data collected on several control units not in the program overall showed no or only a slight increase in productivity from baseline through incentives.

5. Subjective reactions to the system in the form of informal comments were very positive.

6. Work attitudes either improved or remained unchanged during the 15 months of feedback.

7. The units were able to maintain the system themselves after the departure of the research team, and productivity remained as high as it was at the time of our departure.

8. The maintenance unit has continued the system, but the warehouse units have not.

DISCUSSION

Research Conclusions

Several conclusions can be drawn from this research. The productivity measurement system seems to be successful in measuring productivity. Using it as a basis for feedback and for the interventions of goal setting and incentives resulted in very large gains in productivity. For example, using the most conservative figures, the increase in productivity under feedback is 4.2

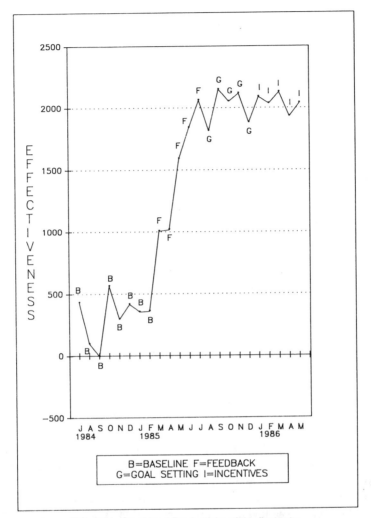

FIG. 8.2. Combined Productivity of the five units.

times as large as the largest effect size for feedback reported by Guzzo, Jette, and Katzell (1985) in their meta-analysis of productivity interventions. In addition, the system worked consistently across five units that varied in the nature of work they did, the technology employed, the nature of the work flow, the type of organizational structure, their size, the level of education of the personnel, and the initial level of productivity when the program started.

There were also two features of the system that were not discussed here that appeared to work quite successfully. First, the system allowed for aggregating the productivity measurement system of the four warehouse units into an overall measure for that organization. Second, the system allowed for direct comparison of the productivity of the different units. These features are discussed in Pritchard et al. (1987).

Motivational Effects

Clearly the interventions increased productivity. If we define motivation to include the amplitude, direction, and persistence of behavior, it seems clear that the system was successful because of an increase in motivation. I want to turn now to a discussion of why and how motivation had such a powerful effect in increasing productivity.

One reason the system seemed to be successful was the use of a *single index* of productivity. Such a single index has the advantage of summarizing the effectiveness of a complex organization into one easily communicable number. Such a single index is motivational because it tells the personnel in an easily understandable way how well they are doing, and whether they are improving or decreasing in productivity. Management, supervision, and incumbents reported that without this summary measure, they would not have been able to derive an overall sense of how the unit was doing.

Another reason for the success of the system was that it was *accepted* by unit personnel. This is a very serious issue for any intervention (Hurst, 1980; Tuttle & Sink, 1984). If the members of the unit do not accept a program, its effects will be limited, and the possibility of it being sabotaged is present. Acceptance of this system was high because unit personnel were heavily involved in the implementation of the system. They identified the products and indicators, they developed the contingencies, and they defended their work to management. Hence, they had a sense of ownership of it.

One apparent conflict is why the system was ultimately discontinued when it was accepted so well and reactions to it were so positive. The reasons had to do with a change in command. Whereas the new manager was positive towards the system and even tried to get it expanded to other units under his control, he had a serious problem with giving some units time off when the other units under his control were not eligible for such an incentive. Furthermore, due to an increased work load, giving the time off incentives became more difficult. Thus, the system was discontinued more because of problems with the incentives rather than problems with the system itself.

The system facilitated *role clarification* (Rizzo, House, & Lirtzman, 1970). The process of developing, refining, and getting approval for the products, indicators, and contingencies forced role clarification. Unit personnel discussed what their objectives should be, disagreements surfaced and were resolved. Expected levels of output were discussed and consensus achieved. Finally, these decisions were reviewed by higher management, debated, and a final resolution was made. When this process was finished, the units had a clear picture of what their objectives were, what they should be focusing on to achieve these objectives, what was expected of them in each area, and what was good and bad productivity in each area.

The use of the system also dramatically increased the amount and quality of the *feedback* unit personnel received. Prior to the system units had some objective feedback on part of their activities. However, the data that was available was known to be influenced by factors beyond the control of the units, and it was not clear what level of output was expected of the units. The formal feedback system from the ProMES should have been effective because it provided more frequent, accurate, and specific feedback (Annett, 1969; Ilgen, Fisher, & Taylor, 1979; Ivancevich, Donnelly, & Lyon, 1970; Pritchard, Montagno, & Moore, 1978), as well as more positive feedback (Feather, 1968; Ilgen & Hamstra, 1972). In addition, the feedback they received contained evaluative information (Dockstader, Nebeker, & Shumate, 1977; Hammond & Summers, 1972).

The positive feedback seemed particularly important. Personnel indicated that the feedback from the system was unusual in that it represented one of the few times they were told they were doing a good job. They indicated that in the past they only heard from management when they made mistakes. This positive feedback also appeared to help them increase their sense of task competence (Ashford & Cummings, 1983; Hackman & Lawler, 1971; White, 1959).

The facilitation of *goal setting* was undoubtedly a significant factor both in the formal goal-setting interventions, and also because the feedback allowed units to much more readily set their own informal goals (Locke, 1968; Locke, Cartledge, & Koeppel, 1968; Locke, Shaw, Saari, & Latham 1981; Tubbs, 1986). As the aforementioned literature has clearly demonstrated, goal setting can have substantial motivational effects.

Another motivational feature of the system is that personnel could *see the results of their efforts*. Most jobs are structured so that doing a better job does not show up in any measurable way. The frequent feedback provided by the system seemed to improve the effort-to-performance expectancy referred to in expectancy theory approaches to motivation (Campbell & Pritchard, 1976; Mitchell, 1974). Specifically, the connection between unit effort and productivity was enhanced. For example, when changes had been made to improve an indicator, the following month there was considerable interest in that indicator. There seemed to be considerable satisfaction when the indicator did improve. This allowed personnel to tell when their effort had resulted in increased productivity.

A very important reason for the effectiveness of the approach seemed to be that it allowed personnel to *focus on the same objectives*. Before the implementation of the system, different supervisors and different levels of management had different things on which they focused effort. Furthermore, what was high priority changed frequently. The process of developing the productivity measurement system and getting all levels of the organization to agree on it seemed to reduce this serious problem dramatically. All had agreed on what should be maximized and a concerted effort could then be maintained to accomplish this.

Another apparent reason for the success of the system was that it provided considerable information on where to direct effort. First, it allowed for the *early identification and diagnosis of problems*. The feedback reports showed personnel when productivity was starting to slip in a given area. This allowed the unit to deal with the problem before it became serious. Second, it allowed the organization to *know when the problems were fixed*. These factors greatly reduced the tendency to ignore problems until they became serious.

The system also allowed for *competition across units*. In the four warehouse units this competition was clearly present between sections, was friendly in nature, and seemed to have a positive effect on productivity.

Another plausible reason for the effectiveness of the system is that it made units *accountable* for their productivity. The regular measurement of productivity and the public nature of the data provided a concrete performance history that was hard for the unit to ignore. The fact that the data existed generated a source of motivation for unit personnel. They wanted to look good and they also knew that they would have to answer for it if they did poorly. This accountability also appeared to make personnel more objective about problem areas. There was much less of a tendency to make excuses and more of a desire to try to find positive solutions.

In conclusion, this short treatment of the ProMES and its application has skimmed over many important issues such as the conceptualization of productivity used, how the scaling of the contingencies is done, the details of the feedback and other treatments, data on many of the findings I presented, and explanation of some of the features of the system to which I only alluded. These issues are discussed elsewhere (Pritchard et al. 1987, 1988, 1989). I can only hope that this chapter serves to increase interest in what I believe is an effective way to measure and enhance productivity.

REFERENCES

Annett, J. (1969). *Feedback and human behavior*. Baltimore, MD: Penguin.

Ashford, S. J., & Cummings, L. L. (1983). Feedback as an individual resource: Personal strategies of creating information. *Organizational Behavior and Human Performance, 32*, 370–398.

Balk, W. L. (1975). Technological trends in productivity measurement. *Public Personnel Management, March–April*, 128–133.

Campbell, J. C., & Pritchard, R. D. (1976). Motivation theory in industrial and organizational psychology. In M. D. Dunnette (Ed.), *Handbook of industrial and organizational psychology* (pp. 63–130). Chicago: Rand McNally.

Dockstader, S. L., Nebeker, D. M., & Shumate, E. C. (1977). *The effects of feedback and an implied standard on work performance* (NPRDC TR 77-45). San Diego, CA: Navy Personnel Research and Development Center.

Feather, N. T. (1968). Change in confidence following success or failure as a predictor of subsequent performance. *Journal of Personality and Social Psychology, 9*, 38–46.

Felix, G. H., & Riggs, J. L. (1983). Productivity measurement by objectives. In W. B. Werther, Jr., W. A. Ruch, & L. McClure (Eds.), *Productivity through people* (pp. 349–356). St. Paul, MN: West.

Guzzo, R. A., Jette, R. D., & Katzell, R. A. (1985). The effects of psychologically based intervention programs on worker productivity: A meta-analysis. *Personnel Psychology, 38*, 275–291.

Hackman, J. R., & Lawler, E. E., III. (1971). Employee reactions job characteristics. *Journal of Applied Psychology, 55*, 259–286.

Hammond, K. R., & Summers, D. A. (1972). Cognitive control. *Psychological Review, 79*, 58–67.

Hurst, E. G. (1980). Attributes of performance measures. *Public Productivity Review, 4*, 43–50.

Ilgen, D. R., Fisher, C. D., & Taylor, M. S. (1979). Consequences of individual feedback on behavior in organizations. *Journal of Applied Psychology, 64*, 349–371.

Ilgen, D. R., & Hamstra, B. W. (1972). Performance satisfaction as a function of the difference between expected and reported performance at five levels of reported performance. *Organizational Behavior and Human Performance, 7*, 359–370.

Ivancevich, J. M., Donnelly, J. N., & Lyon, J. L. (1970). A study of the impact of management by objectives on perceived need satisfaction. *Personnel Psychology, 23*, 139–151.

Kendrick, J. W. (1984). *Improving company productivity*. Baltimore, MD: Johns Hopkins University Press.

Kopelman, R. E. (1986). *Managing productivity in organizations: A practical, people-oriented perspective*. New York: McGraw-Hill.

Locke, E. A. (1968). Toward a theory of task motivation and incentives. *Organizational Behavior and Human Performance, 3*, 157–189.

Locke, E. A., Cartledge, N., & Koeppel, J. (1968). Motivational effects of knowledge of results: Goal-setting phenomenon. *Psychological Bulletin, 70*, 474–485.

Locke, E. A., Shaw, K. N., Saari, L. M., & Latham, G. P. (1981). Goal setting and task performance: 1969-1980. *Psychological Bulletin, 90*(1), 125–152.

Mitchell, T. R. (1974). Expectancy models of job satisfaction, occupation preference, and effort: A theoretical, methodological and empirical appraisal. *Psychological Bulletin, 81*, 1053–1077.

Mali, P. (1978). *Improving total productivity*. New York: Wiley.

Muckler, F. A. (1982). Evaluating productivity. In M. D. Dunnette & E. A. Fleishman (Eds.), *Human performance and productivity: Human capability assessment* (Vol. 1, pp. 13–47). Hillsdale, NJ: Lawrence Erlbaum Associates.

Naylor, J. C., Pritchard, R. D., & Ilgen, D. R. (1980). *A theory of behavior in organizations*. New York: Academic Press.

Norman, R. G., & Bahiri, S. (1972). *Productivity measurement and incentives*. London: Butterworths.

Pritchard, R. D. (in press). Organizational productivity. In M. D. Dunnette (Ed.), *Handbook of industrial and organizational psychology* (2nd Ed., Vol. 4). Palo Alto, CA: Consulting Psychologists Press.

Pritchard R. D., Jones, S. D., Roth, P. L., Stuebing, K. K., & Ekeberg, S. E. (1987). *Organizational productivity measurement: The development and evaluation of an integrated approach* (AFHRL-TR-86-64). Brooks AFB, TX: Manpower and Personnel Division, Air Force Human Resources Laboratory.

Pritchard, R. D., Jones, S. D., Roth, P. L., Stuebing, K. K., & Ekeberg, S. E. (1988). The effects of feedback, goal setting, and incentives on organizational productivity. *Journal of Applied Psychology Monograph Series, 73*, 2, 337–358.

Pritchard, R. D., Jones, S. D., Roth, P. L., Stuebing, K. K., & Ekeberg, S. E. (1989). The evaluation of an integrated approach to measuring organizational productivity. *Personnel Psychology, 42*(1), 69–115.

Pritchard, R. D., Montagno, R. V., & Moore, J. R. (1978). *Enhancing productivity through feedback and job design.* Air Force Human Resources Laboratory Technical Report (AFHRL-TR-78-44, AD-A061703). Brooks AFB, TX: Occupation and Manpower Research Division, Air Force Human Resources Laboratory.

Rizzo, J. R., House, R. J., & Lirtzman, S. I. (1970). Role conflict and ambiguity in complex organizations. *Administrative Science Quarterly, 15*, 150–163.

Tubbs, M. E. (1986). Goal Setting: A meta-analytic examination of the empirical evidence. *Journal of Applied Psychology, 71*, 474–483.

Tuttle, T. C. (1981). *Productivity measurement methods: Classification, critique, and implications for the Air Force* (AFHRL-TR-81-9, AD-A105 627). Brooks AFB, TX: Manpower and Personnel Division, Air Force Human Resources Laboratory.

Tuttle, T. C., & Sink, D. S. (1984). Taking the threat out of productivity measurement. *National Productivity Review*, Winter, 24–32.

Tuttle, T. C., Wilkinson, R. E., & Matthews, M. D. (1985). *Field test of the methodology for generating efficiency and effectiveness measures* (AFHRL-TP-84-54, AD-A158 183). Brooks AFB, TX: Manpower and Personnel Division, Air Force Human Resources Laboratory.

White, R. W. (1959). Motivation reconsidered: The concept of competence. *Psychological Review, 66*, 297–333.

9
Designing Productive Leadership Systems to Improve Both Work Motivation and Organizational Effectiveness

George B. Graen
University of Cincinnati

The temporary improvement in work motivation within competitive organizations can be brought about by a large number of relatively inexpensive programs. In contrast, long-term gains in the motivation to work that contribute to an organization's competitive position in its marketplace appear to be isolated incidents.

For the last 20 years, we have been studying how competitive organizations in the United States and Japan attempt to bring about long-term advantage from their human resources. What we have found leads us to speculate that such long-term competitive advantage requires a complete system comprised of the compatible components of organization, focus, leadership cadre, and workforce (Graen, 1989).

The purpose of this chapter is to review relevant research literature and to speculate on methods of designing productive leadership systems for managers that develop leadership teams through organizational processes. We begin at the dyadic leader–member exchange level, proceed to the level of the organization unit, and reach the level of the management team. This last step draws on research that incorporates the Jacobs and Jaques' (1987) theory of managerial role capabilities.

DYADIC LEADER-MEMBER EXCHANGE (LMX): AN HISTORICAL OVERVIEW

The question of whether or not the unit differentiation process occurs (i.e., In-Group versus Out-Group) was first investigated by Graen, Orris, and

Johnson (1973) in a longitudinal field investigation. Graen and his associates studied new hires from the first day on the job until 4 months later. They found that supervisors established effective LMXs with one group of newcomers and established ineffective LMXs with another group of employees. Moreover, the supervisors imposed a self-fulfilling prophecy on the newcomers. They believed that they could predict which newcomers would stay and which would leave within a few months. And they acted on this belief. For those who they predicted would leave, they invested a minimum of time and energy. At times, they practiced "benign neglect." In contrast, for those who they predicted to stay, they invested a good deal of time and energy in their development and care. The result was two very different types of dyadic exchanges within the same unit. Those predicted by their superior to leave early suffered increased ambiguity about what their supervisor wanted them to do, which began the 2d week, increased the 4th week, and increased again the 7th and 12th weeks. In sharp contrast, those predicted to stay suffered little ambiguity about their supervisor's demands after the 1st week. As might be expected, by the 12th week, most of those treated as "short timers" left the organization and most of those accepted as "long timers" remained. Hence, the differentiation process within units occurred very early in the dyadic interaction process and had significant implications for career outcomes of members 3 months later.

How do Dyads Differ Within Units?

Dansereau, Graen, and Haga (1975) addressed the phenomena of unit differentiation in greater detail. In this study, an entire management hierarchy was investigated longitudinally over 9 months. Fortunately for this study, a company reorganization had left 90% of the direct reporting dyads containing at least one new manager. Hence, the study began at the beginning of the development of 90% of the LMXs and followed this development for 9 months. By systematically administering questionnaires and interviewing both members of each managerial dyad four times over the 9 months (1st, 4th, 7th, and 9th month), the elaboration of unit differentiation was documented.

The results of this investigation of managers developing LMXs from the state of strangers to the state of well-known co-workers were revealing. In sharp contradiction to the conventional leadership theory (Stogdill, 1974) that managers treat all members reporting directly to them in the same manner and hence developed very similar LMXs within the same unit, the results of this longitudinal study demonstrated the development of extremely different LMXs within the same unit. Moreover, this unit differentiation process was the norm; and different LMXs were enacted for different members in all the work units studied. One of the most revealing aspects of this study was that the quality of the LMX was found to be predictable based on information collected during the first month of the dyadic interaction process. Based on the answers to two questions about the quality of the exchange (called Negotiating Latitude in this study), the development over 9 months of the various LMXs could be predicted. Therefore, the value of the LMX was placed on a high-, medium-, or low-quality path very early in the dyadic interaction process (during the first months) and continued to be elaborated over time along whichever path was selected initially.

A second question of interest in this investigation was whether the *relative value* of the quality of LMX within a leader's unit contributed to career outcomes. Relative value was defined as the difference between the dyadic value of the LMX and the average (mean) value of all LMXs of a particular leader (i.e., standard scores within units). The relative value of the LMX was predicted over time (4th, 7th, and 9th months later) by members' responses to the two questions (Negotiating Latitude). The results demonstrated the predictives validity of the relative value measure of LMX. This relative value within work units was predictable over time and also predicted the career outcomes of members 9 months later. Therefore, managers can enact different LMXs with different members of the same unit that become elaborated over time. Also, the relative value of the LMXs within the work unit can also contribute to career outcomes.

What is Negotiated Between Leader and Member?

A study by Graen and Cashman (1975) focused on the issue of whether members can negotiate with managers on issues of unit functioning. In this longitudinal panel investigation, three entire managerial hierarchies were studied over a 9-month period (again, questionnaires and interviews with both members of each dyad were conducted during the 1st, 4th, 7th, and 9th month). The results demonstrated that within most units (with job level partialled out) those members in higher quality LMXs spent more time on administrative duties and less time on routine functioning than those members in lower quality LMXs. In addition, the relative value of the LMX within the unit also showed that the higher relative value members did more administrative and less routine activities than did the lower relative value members of the unit. Moreover, the managers and members negotiated these differences in behavior around issues of unit functioning. Members in the higher relative value LMXs showed greater involvement in the more responsible administrative activities and lower involvement in the less responsible routine activities. This level of involvement was exchanged for greater resources (influence, support, information, latitude) from their managers compared to the members in lower relative value LMXs.

Do Peers and Leaders Know?

This study raised the question of whether or not the quality of the LMX is visible to members outside the dyad, i.e., whether or not peers within the same unit can accurately report on the quality of the LMX. This was also investigated by Graen and Cashman (1975). They asked peers in the same unit as well as the leader of the unit and the focal member to estimate the value of the focal and manager LMX. All members of a unit were asked to indicate for each possible dyad involving the manager how effective the working relationship was in terms of (a) ineffective, (b) effective, or (c) neither ineffective nor effective. The results were compared to the answers to four questions, called Leader–Member Exchange, LMX, which consisted of the original two Negotiating Latitude questions and two new questions about the effectiveness of the working relationship. Results demonstrated that the peers' assessments of the quality of the LMX agreed with managers' focal's perceptions of the Leader–Member Exchange. Moreover, assessments agreed with questionnaire results.

Better Agreement Between Leader and Member?

Although agreement between the manager and the member about the quality of the LMX is related to the perceptions of the manager and the member regarding the effectiveness of the dyadic working relationship, the question remained as to whether or not the quality of the LMX is related to agreement between manager and member concerning aspects of the job situation (e.g., severity of job problems facing the member). Schiemann and Graen (1978) investigated this question and found that agreement between managers and members was related to the quality of the LMX. Those members with lower quality LMXs showed much less agreement than those with higher quality LMXs. Moreover, the threshold for this agreement was rather low. Apparently, above a certain minimal level, the manager and the member shared enough in common to develop adequate agreement about the job situation.

More Frequent Communications Between Leader and Member?

In a study of communications within Leader–Member Exchanges, Schiemann (1977) found that those members with relatively higher quality LMXs communicated more frequently with their managers about administrative and technical matters than did members with relatively lower quality LMXs. These results were cross-validated on a holdout sample of managers. Apparently, there is much more communication in higher quality LMXs than in the lower quality LMXs. Thus, effective communications are an important aspect of the development of high-quality LMXs.

Linking-Pin Effects?

Moving the focus of the discussion to the dyad immediately above the one we have been discussing (between manager as lower member and his/her boss), the question arose regarding whether the LMX between the manager and his-her boss produced resources that were useful to members two levels below the boss. The question of whether linkages of dyadic relationships generate different flows of resources was also investigated. These questions were studied by Graen, Cashman, Ginsburgh, and Schiemann (1978). They found that the value of the upper dyad in this "linking pin" was related to the resources available to members a level below. Those managers who developed higher quality LMXs with their boss produced greater resources for their members than those managers who developed lower quality LMXs. In terms of resource dependency, the particular value of the LMX at the "linking pin" between upper and lower dyads in the management hierarchy appears to be critical. Although the member can have very little impact on the quality of the upper dyad LMX, he/she may benefit or suffer in terms of resource flows that are dependent on its quality. Hence, linking pins were found to vary in amount of resources flowing to members a level below.

Lower Levels of Organization?

Focusing once again on the lower dyad, the question of the generalizability of this process over the organizational hierarchy is relevant. Given that resources exchanged between manager and member are critical and that first-level supervisors have relatively fewer resources to exchange, the question arose as to whether the process of developing LMXs is truncated for the lowest level of supervision. A study by Liden and Graen (1980) addressed this question in a longitudinal investigation comparing these processes for managerial units and foreman units. The results showed no evidence of truncation for the foreman dyads. Hence, the development of high-quality LMXs appears to occur at various levels in the organization.

Between- Versus Within-Leaders' Units?

The next question has received a good deal of attention in the research literature—the question of whether the relative value of the LMX within units can contain validity *over and above* that contained by the total value of the LMX. Although a number of studies have investigated this question (Dansereau et al., 1975; Graen & Cashman, 1975; Katerberg & Hom, 1981; Schiemann, 1977), none of them had employed an experimentally independent criterion. The first to use such a criterion was a study by Graen, Liden, and Hoel (1982), which used turnover as the criterion. In this investigation of information systems professionals, they found that the relative value of the LMX predicted employee turnover 18 months later. The lower the relative value of the LMX (measured 18 months before), the higher the proportion of members who left the organization. The average (mean) value of all LMXs in the unit did not predict turnover; thus, turnover was not related to the manager's average (mean) LMX. All predictable turnover was due to within-unit variation and not between-unit variation. In addition, measures of satisfaction (Job Descriptive Index measures of work, superior, co-worker, pay, and promotion) taken 18 months before failed to predict turnover. Hence, the relative value of LMX (within units) contains validity to predict organizationally relevant outcomes.

Ferris (1985) replicated the Graen, Liden, and Hoel (1982) results. He found that the relative value of the LMX predicted turnover and that the average unit LMX did not. Those persons in dyads with lower LMXs relative to the average of their respective units tended to leave the organization, whereas those with higher relative value LMXs tended to remain. Apparently, the differentiation process at work inside of units produces dyadic differences that have predictable organizational consequences.

Training Leaders

The Graen, Novak, and Sommerkamp (1982) study was a field experiment in which managers of information-processing technicians were trained (experimental condition) or not trained (placebo control condition) in the theory and procedures of the role-making model. During the 26 weeks of the experiment, the managers were trained to use the model specifically with their members and were required to meet with each of their members individually and complete a script that they had role played many times in training. By the end of the 14th week, all individual role-making interviews were completed for the experimental group, and the treatment was in effect from week 15 to week 26.

The results of this field experiment supported the predictive validity of the LMX model. The experimental group (those under the LMX role-making condition) demonstrated large improvements in all areas tested from the 14 weeks before the treatment to the 12 weeks after the treatment compared to the placebo control condition. The areas tested for change from before to after the treatment were (a) hard productivity (quantity and quality or work produced on the computer), (b) work-itself measures (Motivating Potential of the Job, Preferred Work Load, Role Conflict, Role Ambiguity, and Career Relevance of the Job), (c) role making (Leader–Member Exchange from both points of view, Dyadic Loyalty, and Superior Support, and (d) job satisfaction (Overall and Facets: Leader, Work, Pay, Social, and Security). All the preceding measures demonstrated significant improvements for the experimental over the control group with the exception of the satisfaction measures, which only showed significant gains for overall and security satisfaction. Satisfaction with the manager (liking) failed to show a significant result. Hence, it appears that satisfaction with the manager is different from the quality of the LMX.

Moderating Effects

Another question Graen, Novak, and Sommerkamp (1982) investigated in their study was whether individual motivation would moderate the effects of the LMX treatment. Employing Hackman and Oldham's (1975) measure of Growth Need Strength (GNS), they found that GNS moderated the effect of the treatment for productivity and preferred work load as hypothesized. By trichotomizing GNS into lower third, medium third, and higher third, they found that the treatment produced no gains for the lower and medium, but exceedingly strong improvement for the higher third. The higher GNS group showed a 52% improvement in hard productivity improvement attributable to the higher GNS group.

This moderating effect of GNS on the LMX treatment was replicated in a field experiment on a comparable sample of employees conducted by Graen, Scandura, and Graen (1986). In this field experiment, the higher GNS group again showed an outstanding 54% improvement in hard productivity, and the lower and medium GNS groups demonstrated no significant improvements. In addition, quality of production actually improved in this study following the training, as documented by decreases in the number of errors per weekly caseload.

Benefit for the Have-nots

Given that this model, when followed properly, can produce such desirable results, the question becomes whether or not this training will benefit members having initially lower quality LMXs (i.e., out-group members) by offering the opportunity for a higher quality LMX. This question was researched by Scandura and Graen (1984). Controlling for regression effects, this study found that those initially lower in the quality of their LMX improved their productivity more than did those who had initially higher LMXs. Thus, the training resulted in a restructuring of the LMXs within units. Moreover, they demonstrated significant improvements in hard productivity, not at the expense of quality or job attitudes.

First 13 Years in Management

Another question that arises concerns the longer term implications of LMX theory and the possible moderating effects of member's career-relevant abilities. This question was the focus of a study by Wakabayashi and Graen (1984; Wakabayashi, Graen, Graen, & Graen, 1988). In this 13-year panel study of all the college graduates who joined one large corporation, they found that ability assessment taken before entry moderated the predictive relationship between quality of LMX taken during the first 3 years of employment and career progress measures taken over 13 years. Specifically, they found that both speed of promotion and promotability ratings by the company over 13 years were moderated by ability. In what appeared to be a compensatory fashion, those young managers who were higher on either or both quality of LMX or ability showed faster promotions and higher bonuses than those who were lower on both. Hence, there appeared to be two separate paths to career success—high ability or high-quality LMX. To have both demonstrated no special advantage, but to have neither showed a clear disadvantage. This study demonstrated the importance of role making for career progress.

BEYOND THE DYADIC EXCHANGES

To this point, our discussion has focused on two particular types of dyadic relationships: In-Group Track and Out-Group Track. Research on dyadic organizing has shown that these two groups emerge and become differentiated over time (Dansereau, Graen, & Haga, 1975; Graen & Cashman, 1975) and that the status of these relationships predicts outcomes of employees turnover (Graen, Liden, & Hoel, 1982) and employee productivity and satisfaction (Graen, Novak, & Sommerkamp, 1982). Although the stability of dyadic relationships has been documented, research, is needed in which In-Group and Out-Group relationships are simultaneously examined as components of a dyadic work-unit structure. Following Weick (1979), the dyad can be conceptualized as the basic unit of social organization in which there is interdependence, reciprocal behavior, and the necessity for accommodation to another person.

As stated previously, research on the Dyadic Organizing model has shown that managerial work units become differentiated into dyadic working relationships that are collaborative and those that are not (Dansereau, Graen, & Haga, 1975; Graen, 1976; Graen & Scandura, 1987; Lindholm, 1982). Over time, certain members of the unit form an In-Group whereas others remain in the Out-Group with respect to the unit manager (superior). Given that some managers experience collaborative relationships with their immediate superior and others do not, an important question is that of selection. In other words, what do superiors look for when seeking a member with whom to collaborate?

Managers' Views

A sample of 50 managers was asked to describe two of their present members who were comparable in promotion potential, education, sex, and race, but who differed in terms of the managers' professional investment. It is notable that 80% of these managers were able to differentiate between subordinates in terms of the degree to which they were investing in their careers. Further, clear differences were found between the identified In-Group and Out-Group members based on responses to the University of Cincinnati Employee Development Survey (EDS). Those members who were selected by their superiors for such investment were described as (a) being more likely to make the same decisions as their superior on complex problems, (b) being more likely to complete an assignment started by their superior when needed, and (c) having built a more effective working relationship with the superior. Although these factors appear to describe outcomes of the executive development process, they suggest the kind of characteristics that are likely to be attractive to the superior. Superiors appear to select those members who are similar to them in decision making, who are dependable in the sense that they can be counted on to complete the superior's task when necessary, and who effectively collaborate.

A second question addressed in this study with respect to this differentiation process within units involves what types of activities superiors and subordinates engage in during "on-the-job" management development. In this study, managers' development of their In-Group Track members clustered into four broad categories: (1) Collaboration, (2) Sponsorship, (3) Counseling, and (4) Visibility. The first category, Collaboration, involves the necessary exchange of valued resources and skills that takes place between the manager and the subordinate. Such collaboration involves exchange of important responsibilities, confidential or special information, challenging assignments, and exposure to the functions of other departments in the company. This exchange of resources is at the heart of the Leader–Member Exchange model and is critical to the unit's functioning and the development of the subordinate. The second development activity taking place in the managerial dyads is Sponsorship. Here, managers arrange for collaborators to meet people in the company, provide advice on long-range career plans, and serve as confidant to the subordinate. In addition, the superiors might play "devil's advocate" for the subordinate's new ideas. The third developmental activity is Counseling. Specific development activities in this category include giving specific and constructive criticism as well as praise. In addition, managers may include the person's input on critical decisions. The fourth type of developmental activity is providing Visibility. This involves the senior manager promoting the career of the subordinate in various ways. One way managers provide visibility is by arranging for the subordinate to attend a business conference. A second developmental activity might be for the manager to arrange for the person to make presentations to higher management. Other activities promoting visibility include reviewing written reports and memoranda of the subordinate, discussion of current tasks, and encouragement of the subordinate's new ideas.

TABLE 9.1
Actions of Boss Toward In-Group
and Out-Group Members

	In Group	Out Group
1. Provide special information through which the member can better learn company strategies . . .	75%	30%
2. Expose the member of various aspects of sister department's functions within the company . . .	60%	20%
3. Give the member challenging assignments . . .	83%	44%
4. Talk about the member's strengths with higher management . . .	58%	20%
5. Prepare the member for difficult situations . . .	60%	25%
6. Advise the member on long-range career plans . . .	47%	12%
7. Delegate important responsibilities to the member when the boss' workload is heavy . . .	83%	44%
8. Advise the member on promotional opportunities . . .	46%	14%
9. Serve as condidant to the member about career problems . . .	45%	15%
10. Include the member's input in decisions for which only the boss is responsible . . .	78%	50%

Top 10 Ways

To illustrate the differentiation process occurring within these managerial units, the percentages of the managers that reported engaging in these activities for the In-Group and the Out-Group are shown in Table 9.1. Examination of these top 10 items reveals that the managers do engage in differential treatment between In-Group and Out-Group members. Further, this differential treatment encompasses a broad range of behavior from the provision of special information and challenging assignments to the managers giving advice on long-range career plans and promotional opportunities.

A Model of Development

The study just described served to (a) verify that managers can differentiate between collaborative relationships and other relationships in their unit when asked to do so, (b) identify some of the selection factors managers use to identify that In-Group, and (c) identify some of the developmental activities that take place in these dyads. These results suggest that there are dual tracks of management development. Based on various input factors (demographics, abilities, trust, and involvement), superior–subordinate similarity and the outcomes of the role-taking process, two very different management development tracks emerge, as shown in Fig. 9.1. These tracks are labeled "In-Group Track" and "Out-Group Track" in the figure and reflect the differentiation process that occurs within units. Those on the In-Group Track are given differential treatment with respect to management development. Based on the data in Table 9.1, they receive support, special information, preparation, decision-making influence, and more challenging assignments than Out-Group members. Both types receive equivalent attention from their superiors on goal setting, performance monitoring, and performance–evaluation activities.

The degree of challenge on the job is a key variable to the development of the In-Group Track. Challenging tasks can be considered to be somewhat more unstructured and, hence, provide more opportunities for new learning on the job. Results from a number of different studies on the management progress model (Berlew & Hall, 1966; Hall & Lawler, 1969; Schein, 1967) show clearly that initial job challenge is very important to the way a person's career develops. A study of young male managers (Berlew & Hall, 1966) followed managers for 5 years and for 7 years. Performance was evaluated by salary scale and ratings from supervisors and other persons who were in a position to evaluate them. Results of this study showed that the more challenging a person's first job, the more effective and successful he or she was even 5 or 7 years later. Moreover, these predictive relationships between job challenge and career progress were significant after ability differences were controlled. Thus, the challenge found in unstructured tasks is an important aspect of the development of the In-Group Track.

Some of the predicted outcomes of the management development process are also shown in Fig. 9.1. These outcomes include mobility, professional growth, performance, as well as the developmental activities of collaboration, sponsorship, counseling, and visibility. Whereas these outcomes are shown to result for both In-Group and Out-Group Tracks, the model predicts that the Out-Group Track will experience these outcomes to a lesser degree than the In-Group Track. In other words, the In-Group Track experiences an accelerated pace of management development.

Also shown in the figure are arrows indicating movement between the In-Group Track and the Out-Group Track. These arrows indicate that these groups are fluid and that managers can move from one group to the other. Evidence for this movement was presented by Scandura and Graen (1984). The results of this field experiment indicated that those initially in the Out-Group improved their productivity more than those initially in the In-Group when their immediate superiors received training in role-making skills controlling for regression effects. Thus, the training resulted in a restructuring of dyadic relationship within units. Those initially in the Out-

144

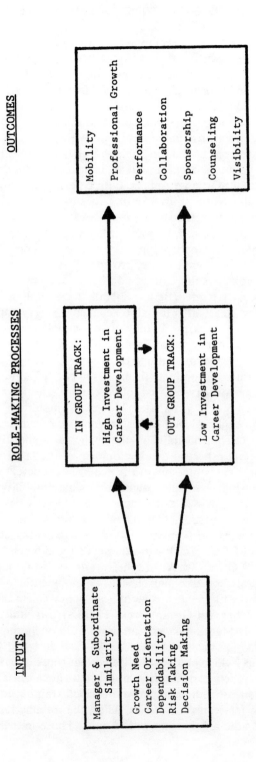

FIG. 9.1   Dual tracks in management development.

Group were able to achieve In-Group status as the high performers in the units studies.

A Fast-Track Investigation

To illuminate the differentiation process, the career progress of 50 more successful and 50 less successful managers were randomly selected for study. These managers were all college graduates with at least 3 years' tenure with the company and represented a vertical slice of the management hierarchy.

Focusing on the first four jobs since joining the organization, the job experiences that separated the fast track from their slower moving colleagues can be seen in Table 9.2 (all differences are statistically significant). As shown, the fast-track members were encouraged to begin making contributions in their first job and to continue while learning by doing under the masters. Note that the fast track were invested in by at least one of their immediate superiors and that their career development was opportunistic and active. Moreover, this study suggested that if they failed to experience the fast track during their first four job assignments, they were unlikely to be in the fast track group years later.

Those who experienced the selected member treatment at least once during their first four job assignments tended to be more successful years later than those who were never selected. This suggests that early experiences are especially relevant to later career progress. This critical early experience was further supported by the second study of 13 years in managment.

13 Years in Management Study

To clarify our understanding of the contribution of early experiences to later career progress in management, a panel study was begun in 1972. This study selected all the college graduates who joined the company that year and proposed to follow them throughout their careers with the company (Wakabayashi & Graen, 1984; Wakabayashi, Graen, Graen, & Graen, 1988).

The focus of this study was on the ability and job experiences of members during the first 3 years on the job as predictors of career success at the end of 13 years.

The results demonstrated that the early treatment by the boss was predictive of later career success. As shown in Table 9.3, the immediate superior mediated more of all nine of these jobs experiences to those who were more successful after 13 years (all differences were statistically significant). In other words, the experience of being selected at least once during the critical first 3 years was instrumental to career success.

The similarity of the critical factors in Table 9.3 and the top 10 job opportunities of the In-Group Track (listed before) should be noted. Clearly,

TABLE 9.2
Early Fast-Track Job Experience

	Career Track	
	Fast	Slow
Applied their school learning in their first job . . .	More	Less
Moved to different job assignments at appropriate intervals . . .	More	Less
Careers were invested in by at least one immediate superior . . .	More	Less
Careers were influenced in a positive manner by an average of four "masters" . . .	More	Less
Gained technical expertise from early masters . . .	More	Less
Learned how to influence others including team leadership from later masters . . .	More	Less
Career development was opportunistic and active regarding specific job experiences . . .	More	Less

Note: A study of 50 high performers and 50 low performers in one of *Fortune's* best run companies is the source for this table.

TABLE 9.3
Clinical Factors During the First 3 Years on the Job

	Career Track	
	Fast	Slow
Providing special information through which the member can learn how the company really operates . . .	More	Less
Exposing the member to information regarding changes to be made . . .	More	Less
Giving the member challenging assignments . . .	More	Less
Preparing the member for difficult assignments . . .	More	Less
Delegating to the member enough authority to complete important assignments . . .	More	Less
Allowing the member to put some of his/her ideas into assignments . . .	More	Less
Including the member's input in decisions for which only the boss is responsible . . .	More	Less
Supporting the member's actions through clear expectations, attention to work progress, willingness to help, and constructive guidance . . .	More	Less
Developing a trusting relationship . . .	More	Less

Note: A study of 71 managers over the first 13 years since joining their company supplied the information for this table.

this treatment can make a significant contribution to career progress in management.

In addition to the job opportunities present in Table 9.3, the more successful managers evaluated their working relationships with their immediate superiors during the first 3 years as much more positive than the less successful managers on the following: recognition of potential, understanding of problems, sharing of expectations, willingness to collaborate,

TABLE 9.4
Variable Assessment Schedule

| | Years of Tenure | | | | |
Measure	1–3	7	9	10	13
Assessed Management Potential . . .	X				
Leader–Member Exchange . . .	X[a]				X
Organizational Commitment . . .	X[a]				
Performance Appraisal . . .	X[a]				X
Speed of Promotion . . .		X		X	X
Job Satisfaction . . .					X
Satisfaction with Supervisor . . .					X
Management Resources:					
Subordinate View . . .					X
Superior View . . .					X

X indicates variable assessed.
[a]indicates average over six separate measures during the first 3 years.

attitude toward changing job definition, monitoring of performance, and social activities.

Contribution of Early Dyadic Development to Later Career Outcomes

The design of the 13-year follow-up study is shown in Table 9.4. The predictors from the first 3 years in management to the 13th year were Assessed Management Potential (AMP), Performance Appraisal (PA), Organizational Commitment (OC), and Leader Member Exchange (LMX), and the pairwise combinations. Results shown in Table 9.5 show that LMX and

TABLE 9.5
Strength of Unique Contribution Estimates
for Predictors (N = 71)

| 13-Year Leadership Situation Criterion | Unique Variance Contribution | | |
	LMX	AMP × LMX	OC × LMX
Overall Job Satisfaction . . .	9.8%	8.2%	2.1%
Satisfaction with Sup . . .	9.3%	5.7%	8.3%
Management Resources (Sub.) . . .	22.1%	6.8%	6.6%
Management Resources (Sup.) . . .	6.6%	12.9%	2.4%
L–M Exchange (Sub.) . . .	19.5%	10.4%	4.4%
L–M Exchange (Sup.) . . .	1.0%	6.5%	4.8%
Performance Appraisal	4.8%	12.2%	8.5%

Note: Unique variance contribution is estimated by Eta^2 values of variable entered last in 10-variable hierarchical regression.

TABLE 9.6
Strength of Unique Contribution Estimates
for Predictors (N = 71)

Career Progress Measure	Unique Variance Contribution		
	LMX	PA	AMP × LMX
Speed of Promotion:			
First-Level (7 years) . . .	3.3%	10.9%	2.2%
Second-Level (10 years) . . .	6.4%	6.4%	2.6%
Third-Level (13 years) . . .	4.3%	7.2%	3.4%
All three . . .	6.3%	11.0%	3.9%
Promotability:			
9 years . . .	2.7%	8.2%	1.8%
10 years . . .	7.3%	13.6%	5.5%
13 years . . .	9.9%	8.4%	7.6%
All three . . .	8.3%	13.2%	6.2%

Note: Unique variance contribution is estimated by Eta^2 values of variable entered last in 10-variable hierarchical regression.

combinations of LMX × AMP and LMX × OC predicted the 13-year management situation. Moreover, as shown in Table 9.6 career progress over 13 years was predicted by LMX, PA, and the combination of LMX × AMP.

These studies suggest the nature of the dyadic role-development process in management and the implications of this process for career development and contribution. Clearly young managers acquire critical leadership skills early in their careers that serve them well a decade later. The process by which this occurs involves the investment in their dyadic development by immediate superiors as discussed earlier. We hypothesize that, once engaged in a productive leadership system, managers experience its effectiveness and motivating potential and in the future will work to replicate it in each new job situation throughout their careers.

MOVING TO TEAM FOCUS

The focus now turns to the question to designing Productive Leadership Systems for managers that develop leadership teams through organizational processes that improve both long-term work motivation and organizational effectiveness. Let us state with a definition. Productive Leadership Systems (PLS) involve the expansion of total influence and commitment in a unit through dyadic role development directed at capitalizing on available opportunities and resources of the unit and the unique set of abilities and motivations of available unit members, in such a way that dyadic roles are integrated into cohesive, coordinated, and adaptable management teams and into larger competence networks. Such teams are expected to manage greater authority and responsibility than traditionally developed units.

Let us unpack this definition of Productive Leadership System. First, the objective is to expand the total influence and commitment in a unit through dyadic role development. This means that dyadic role development must tap into the individual motivations of unit members to transform their current job interests into larger organizational and career interests. Thus, dyadic role development must create opportunities for progress toward relevant organizational and career outcomes that are superior to traditional role development. Second, dyadic role development is directed at capitalizing on the opportunities and resources of the unit and the unique set of ability and motivations of available unit members. This implies that dyadic role development is restricted to members within the unit and the opportunities and resources that can be obtained by the unit. Moreover, the abilities and motivations of unit members, including the leaders, are to be identified and engaged according to some design. This implies that a good deal of this dyadic role development occurs in the unit while performing the functions of the unit. Third, dyadic role development is performed in such a way that dyadic roles are integrated into cohesive, coordinated, and adaptable teams and into larger competence networks. The objectives of this system are to construct organizational processes that tap into individuals' motivations and transform job incumbents into cohesive, coordinated, and adaptable team members within their current unit and into effective team contributors in successively more responsible units from project level, through middle management, to the executive level. At each level, the teams are designed to be cohesive, coordinated, and adaptable and integrated into competence networks that reach outside the unit.

With this working definition of PLS, let us turn to several propositions derived from Jacobs and Jaques' (1987) theory of critical managerial skills. They define three different types of organizational functions that require unique role capabilities. We have taken these three functions and derived propositions involving Productive Leadership Systems.

Project Leadership. Influence is added based on interpersonal and technical skills, project authority and support, and the emergence of potential within a work group context.

Middle Management Leadership. Influence is added based on interpersonal and organizational skills, organizational authority and support, and the emergence of potential for: (a) improving the stability of project environments by decreasing uncertainty; (b) coordinating the actions of interdependent units; and, (c) linking transactions between parts of their organization and environments.

Executive Leadership.   Influence is added based on interpersonal and system skills, executive authority and support, and the emergence of potential for: (a) producing more stable environments for subordinate units by interacting with external environments (impacting on and getting and interpreting information from), and (b) creating critical resource masses for the future.

AN INTEGRATION OF JAQUES' THEORY
AND LEADER-MEMBER EXCHANGE

Jacques' (1986) general theory hypothesizes predictable growth over time of capabilities to perform at high levels based on motivational processes related to growth of cognitive development. Predictable growth of such capability implies some sequences of growth experience that enhance the development of executive ability, and other sequences that may deny these growth opportunities. Graen and Scandura (1987) posit that some of these sequences of growth experience are products of leader-member exchanges in which the subordinate manager contributes the acceptance of leadership in exchange for sequences of growth experience for the superior manager. Acceptance of leadership from a superior consists of accepting a leader's purpose (direction and rationale) for the unit and cooperating in the mobilization of energy to achieve the aforementioned purpose in relation to system effectiveness (Jacobs & Jaques, 1987). Clearly, leadership must be accepted by subordinate(s) or it is only the superior's behavior—a single person influencing his or her own behavior cannot, by definition, be social influence. Moreover, only a single subordinate need accept leadership for it to exist in a unit. If more than one accepts leadership, then the magnitude of leadership in the unit is increased. In the Graen and Scandura (1987) model, leadership exchange for a superior manager would be beneficial when the net increment in his or her value added to the unit by the acceptance of leadership relationship by a subordinate proportionally exceeds the investment needed to supply sequences of growth experiences to the accepting subordinate. Proportionality means that for every X value invested by the superior, the subordinate eventually returns X plus Y value to the superior. In contrast, nonaccepting subordinates (Out-Group) may offer too little potential value added.

This implies that the acceptance of leadership (In-Group) and the delivery of sequences of growth experience are activities of like kind that may be invested. In addition, such investments may not involve all subordinates in a unit. This differentiation of sequences of growth experiences between In-Group and Out-Group is suggested by the research summarized in Graen and Scandura (1987). The trick is to identify the In-Group and Out-Group Track early (say, during the first 3 years of job tenure), so that those experi-

TABLE 9.7
Responsibility Statement Guidelines

Responsibility Statement Should Prescribe A Direct Reporting Relationship in the Following Manner:

Individualized (you and your direct report)
Normative (should, ought, must)
Future Oriented (investments in long term)
Growth directed (capability acquisition)
Empowerment specified (authority and latitude)
Accountability and coordination detailed (monitoring content and process)
Collaboration addressed (shared responsibility for larger unit)
Exhaustive (major areas)
Template provided for different types of relationships and
incorporates new organizational design and new focus
Drafted by member with assistance of counselor
Negotiated between member, leader, and counselor
Signed and dated by both parties
Executed on signing
Monitoring at 3 months, 6 months, 12 months

encing lower levels of career investment can be enabled to shift to the In-Group Track, if they so desire. As we have seen, one variable that has been shown to empirically differentiate these two groups (In vs. Out) during the early years of development is Leader–Member Exchange (Graen & Scandura, 1987).

RESPONSIBILITY STATEMENT PROGRAM

The question that arises is how can organizations facilitate the emergence of this dyadic role-development process that we call the Productive Leadership System? One method for accomplishing this is presently under investigation in a large corporation. In this study, all direct reporting relationships from the Chairman of the Board down to the lowest cadre manager are undergoing a process of contracting dyadic role development. The guidelines for this contracting are show in Table 9.7. As can be seen in these guidelines, the two parties are negotiating the terms of their new dyadic relationship with the aid of a counselor. The major elements of these contracts that are signed and published are presented in Table 9.8. These elements cover the critical parameters and objectives of dyadic development.

Three Basic Issues

For any work involving superiors and subordinates to be done well, there must be agreement on three basic issues: (1) what the subordinate needs from the supervisor to do the job; (2) what the supervisor needs from the

TABLE 9.8
Major Elements

1. Strategic and tactical planning.
2. Annual planning and budgeting cycles.
3. Regular updating and periodic review of operations against budget with superior(s).
4. Ensure, within approved plans and budgets, that your direct reports have needed resources available to them.
5. Ensure that staffing and funding levels are reasonable in terms of recognized industry standards.
6. Approve addition, transfer, termination, and replacement of staff.
7. Foster communications and coordination up, down, and laterally.
8. Provide your staff with encouragement, leadership, counseling, training, guidance, and opportunities necessary to maximize their productivity and individual career development.
9. Ensure that your staff is aware of and understand the professional management system concept and employ it effectively in their daily activities.
10. Review and evaluate the performance of your staff on a periodic basis.
11. Maintain and administer, within guidelines approved by senior management, a salary administration program.
12. Spending limits.
13. Keep superiors abreast of changes in technology and business practices in your area.
14. Be aware of your competition and their products, services, and costs.
15. Negotiate with customers to arrive at an agreement on acceptable levels of service.
16. Affiliates.

subordinate to do the job; and (3) what the job is. If there is no agreement on these fundamental issues of the reporting relationship, the company almost certainly will falter in its mission (Graen, 1989).

The first issue concerns the authority that the supervisor delegates to the subordinate to get things done. Authority is the energy source that allows action to be taken. When there is agreement on authority issues, three outcomes may occur: (1) Only one party takes action, (2) both act independently, or (3) neither acts but both assume the other acted. Outcomes (2) and (3) may have unfortunate consequences. With (2) they may trip over each other. With outcome (3) the appropriate action may not be taken.

The second issue, what the supervisor needs from the subordinate to do the job, concerns accountability. Unless the supervisor is kept adequately informed about the subordinate's progress on various programs, he or she cannot be confident that the programs are functioning properly. Clearly, from a supervisor's viewpoint, there are no pleasant surprises. Moreover, supervisors are reluctant to delegate authority unless they feel confident that they have adequate accountability.

The third issue, what the job is, concerns responsibilities. The functions the subordinate performs and the objectives of these functions are his/her responsibilities. Without agreement with the supervisor, the subordinate is in danger of doing a great job without fulfilling the supervisor's confidence and perhaps a downward spiral in the working relationship occurs.

Our procedure involved all subordinates. Each was asked to draft a "Responsibility Statement" detailing the three fundamental issues aforementioned. We first held small group training sessions, during which we discussed the issues and used a concrete example as a guide. The subordinates drafted their statements, showed them to us for suggestions and refinements, and finally gave their revised statements to their respective supervisors.

This was the first time that the supervisor had seen the draft. Finally, the subordinates and the supervisor negotiated the statement with our assistance. We made sure that both parties addressed the major issues in detail. We also acted as impartial witnesses to the written contract that was negotiated, dated, and signed by both parties.

The object of this process was to improve agreement between subordinates and supervisors. Next, we dealt with peer relations. In this step, all subordinates who reported to the same supervisor met with that supervisor and with us. We reviewed all their statements and negotiated any problems or issues making sure that nothing was omitted.

Finally, senior management and all other cadre members reviewed these sets of statements. A permanent collection of the statements was made available to all cadre members.

Jacobs and Jaques' Theory

The three different types of organizational functions that require unique role capabilities that we derived from Jacobs and Jaques (1987) were represented in this study.

Executive leadership capabilities were specified in the "Responsibility Statements" for the most senior officers (the top levels of the organization). For those immediately below the most senior officers, the middle management leadership capabilities were required. Finally, for the lowest level in the cadre, project leadership capabilities were specified in their "Responsibility Statements."

An example of this specification for project leadership capabilities is as follows. Suppose we have two project managers, Adam and Alex, reporting to the same supervisor. Adam is quite skilled as a technician but needs to develop his team leadership skills. Alex is the reverse, a good team leader but technically a bit weak. Their respective "Responsibility Statements" would reflect these differences. Adam would be encouraged and supported to grow out of his job by developing his team leadership skills. In contrast, Alex would be encouraged and supported to grow out of his job by developing his technical skills.

This may appear at first glance to be the same as Management by Objectives (MBO), a form of goal setting. However, on further reflection, it should be clear that the focus is the development of effective dyadic working relationships and team effectiveness. Agreement on expectations is but one component of the larger system. Equally important additional components include: reciprocal trust between leader and member, complimentary dyadic negotiating skills, mutual value-added potential, and boundary conditions (Graen, 1989).

It is one thing to attain agreement on expectations in a "Statement of Responsibility" and quite another to function as an effective team. The next step is to refine the "Statements" to specify expected team behavior of both supervisor and subordinate. The final step is reached when team behavior drives the "Responsibility Statements" rather than the reverse.

The theory underlying this program is that managers can learn to expand the total influence and commitment of their units through dyadic role development by utilizing the opportunities and resources of their units to capitalize on the underemployed abilities and motivations of people within their units in ways that people grow out of their former prescribed roles and into dyadic roles that are integrated into cohesive, coordinated, and adaptable teams and into large competence networks. One postulate of this theory is that contracts negotiated between direct reports can specify the necessary responsibilities to produce the needed team relationships between peers (horizontal dyads) and between members and higher or lower level employees (diagonal dyads).

Note that these dyadic contracts are subject to renegotiation whenever appropriate. When either party feels that an item in the contract should be improved, he or she can call for a renegotiation of that item. The basic intent is that such contracts improve effectiveness and adaptability by reducing ambiguity, offering challenge and growth, and prescribing team management.

Finally, recall that as mentioned in the introduction the other elements within the organization must be compatible with the productive leadership system (Graen, 1989).

Conclusion

Much of modern organization theory assumes that organizations are peopled by managers who do not grow out of their prescribed roles in terms of contribution and commitment to organizational objectives. These people are assumed to comply with the stated requirements by employing a minimum personal cost strategy. Their reason for not doing something that needs to be done and that they could do is that "it's not my job—it's outside of my role."

In contrast, PLS assumes that managers can and do grow out of their prescribed roles under the appropriate conditions. We are attempting to demonstrate that not only does dyadic role development happen in modern organizations, but that it can be facilitated by well-designed and implemented Productive Leadership Systems.

ACKNOWLEDGMENTS

The author would like to thank Mitsuru Wakabayashi for his insightful contributions to this chapter, Joan Graen, Marty Graen, Mike Graen, and Terri Scandura for their scholarly assistance, and the comments of two anonymous reviewers.

REFERENCES

Berlew, D. E., & Hall, D. T. (1966). The socialization of managers: Effects of expectations on performance. *Administrative Science Quarterly, 11*, 207–223.

Dansereau, F., Graen, G., & Haga W. J. (1975). A vertical dyad linkage approach to leadership within formal organizations. *Organizational Behavior and Human Performance, 13*, 46–78.

Ferris, G. R. (1985). Role of leadership in the employee withdrawal process: A constructive replication. *Journal of Applied Psychology, 70*, 777–781.

Graen, G. (1976). Role-making processes within complex organizations. In M. D. Dunnette (Ed.), *Handbook of industrial and organizational psychology* (pp. 1201–1246). Chicago: Rand-McNally.

Graen, G. B. (1989). *Unwritten rules for your career.* New York: Wiley.

Graen, G., & Cashman, J. (1975). A role-making model of leadership in formal organizations: A development approach. In J. G. Hunt & L. L. Larson (Eds.), *Leadership frontiers* (pp. 143–166). Kent, OH: Kent State University Press.

Graen, G., Cashman, J. F., Ginsburgh, S., & Schiemann, W. (1978). Effects of linking-pin quality upon the quality of working life of lower participants: A longitudinal investigation of the managerial understructure. *Administrative Science Quarterly, 19*, 491–504.

Graen, G., Liden, R., & Hoel, W. (1982). The role of leadership in the employee withdrawal process. *Journal of Applied Psychology, 67*, 868–872.

Graen, G., Novak, M., & Sommerkamp, P. (1982). The effects of leader–member exchange and job design on productivity and job satisfaction: Testing a dual attachment model. *Organizational Behavior and Human Performance, 30*, 109–131.

Graen, G., Orris, D., & Johnson, T. (1973). Role assimilation processes in a complex organization. *Journal of Vocational Behavior, 3*, 395–420.

Graen, G. B., & Scandura, T. A. (1987). Toward a psychology of dyadic organizing. In B. M. Staw & L. L. Cummings (Eds.), *Research in organizational behavior* (pp. 175–208). Greenwich, CT: JAI Press.

Graen, G. B., Scandura, T. A., & Graen, M. R. (1986). A field experimental test of the moderating effects of GNS on productivity. *Journal of Applied Psychology, 71*, 484–491.

Hackman, J. R., & Oldham, G. (1975). Development of the Job Diagnostic Survey. *Journal of Applied Psychology, 60*, 159–170.

Hall, D. T., & Lawler, E. E., III. (1969). Unused potential in research and development organizations. *Research Management, 12*, 339–354.

Jacobs, T. O., & Jaques, E. (1987). Leadership in complex systems. In J. A. Zeidner (Ed.), *Human productivity enhancement (Vol. 2. pp. 2–44) Organizations and personnel.*

Jaques, E. (1986). Stratification of cognitive power. *Journal of Applied Behavioral Science, 22*, 361–383.

Katerberg, R., & Hom, P. W. (1981) Effects of within-group and between-group variation in leadership. *Journal of Applied Psychology, 66*, 218–223.

Liden, R., & Graen, G. (1980). Generalizability of the vertical dyad linkage model of leadership. *Academy of Management Journal, 23*, 451–465.

Lindholm, J. (1982). Mentoring: The mentor's perspective. *ONR Technical Report* No. TR-ONR-9, MIT, Cambridge, MA.

Scandura, T. A., & Graen, G. B. (1984). Moderating effects of initial leader–member exchange status on the effects of a leadership intervention. *Journal of Applied Psychology, 69*, 428–436.

Schein, E. H. (1967). Attitude change during management education: A study of organizational influences on student attitudes. *Administrative Science Quarterly, 11*, 601–628.

Schiemann, W. (1977). *Structural and interpersonal effects on patterns of managerial communication: A longitudinal investigation*. Unpublished doctoral dissertation, University of Illinois.

Schiemann, W., & Graen, G. (1978). Leader–member agreement: A vertical dyad linkage approach. *Journal of Applied Psychology, 63*, 206–212.

Wakabayashi, M., & Graen, G. B. (1984). The Japanese career progress study: A seven-year follow-up. *Journal of Applied Psychology, 69*, 603–614.

Wakabayashi, M., Graen, G. B., Graen, M. R., & Graen, M. G. (1988). Japanese management progress: Mobility into middle management. *Journal of Applied Psychology, 73*, 217–227.

Weick, K. (1979). *The social psychology of organizing*. Reading, MA: Addison-Wesley.

10
Motivational Determinants of Absence Behavior

Hans-Henning Quast*
Rohrer, Hibler & Replogle International (Europe) Company

Uwe Kleinbeck
Sieglinde Stachelhaus
University of Wuppertal, Wuppertal, West Germany

Absence behavior is a serious problem of organizations that cuts across industries and national boundaries. On a typical day between 2 and 4% of Americans fail to show up for work, which does not sound like a high rate of absence, but more time is lost because of absence behavior than through strikes and lockouts (Johns, 1987, p. 30).

The yearly costs of absence behavior in the United States are estimated to be $30 billion and a change of 5% in the national absence rate changes the gross national product (GNP) by $10 billion (Steers & Rhodes, 1984, p. 233).

In Europe, Italy ranks first with an absence rate of 14%, followed by France. The lowest rate is found in Switzerland with 1% (Yankelovich, 1979).

A great number of studies were done to identify the determinants of absence behavior. Steers and Rhodes (1984) have counted 209 variables that were investigated with regard to their influence on absence behavior. Although many variables were found to be significantly related to indices of absence, the results appear to be unstable across situations and time. At the end of their literature review, Steers and Rhodes (1984) concluded: "It should be clear from this review of the literature on employee absenteeism, that we know far less about absenteeism than we would like to" (p. 263).

A comprehensive model capturing the key motivational variables that are effective in the work place was developed by Hackman and Oldham (1975,

*This research was done when the first author held a position as an assistant professor of industrial and organizational psychology at the University of Wuppertal.

157

1976). It is called the Job Characteristics Model (JCM) and has been investigated in a number of studies and has often served as a tool to solve practical problems in the workplace (Hackman, 1977; Hackman & Oldham,
1980; Hackman, Oldham, Janson, & Purdy, 1975).

The basic assumption of the model is that motivation, satisfaction, and
work performance are determinated by three "critical psychological states"
(experienced meaningfulness of work, experienced responsibility for outcomes of the work, and knowledge of results) that are in turn influenced by
five "core job dimensions" (skill variety, task identity, task significance, autonomy, and job feedback). Individual differences (e.g., Employee Growth
Need Strength) are supposed to moderate the relationship between the core
job dimensions and critical psychological states and the relationship between critical psychological states and outcome variables. Hackman and
Oldham (1975, 1976) developed a formula that combines the five core job
dimensions into a total "Motivating Potential Score" (MPS).

In an extensive review Algera (this volume) discussed a number of empirical and methodological studies concerning the dimensionality of the job
characteristics, the role of the critical psychological states, the effects of
moderator variables, the relationship between job characteristics and outcomes and issues with regard to the dependent variables in the model.

In the original model absence behavior and turnover were dependent on
outcome variables besides work satisfaction, quality of work performance,
and internal work motivation. In their revised Job Characteristics Model
(JCM) (Hackman & Oldham, 1980), the outcome variables absence behavior and turnover disappeared, and quality of work performance was replaced by work effectiveness.

In an earlier study Hackman and Lawler (1971) had found a significant
negative relationship between job involvement and absence frequency, but
this relationship was not moderated by Growth Need Strength (GNS) as assumed. Spector (1985) conducted a meta-analysis to test the moderating effect of higher order need strength (GNS) on the relationship between job
scope and employee outcomes. He combined 20 samples and found some
evidence for a moderator effect for a number of outcome variables but not
for absence behavior and involvement. Concerning the outcome variables
studied, Algera (this volume) pointed out that there had been more studies
on personal outcomes (satisfaction, internal work motivation) than on
work outcomes (performance, absence behavior, turnover).

Fried and Ferris (1987) made a comprehensive review of about 200 relevant studies on the JCM model and applied meta-analytic procedures to a
large portion of the data. They concluded that the relationship between job
characteristics and behavioral outcomes were more meaningful and more
consistent than argued by critics. Although in the number of studies that
had been investigated the relationship between JCM-variables and absence

behavior was small ($N = 3$), they see the linkage proposed by the JCM supported. In their analysis growth need strength (GNS) moderated the MPS–job performance relationship, suggesting that in the group of people with high GNS the correlation between MPS and performance was substantially larger than among people with low GNS. Unfortunately, this analysis was not done for the MPS–absence behavior relationship and other moderating variables. In general, very few studies have investigated the effects of other moderating variables on absence behavior. As there is some evidence for the task characteristics (MPS)–work outcome (performance, absence behavior) relationship, more systematic research on moderating variables is needed.

With regard to the JCM we think an adequate moderating variable should be conceptually related to the qualities of the workplace that are represented in the task characteristics and summarized in the Motivating Potential (MPS). Furthermore, the moderating variable should be linked to the outcome variable of the model.

Such a moderating variable was proposed by Kleinbeck and Schmidt (1979) and Kleinbeck, Schmidt, Donis, and Ballé (1983) and is called *Instrumentally of Absence Behavior*. This notion of the "Instrumentality of Absence Behavior" was based on Vroom's (1964) concept of instrumentality. He distinguished "instrumentality" from "expectancy" by defining the first one as an outcome–outcome association and the later one as an action–outcome association. Our research focuses on the anticipated consequences (second outcome) of absence behavior (first outcome) and does not consider the various actions leading to absence behavior. In terms of absence behavior, the Instrumentality of Absence Behavior was defined as the perceived negative consequences of being absent (absence behavior) with respect to the qualities of the workplace that are addressed in the task characteristics (MPS).

The study reported here was done to investigate three things: first to test the MPS–absence behavior relationship with regard to different measures of absence behavior, second to test the moderating effect of GNS, and third to test the moderating effect of the variable, Instrumentality of Absence Behavior.

The lack of empirical support for the relationship between task characteristics and absence behavior (respectively, critical psychological states and absence behavior) is undoubtedly related to the problem of defining adequate indicators of absence behavior. Hammer and Landau (1981), Atkin and Goodman (1984), Avery and Hotz (1984), and Landy, Vasey, and Smith (1984) have demonstrated the substantial theoretical and methodological problems of defining and measuring absence behavior and analyzing data of absentee behavior. Therefore, one should define different indicators of absence behavior and inspect the distributions of the absence data carefully.

METHOD

Sample and Research Site

The subjects were drawn from a medium-sized plant in West Germany that packed and distributed tools. The plant was located at the edge of a major industrial area in the western part of the country. The sample consisted of 81 employees. Ninety two percent were German; the others had different nationalities. Forty eight percent of the sample were female, 52% male employees. Forty six percent were married, 54% single, divorced, or widowed. The average age was 33.3 (SD = 12.1). Mean plant tenure was 5.8 years (SD = 3.4) and mean work assignment was 4.1 years (SD = 2.8). Seventy five percent had completed junior high school and 66% were trained during their apprenticeship. The kind of work done by the 81 employees can be categorized as low-level routine work.

Measures

From the personnel records individual sheets were prepared including the dates of absence for the last 12 months. A battery of instruments contained among other scales the Job Diagnostic Survey (Hackman & Oldham, 1975) and the scale measuring the Instrumentality of Absence Behavior (Kleinbeck, Schmidt, Donis, & Ballé 1983). The participants were asked to indicate to what extent absence behavior would have negative consequences for participation and decision latitude, style of leadership, cooperation and communication with colleagues, etc. The internal consistency of the Instrumentality scale was Cronbach's Alpha = .85.

The items of the scale were put the following way: When you are ill or absent from work for other reasons, what does it mean with regard to the following consequences?

Being absent has negative consequences for:

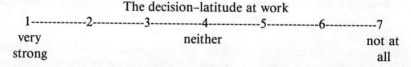

The decision–latitude at work

1-------------2------------3------------4------------5------------6------------7
very   neither   not at
strong   all

Procedure

Questionnaires containing these measures were distributed to employees and had to be completed in 10 groups of people of different sizes. Each participant received his or her personal sheet including the dates of absence. To assure anonymity the employees were asked to cut off their names from the sheets and to attach them to the questionnaires that did not have their names. The employees completed the questionnaires during their working time.

TABLE 10.1
Intercorrelations Among Motivational Variables and Indicators
of Absence Behavior

	Motivating Potential	Growth Need Strength	Instru- mentality	Total Days	1 or 2 Days	3 to 7 Days	1 to 2 Weeks	Number of Periods
Motivating Potential	---							
Growth Need Strength	.15	---						
Instrumentality	.27*	− .08	---					
Total days	− .23*	− .08	− .19	---				
1 or 2 days	− .12	.00	− .16	.20	---			
3 to 7 days	− .19	− .03	− .15	.43***	.10	---		
1 to 2 weeks	− .09	− .11	− .22*	.65***	− .09	.04	---	
Number of periods	− .28**	− .05	− .27*	.83***	.67***	.45***	.44***	---

$^*p < .05$
$^{**}p < .01$
$^{***}p < .001$

Results

An overall score of the "Motivating Potential" of the work setting was calculated according to Hackman and Oldham (1975) on the basis of the scale scores of the four task characteristics (Skill Variety, Task Identity, Task Significance, and Feedback) in the Job Diagnostic Survey. The mean Motivating Potential Score was 116.8 (SD = 62.5), 5.4 (SD = 1.4) for the Growth Need Scale, and 3.6 (SD = 1.3) for the Instrumentality Scale. Five indicators of absence behavior were developed to see if different kinds of absence behavior would be affected differently by motivational variables. The measures of absence behavior were total days absent, number of 1 or 2 days absence from work, number of 3 to 7 days absence from work, number of 1 to 2 weeks of absence from work, and finally the number of all 1 or 2 days, 3 to 7 days, and 1 to 2 weeks missed. Measures of absence behavior turn out to be positively skewed (Hammer & Landau, 1981; Landy, Vasey, & Smith, 1984), which limits inferences made from statistical analyses of untransformed variables. As the positive skewness of the variables was severe, a logarithmic transformation was applied. All multiple regression analyses reported here were done with the transformed (dependent) variables of absence behavior. Table 10.1 presents the correlation matrix of the variables included in the multiple regression analysis.

To test the assumption that the Instrumentality of Absence Behavior was a better moderating variable than Growth Need Strength with regard to the influence of the Motivating Potential on different indicators of absence behavior, two sets of five multiple regression analyses were computed. To determine the moderating strength of Growth Need Strength and Instru-

TABLE 10.2
Summary Table of the Moderated Multiple Regression Analyses
Predicting Absence Behavior from Motivating Potential and Growth
Need Strength ($N = 81$)

Dependent Measure	Step	Predictor Added	F to Enter	p	R	R^2	R^2 Change	Overall F	p
Total days	1	MPS	4.37	.04	.23	.05	.05	4.37	.04
	2	GNS	.14	.70	.23	.05	.00	2.23	.11
	3	Interaction	.51	.47	.25	.06	.00	1.65	.18
1 or 2 days	1	MPS	1.11	.29	.12	.01	.01	1.11	.29
	2	GNS	.02	.87	.12	.01	.00	.56	.57
	3	Interaction	1.08	.30	.17	.03	.02	.73	.53
3 to 7 days	1	MPS	3.05	.09	.19	.04	.04	3.05	.09
	2	GNS	.00	.98	.19	.04	.00	1.50	.22
	3	Interaction	.32	.57	.20	.04	.00	1.10	.35
1 to 2 weeks	1	MPS	.58	.45	.09	.00	.00	.58	.45
	2	GNS	.69	.41	.13	.02	.00	.63	.53
	3	Interaction	.67	.42	.16	.02	.00	.64	.59
Number of periods	1	MPS	6.70	.01	.28	.08	.08	6.70	.01
	2	GNS	.00	.93	.28	.08	.00	3.31	.04
	3	Interaction	.90	.35	.30	.09	.01	2.50	.06

mentality of Absence Behavior, hierarchical multiple regression analyses were performed entering Motivating Potential (MPS) first, then Growth Need Strength (GNS) or Instrumentality of Absence Behavior (INST), and finally the interaction term Motivating Potential by Growth Need Strength, or the interaction term Motivating Potential by Instrumentality. Table 10.2 presents the results of five moderated multiple regression analyses for Motivating Potential and Growth Need Strength with regard to the different measures of Absence Behavior. Table 10.3 contains the results for Motivating Potential and Instrumentality of Absence Behavior as predictors for the same dependent measures.

As can be seen in Table 10.2, "Motivating Potential" has an influence on the number of total work days missed ($F(1, 79) = 4.37$; $p < .04$), 3 to 7 days of absence ($F(1, 79) = 3.05$; $p < .09$), and number of absence periods ($F(1, 79) = 6.70$; $p < .01$). That means that a higher Motivating Potential leads to a lower rate of absence behavior (measured by these three indicators). The absence period of 1 or 2 days absent from work and absence time of 1 to 2 weeks were not determined by the Motivating Potential. Growth Need Strength did not explain additional variance in absence behavior after entering in the equation in the second step. Furthermore, Growth Need Strength did not moderate the influence of the Motivating Potential at all, as the insignificant results for the interaction terms reveal.

In contrast, a clear direct as well as moderating effect was found for Instrumentality of Absence Behavior. As mentioned before, Motivating Potential had a significant effect on number of work days missed. Instrumen-

TABLE 10.3
Summary Table of the Moderated Multiple Regression Analyses
Predicting Absence Behavior from Motivating Potential and
Instrumentality of Absence Behavior ($N = 81$)

Dependent Measure	Step	Predictor Added	F to Enter	p	R	R²	R² Change	Overall F	p
Total days	1	MPS	4.37	.04	.23	.05	.05	4.37	.04
	2	INST	1.40	.24	.26	.07	.02	2.89	.06
	3	Interaction	2.45	.12	.31	.10	.03	2.78	.04
1 or 2 days	1	MPS	1.11	.29	.12	.01	.01	1.11	.29
	2	INST	1.37	.25	.18	.03	.02	1.24	.29
	3	Interaction	4.10	.05	.28	.08	.05	2.23	.09
3 to 7 days	1	MPS	3.05	.09	.19	.04	.04	3.05	.09
	2	INST	.86	.36	.22	.05	.01	1.95	.15
	3	Interaction	.37	.55	.23	.05	.00	1.41	.25
1 to 2 weeks	1	MPS	.58	.45	.09	.01	.01	.58	.45
	2	INST	3.60	.06	.23	.05	.04	2.10	.13
	3	Interaction	.02	.89	.23	.05	.00	1.39	.25
Number of periods	1	MPS	6.71	.01	.28	.08	.08	6.71	.01
	2	INST	3.57	.06	.34	.12	.04	5.25	.007
	3	Interaction	3.01	.09	.39	.15	.03	4.59	.005

tality did not affect this measure of absence behavior but tended to moderate the influence of the Motivating Potential ($F(1, 78) = 2.45$; $p < .12$). The multiple regression coefficient for these three predictors was $R = .31$ and explained 10% of the variance ($F(3, 77) = 2.78$; $p < .04$). For the absence measure 1 or 2 work days missed, a slightly different result was obtained. This time, the Motivating Potential did not have a direct effect on the criteria, but the interaction between Motivating Potential and Instrumentality was significant ($F(1, 77) = 4.10$); $p < .05$). The R for the full model was $R = .28$, explaining 8% of the variance ($F(3, 77) = 2.23$; $p < .09$). For the absence measures 3 to 7 days of absence and 1 to 2 weeks of absence, Motivating Potential ($F(1, 79) = 3.05$; $p < .09$), and Instrumentality ($F(1, 78) = 3.6$; $p < .06$) tended to influence absence behavior, suggesting that higher scores in either scales resulted in fewer work days missed. However, the multiple regression coefficient for the full model was not significant. The best prediction could be made for the criteria number of periods missed. The Motivating Potential ($F(1, 79) = 6.71$; $p < .01$) and Instrumentality ($F(1, 78) = 3.57$; $p < .06$) entered in the second step were significant predictors of this indicator of absence behavior. In addition, to the variance explained by these two variables the interaction between Motivating Potential and Instrumentality added another 3% of variance explained ($F(3, 77) = 3.01$; $p < .09$). In other words, these were parts of the variance that could not be explained by the two variables individually but were due to the interaction effect between them or in the terms of the model due to the moderating effect of Instrumentality. The multiple correlation coefficient was $R = .39$, explaining 15% of the variance ($F(3, 77) = 4.59$; $p < .005$). In sum, the simple effects of Motivating Potential and Instrumentality and their interaction effect was most obvious for the indicator of absence behavior measuring the number of periods missed.

For illustrative purpose regression lines for high versus low Instrumentality were plotted for the regression on two measures of absence behavior by three levels of Motivating Potential (one standard deviation below and above mean). In Fig. 10.1 and 10.2 these lines are depicted for number of periods missed and 1 or 2 work days missed. The number of periods missed decreased for employees with a high score in Instrumentality as the Motivating Potential of the workplace increased ($F(1, 37) = 4.86$; $p < .03$). No changes with regard to different levels of Motivating Potential was observed

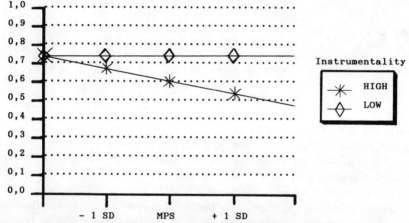

FIG. 10.1   Regression lines predicting number of periods missed (logarithmic transformation) from Motivating Potential (MPS) and Instrumentality of Absence Behavior.

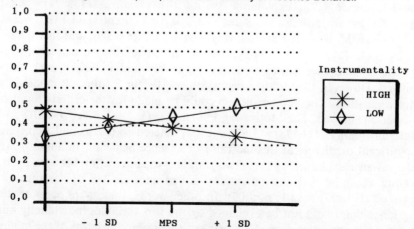

FIG. 10.2   Regression lines predicting 1 or 2 days of absence (logarithmic transformation) from Motivating Potential (MPS) and Instrumentality of Absence Behavior.

for people scoring low in Instrumentality (Fig. 10.1). For the absence behavior measure 1 or 2 work days absent, the interaction between Motivating Potential and Instrumentality turned out to be two-fold, as can be seen
in Fig. 10.2. For employees with a high score in Instrumentality, periods of
1 or 2 work days missed decreased as the Motivating Potential increased
($F(1, 37) = 3.4$; $p < .07$). In the low Instrumentality group a higher Moti-
vating Potential led to significantly more 1 or 2 days of absence ($F(1, 40) = 4.35$; $p < .04$), and the correlation between Motivating Potential and
absence behavior was positive ($r = .33$) in this group. In contrast, in the
groups of employees with high scores in Instrumentality, the correlation between Motivating Potential and different measures of absence behavior was
always negative (ranging between $r = -.29$ and $r = -.34$). In other words,
improving the Motivating Potential of the work place would have a negative effect for people scoring low in Instrumentality, and it would have a
positive influence on people with high scores in Instrumentality (with regard to absence of 1 or 2 days).

Discussion

The analyses showed that the indicator of absence behavior, "Number of
Periods missed," had the strongest relationship with the motivational variables studied. In other studies "Frequency of Absence" has also turned out
to be the best indicator of absence behavior with regard to the influence of
psychological variables (Clegg, 1983; Hammer & Landau, 1981; Keller,
1983). The second most relevant measure of absence behavior was "total
days absent," but in this case the effect of the moderating variable was not
as strong. However, the multiple regression coefficient reached $R = .31$ with
only three predictors in the model. A moderating effect of Instrumentality
could be observed for the absence measure "1 or 2 days of absence," but
the multiple correlation coefficient only reached $R = .28$. The differing
results obtained for the indicators of absence behavior are reflected in the
varying strength of association among these absence measures (Table 10.1).
This underscores the necessity to differentiate between indicators of absence behavior. Furthermore, the results of the study indicate that there is a
direct relationship between job characteristics (MPS) and work outcomes in
terms of absence behavior (total days, 3 to 7 days, number of periods). This
finding is in line with an analysis made by Wall, Clegg, and Hackson
(1978), who found evidence for a direct causal relationship between job
characteristics and outcome variables. The critical psychological states only
seem to have a mediating effect with regard to personal outcomes (e.g., internal work motivation, general job satisfaction) but not with respect to
work outcomes (e.g, performance, absence behavior). Our analyses clearly
demonstrated that growth need strength (GNS) did not have a moderating
effect for any of the defined measures of absence behavior. Roberts and

Glicks (1981) had questioned the quality of GNS as a moderating variable too. We think it is safe to say that growth need strength is not an adequate moderating variable for the outcome variable, absence behavior. In contrast, Instrumentality proved to be a suitable moderating variable, as it is conceptually related to the content of the task characteristics (MPS), which is underscored by the significant positive correlation between both measures ($r = .27$). Furthermore, there is a direct link to the criterion Absence Behavior.

If absence behavior shall be considered in the JCM in the future (and not be dropped as proposed by Hackman and Oldham, 1980) the Instrumentality of Absence Behavior should be incorporated as the crucial moderating variable. This line of reasoning leads to the conclusion that all moderating variables in this model should on the one hand be conceptually (and empirically) related to the task characteristics (MPS) and on the other hand be linked to the outcome variable in a question. Growth Need Strength is conceptually related to the task characteristics (however, in our study this relationship did not reach the $p < .05$ level of significance), but it is not conceptually and empirically linked to absence behavior at all. This explains why it has not been an effective moderating variable with regard to absence behavior and why it disappeared in the latest version of the Job Characteristics Model. We would like to argue for keeping absence behavior (absenteeism) in the Job Characteristics Model and for incorporating Instrumentality of Absence Behavior as a moderating variable with regard to absence behavior.

ACKNOWLEDGMENTS

The authors wish to thank Jen Algera, Gary Latham, Henk Thierry, and Rainer Wieland-Eckelmann for their helpful comments on an earlier version of this chapter, and our students Martina Przygodda and Ronald Schwarz for their assistance.

REFERENCES

Atkin, R. S., & Goodman, P. S. (1984). Methods of defining and measuring absenteeism. In P. S. Goodman & R. S. Atkin (Eds.), *Absenteeism: New approaches to understanding, measuring and managing employee absence* (pp. 47–109). San Francisco: Jossey Bass.

Avery, R. B., & Hotz, V. J. (1984). Statistical methods for analyzing absentee behavior. In P. S. Goodman & R. S. Atkin (Eds.), *Absenteeism: New approaches to understanding, measuring and managing employee absence* (pp. 158–193). San Francisco: Jossey Bass.

Clegg, C. W. (1983). Psychology of employee lateness, absence and turnover: A methodological critique and an empirical study. *Journal of Applied Psychology, 68*, 88–101.

Fried, Y., & Ferris, G. R. (1987). The validity of the Job Characteristics Model: A review and meta-analysis. *Personnel Psychology, 40*, 287–322.

Hackman, J. R. (1977). Work design. In J. R. Hackman & J. L. Suttle (Eds.), *Improving life at work: Behavioral science approaches to organizational change* (pp. 96–162). Santa Monica, CA: Goodyear.

Hackman, J. R., & Lawler, E. E., III (1971). Employee reactions to job characteristics. *Journal of Applied Psychology* (Monograph), *55*, 259–286.

Hackman, J. R., & Oldham, G. R. (1975). Development of the job diagnostic survey. *Journal of Applied Psychology, 60*, 159–170.

Hackman, J. R., & Oldham, G. R. (1976). Motivation through the design of work: Test of a theory. *Organizational Behavior and Human Performance, 16*, 250–279.

Hackman, J. R., & Oldham, G. R. (1980). *Work redesign.* Reading, MA: Addison–Wesley.

Hackman, J. R., Oldham, G. R., Janson, R., & Purdy, K. (1975). A new strategy for job enrichment. *California Management Review, 17*, 57–71.

Hammer, T. H., & Landau, J. (1981). Methodological issues in the use of absence data. *Journal of Applied Psychology, 66*, 574–581.

Johns, G. (1987). The great escape. *Psychology Today, 10*, 30–33.

Keller, R. T. (1983). Predicting absenteeism from prior absenteeism, attitudinal factors and nonattitudinal factors. *Journal of Applied Psychology, 68*, 536–540.

Kleinbeck, U., & Schmidt, K.-H. (1979). Aufgabenwahl im Ernstfall einer betrieblichen Ausbildung: Instrumentalitätstheoretische Ergänzung zum Risikowahlmodell [Choice of task in real life situations in training on the job: extension of the choice of risk model through the aspect of instrumentality]. *Zeitschrift für Entwicklungspsychologie und Pädagogische Psychologie, 11*, 1–11.

Kleinbeck, U., Schmidt, K.-H., Donis, R., & Ballé, W. (1983). Untersuchungen über den Zusammenhang zwischen leistungsthematischer Motivation und betrieblichen Fehlzeiten [Studies on the relationship between achievement motivation and absenteeism.] *Zeitschrift für Experimentelle und Angewandte Psychologie, 30*, 425–441.

Landy, F. J., Vasey, J. J., & Smith, F. D. (1984). Methodological problems and strategies in predicting absence. In P. S. Goodman & R. S. Atkin (Eds.), *Absenteeism: New approaches to understanding, measuring and managing employee absence* (pp. 110–157). San Francisco: Jossey Bass.

Roberts, K. H., & Glicks, W. H. (1981). The job characteristics approach to task design: A critical review. *Journal of Applied Psychology, 66*, 193–217.

Spector, P. E. (1985). Higher order need strength as a moderator of the job scope-employee outcome relationship: A meta-analysis. *Journal of Occupational Psychology, 58*, 119–127.

Steers, R. M., & Rhodes, S. R. (1984). Knowledge and speculation about absenteeism. In P. S. Goodman & R. S. Atkin (Eds.), *Absenteeism: New approaches to understanding, measuring and managing employee absence* (pp. 229–275). San Francisco: Jossey Bass.

Vroom, V. H. (1964). *Work motivation.* New York: Wiley.

Wall, T. D., Clegg, C. W., & Hackson, P. R. (1978). An evaluation of the Job Characteristics Model. *Journal of Occupational Psychology, 51*, 183–186.

Yankelovich, D. (1979). "We need new motivational tools." *Industry Week, 8*, 52–63.

11

Increasing Job Attendance Through Training in Self-Management: A Review of Two Field Experiments

Gary P. Latham
University of Washington

Collette A. Frayne
University of Western Ontario

Low job attendance, or absenteeism, is a chronic problem in many organizational settings (Goodman & Atkin, 1984). The annual cost of absenteeism in the United States is approximately thirty billion dollars (Steers & Rhodes, 1984). This is because employee absences can disrupt work schedules, increase costs, and decrease productivity.

In 1962, As argued that employee absenteeism is a social fact in need of a theory. Twenty years later, Johns and Nicholson (1982) found that despite a heavy investment of research effort no major breakthrough in the prediction, understanding, and control of absenteeism had occurred.

There are at least two explanations for this impasse. The first is the measurement problem. Latham and his colleagues (Latham & Frayne, 1987; Latham & Napier, 1984; Latham & Pursell, 1975, 1977) have maintained that the primary interest of researchers should be to find a stable measure on which to build theory, on which to evaluate the validity of predictors or the effectiveness of interventions. For this reason, they argued the necessity of measuring job attendance in addition to, if not in place of, absenteeism. This argument was based on findings from four samples of employees that test–retest reliability coefficients of job attendance are significantly higher than typical measures of absenteeism (Latham & Frayne, 1987; Latham & Pursell, 1975). This occurs because absenteeism measures are almost always contaminated heavily by human judgment. The measures reflect the categorization behavior (e.g., jury duty, illness, injury, bereavement, vacation) of the recorder rather than the measurements of the researcher. Conversely, the recording of job attendance is relatively straightforward. The measurement is based on observations of employee presence at the work site.

For reasons that are not altogether clear, Nicholson and his colleagues

(Chadwick-Jones, Nicholson, & Brown, 1982; Johns, 1984; Johns & Nicholson, 1982) have argued against relying on traditional test–theory concepts such as test–retest reliability when studying a low base rate construct such as absenteeism. Arguments similar to Nicholson's have been put forth by Ilgen (1977) in explaining why interobserver reliability coefficients should be calculated in place of test–retest reliability. This de-emphasis of the importance of stable measures (test–retest reliability) because of the difficulty in obtaining them is a straightforward explanation of why prediction of, let alone controls for, absenteeism have often proven to be elusive. Lack of stability in measurement increases the likelihood of Type II measurement error, namely, the erroneous conclusion that the predictor is not valid or the intervention is not effective in bringing about a behavior change.

Work by Nicholson and his colleagues (Chadwick-Jones et al., 1982; Johns, 1984; Johns & Nicholson, 1982) suggests a second explanation for the lack of progress in research of absenteeism, namely, a focus on the individual employee to the exclusion of the social dynamics affecting employee absences. Nicholson and Johns (1982) interpreted their data as indicating the existence of absence cultures within organizations. The result is group norms that affect attendance behavior. In reviewing this research, Johns (1984) concluded that it is unlikely that cost-effective interventions exist for solving absenteeism *at the level of the individual employee.* Moreover, where such an intervention is used, symptom substitution is likely.

Based on work by Kanfer in clinical psychology, these two conclusions would appear unwarranted. Kanfer's (1970, 1975, 1980) training in self-management teaches people to assess problems, set specific hard goals in relation to those problems, monitor ways in which the environment facilitates or hinders goal attainment, and identify and administer reinforcers for working toward and punishers for failing to work toward goal attainment. In essence, this training teaches people skills in self-observation, to compare their behavior with the goals that they set, and to administer reinforcers and punishers to bring about and sustain goal commitment (Karoly & Kanfer, 1982). The reinforcer or punisher is made contingent on the degree to which their behavior approximates the goal. Kanfer views these two outcome variables in terms of informational as well as emotional feedback to account for cognitive as well as motoric and autonomic effects. Essentially, however, this represents a broadening rather than a change of the reinforcement contingency concept.

Training in self-regulation has been evaluated rigorously in both laboratory and clinical settings. Positive results have been obtained with regard to teaching oneself to stop smoking (Kanfer & Phillips, 1970), to overcome drug addiction (Kanfer, 1974), to reduce weight (Mahoney, Moura, & Wade, 1973), to improve study habits (Richards, 1976), and to enhance academic achievement (Glynn, 1970).

One theory that explains the effectiveness of training in self-management is social learning theory (Bandura, 1977a, 1986). This theory emphasizes the role of self-reactive influences in motivating and guiding one's behavior. The theory states that by arranging environmental contingencies, establishing specific goals, and producing consequences for their actions people can be taught to exercise control over their behavior.

Two social learning theory constructs that may underlie the effectiveness of training in self-management are perceived self-efficacy and outcome expectancies. Perceived self-efficacy refers to the strength of one's belief that he or she can successfully execute the behaviors required (Bandura, 1982). Such self-beliefs influence what people choose to do, how much effort they mobilize, and how long they will persevere in the face of real or perceived obstacles. For example, people who judge themselves as inefficacious in coping with environmental demands may imagine their difficulties (e.g, family obligations, transportation issues) as more formidable than they are in fact. In contrast, people who have a strong sense of self-efficacy focus their attention and effort on the demands of the situation and are spurred to an increase in effort by perceived obstacles (Bandura, 1982).

Outcome expectancies refer to beliefs concerning the extent to which one's behavior will produce favorable or unfavorable outcomes. People are prone to act on their self-precepts of efficacy when they believe that their actions will produce outcomes that are beneficial to them (Bandura, 1982). However, they are unlikely to change their behavior when they believe they can perform competently, but that the environment (e.g., supervisory or peer evaluation) will be unresponsive to their improved performance.

With regard to job attendance, some people may judge themselves as inefficacious in coping with environmental demands that prevent them from coming to work. Support for this assumption can be found in the revision of the Steers and Rhodes (1984) model. These authors introduced perceived inability to come to work as a critical variable affecting employee attendance. In addition, Chadwick-Jones, Nicholson, and Brown (1982) showed how cultural and normative variables can affect attendance negatively. Even a variable so straightforward as one's work schedule (flexible for most white-collar jobs; inflexible for most blue-collar jobs) can have a positive or negative effect on an employee's attendance. For example, people in a blue-collar unionized job may find it extremely difficult to take an hour off in the middle of the workday to accompany a child to a medical doctor's office, whereas most people in white-collar jobs can do this with relative ease. Thus the former person may take the day off to accomplish what the latter person can do in 2 or 3 hours.

On the other hand, employees may believe that neither managers nor peers will change their low opinion of them (outcome expectancy) even if they do increase their attendance. Support for this is based on anecdotal evidence obtained in industry. Many people feel that once they have been labeled "poor employees" it is difficult for them to change their reputation.

Support for this belief can be found in research on attitude perseverance in the face of contradictory evidence (Ross, 1977).

This chapter describes research that evaluated training in self-management in terms of its effects on job attendance. This training was used for three reasons. First, training in self-management is cost effective in that it requires minimal trainer time. Second, evidence from clinical psychology showed that this training is effective in the treatment of substance abuse behavior (Kanfer, 1986) that often occurs within a culture that maintains and strengthens it. Thus, it was hypothesized that training in self-management should also be effective in increasing job attendance despite a culture that may reinforce absenteeism. Third, the implicit theory underlying this intervention was that people who come to work judge themselves as efficacious (Bandura, 1986) in coping with environmental demands (e.g, supervisory conflict, peer pressure, family obligations, transportation issues, illness), whereas those who do not come to work perceive themselves as inefficacious. It was thus hypothesized that training in self-management would increase one's perceived self-efficacy with regard to responding effectively to those demands, which in turn would increase one's job attendance. The method used to test this hypothesis is described next.

METHOD

Sample

Forty unionized, state, government employees employed as carpenters, electricians, and painters in a maintenance department participated in the two studies. The union agreed to support the training if certain conditions were agreed on by management, namely, no employee would be required to receive the training, no monetary incentive would be offered for increasing one's attendance, and the course would be offered during normal work hours.

Employees who had used 50% or more of their sick leave received a memo from the Personnel Department inviting them to participate in this study. In an attempt to minimize attrition rates reported in other studies (e.g., Harris & Ream, 1978), the memo stressed that only persons who would commit themselves to eight 1-hour weekly group sessions and eight 30-minute weekly one-on-one sessions should volunteer for the training. Further, people who had scheduled vacation time should not enroll in the training at this time. Finally, people who were on disciplinary probation could not participate in the training.

Of the 50 individuals who were contacted, 42 volunteered to receive the training. Of the 42, two individuals stated that they would not be able to attend all eight sessions due to scheduled vacation time. The remaining 40 were randomly assigned to an experimental ($n = 20$) or a control group

($n = 20$). The people in the control group were told that they would be trained at a later date.

The mean age of the 40 employees was 44.33 ($SD = 11.4$). Seventy percent of them were male. The mean number of years they had worked for the state was 7.41 ($SD = 3.14$). None of these people dropped out of the training program.

Procedure

The control group, like the experimental group, was exposed to ongoing organizational sanctions regarding absenteeism (e.g., 2 or more days off per month without a medical slip, failure to call in). These sanctions consisted of an oral warning, a written warning, being placed on 3 months probation, and termination. The incentive for job attendance was that employees earned 8 hours sick leave each month. Hours that were not used by the end of the year would be applied to the next year. People were given compensation on retirement for the total number of sick leave hours that were not used. These policies had been in existence for 12 years. Nevertheless, the mean recorded absenteeism due to sick leave was 5.26 employee hours per week ($SD = 3.61$) in the experimental group and 4.96 employee hours in the control group ($SD = 2.16$).

The training program itself consisted of eight weekly 1-hour group sessions followed by eight 30-minute one-on-one sessions. Each training group consisted of 10 people. The one-on-one sessions were conducted to tailor the training to the specific concerns of each individual and to discuss issues that the person might have been reluctant to introduce in a group setting.

Group Sessions

The first week an orientation session was conduced to explain the principles of self-management. In the second week, the reasons given by the trainees for using sick leave were listed and classified into nine categories, namely: legitimate illness, medical appointments, job stress, job boredom, difficulties with co-workers, alcohol and drug related issues, family problems, transportation difficulties, and employee rights (i.e., "sick leave belongs to me"). Of these nine, family problems, incompatibility with supervisor or co-workers, and transportation problems were listed most frequently. Sick leave was the focus of discussion in this session because it accounted for 49.8% of the recorded absenteeism in the organization. This is because the norm in the organization among these employees was to state that they were sick when they wanted a day off.

The trainees were taught to develop a description of the problem behaviors (e.g., difficulty with supervisor), to identify conditions that elicited and maintained the problem behaviors, and to identify specific coping strategies. This constituted the session on self-assessment. In this session, as in all sessions, the employees were assured that their comments would not be shared with anyone outside the training group.

The third week focused on goal setting. The distal goal was to increase one's attendance within a specific time frame (e.g., 1 month/3 months). The proximal goals were the specific behaviors that the respective individual had to engage in to attain the distal goal.

The fourth week focused on the importance of self-monitoring one's behavior. Specifically, the trainees were taught to record (a) their own attendance, (b) the reason for missing a day of work, and (c) the steps that were followed to deal with the constraint(s) to subsequently get to work. This was done through the use of charts and diaries. Emphasis was placed on the importance of daily feedback for motivational purposes as well as accuracy in recording.

In the fifth week, the trainees identified reinforcers and punishers to self-administer as a result of achieving or failing to achieve the proximal goals. The training emphasized that the reinforcer must be powerful and easily self-administered (e.g., self-praise, purchasing a gift). The punisher was to be a disliked activity, easily self-administered (e.g., cleaning the garage). Each individual developed specific response-reward contingencies.

The sixth week was essentially a review of the previous five sessions. This was accomplished by asking the trainees to write a behavioral contract with themselves. Thus, each trainee specified in writing the goal(s) to be achieved, the time frame for achieving the goal(s), the consequences for attaining or failing to attain the goal(s), and the behaviors necessary for attaining the goal(s).

The seventh week emphasized maintenance. Discussion focused on issues that might result in a relapse in absenteeism, planning for such situations should they occur, and developing coping strategies for dealing with theses situations.

During the last week of training, the trainer reviewed each technique presented in the program, answered questions from the trainees regarding these skills, and clarified expectations. The measure of goal commitment was taken at the end of this session.

The theoretical rationale for combining these variables into one treatment package can be found in Bandura (1977b). The assumption underlying training in self-management (Azrin, 1977) is that the treatment package should "include as many component procedures as seem necessary to obtain, ideally, a total treatment success" (p. 144). Empirical support for combining goal setting, feedback, and self-monitoring into one treatment package can be found in both the organizational behavior and clinical psychology literatures. For example, Erez (1977) found that goal setting in the absence of feedback has no effect on behavior. Latham, Mitchell, and Dossett (1978) found that feedback in the absence of goal setting has no effect on behavior subsequent to a performance appraisal. Similarly, Simon (1979) showed that self-monitoring in the absence of goal setting has no effect on behavior. Campbell (1982) concluded that little would be gained from further attempts to tease apart the relative effects of goal setting, feedback, and reinforcers.

Research Design

Reaction, learning, cognitive, and behavioral measures were taken 3 months, 6 months, and again 9 months subsequent to the training to evaluate its effects over time. The purpose of the reaction measures was to assess whether employee affect for the training diminished over time. In addition, the employees were interviewed to determine whether the reasons given for absenteeism changed. The measure of learning was collected to determine whether the employees retained the knowledge disseminated in the training program. If the knowledge was not retained, it could explain any return to pretraining levels of job attendance that might exist. The cognitive measure, perceived self-efficacy, was measured to determine its importance as a psychological variable affecting job attendance. A decrease in the trainees' self-efficacy also would explain any decrease in job attendance that may have occurred. Finally, both job attendance and employee sick leave were measured. Sick leave was measured because it accounted for 49.8% of the organization's categorized reasons for absenteeism. Measuring both job attendance and categorized sick leave permitted multiple operationalism of the dependent variable of primary interest, namely, employee presence at the work site.

Subsequent to the 9-month follow-up assessment, the employees in the control group also received the training in self-management. The only difference between the two studies was the trainer. Frayne conducted the first training program; a person in the organization's personnel department, trained by Frayne, was the trainer in the replication study. The data for this second experiment were collected 3 months subsequent to the training of the control group. The results were compared with those collected from the original experimental group 3 months after it had been trained.

RESULTS

Manipulation Checks

Goal Commitment. Goal commitment lies at the core of self-management training. In this study, if the employees had not been committed to improving their attendance, the training could not have been successful. The internal consistency of a 4-item commitment measure (e.g., "To what extent will you strive to attain the goal?" "How important is it to you to at least attain the goal that was set?") administered during the final week of training to the experimental group was satisfactory (coefficient alpha = .81). The mean of the responses to these 5-point Likert-type items was extremely high ($\overline{X}$ = 4.73; SD = .22). This restriction in range for uniformly high commitment precluded significant correlations between goal commitment and performance on the learning test, or job attendance. Similarly, the internal consistency of this 4-item scale in the subsequent training of the replication group 1 year later was .84. The mean of the responses to the 5-point Likert-type items ($\overline{X}$ = 4.81; SD = .25) in this second sample was also extremely high and was not significantly different from that of the original experimental group.

Criterion Measures

Reaction Measures. Assessing employee reactions to the training was important because many trainees had argued that sick leave is a "privilege that belongs to me." Moreover, in the initial session, the trainees in the original experimental group expressed hostile reactions to the training in the form of self-deprecating and aggressive comments (e.g., "I guess we are the delinquent bunch"; "The trainer is a spy for management"). A fist fight occurred in the first class as a result of name calling between two trainees. Thus it was important to determine what the trainees perceived was especially effective or ineffective about the program.

A 5-point 5-item Likert-type questionnaire (e.g., "The training I received helped me overcome obstacles preventing me from coming to work") was completed 3 months after the training to measure employee reactions to the training. The coefficient alpha for this questionnaire was .73. In the replication sample, it was .74. The test–retest reliability of this measure over a 3-month period was .81; in the replication sample it was .84.

The employee reactions to the training were very positive immediately after training ($\overline{X}$ = 4.32; SD = .55). The employees expressed the same positive reaction 3 months ($\overline{X}$ = 4.46; SD = .41), 6 months ($\overline{X}$ = 4.48; SD = .46), and 9 months later ($\overline{X}$ = 4.47; SD = .43). The differences among these values are not statistically significant. Thus, employee affect toward the training program remained highly positive.

The employee reactions in the replication sample 3 months after receiving the training from a person in the personnel department were also high ($\overline{X}$ = 4.45; SD = .43). A t-test revealed no significant difference between this value and the value obtained from the original training group 3 months after the training had taken place.

Specifically, the trainees in both the original and replication groups reported that the training enabled them to identify obstacles preventing them from coming to work, helped them overcome these obstacles, led them to set specific goals for increasing job attendance, and increased their confidence in their ability to control their own behavior.

Learning Measure.   An important issue is to understand in what way the training was effective. One criterion is learning (Kirkpatrick, 1976; Wexley & Latham, 1981). Did the trainees learn ways of responding to attendance related issues? Did they acquire problem-solving principles that enabled them to deal with coming to work effectively? To answer these questions, a learning test was developed on the basis of interviews with the supervisors of the employees.

The learning test consisted of 12 situational items with a scoring guide. A sample item is: "The reason I can't come to work is that I do not get along with a particular person with whom I work. Whenever she is on shift, I call in sick. I noted that when I do have contract with her on the job, we get into arguments. I decided to set a goal of "getting along with her," but it does not seem to be working. What should I do?"

This methodology is based on the situational interview (Latham & Finnegan, 1987; Latham & Saari, 1984; Latham, Saari, Pursell, & Campion, 1980). The test was administered and scored prior to training (coefficient alpha = .74) and again 3 months after the training (coefficient alpha = .82) by two judges who were blind as to whether the responses were from people in the training or the control group. The test–retest reliability of responses to the items was .85.

An analysis of variance revealed no significant difference between groups prior to training. However, the difference between groups was highly significant subsequent to training ($F[1, 38] = 6.30$; $p < .02$). The mean of the training group's performance on this test was 29.95 ($SD = 7.0$); the mean of the control group was 16.4 ($SD = 2.9$). The correlation between the learning test scores and job attendance was .77 ($p < .05$). This indicates that the knowledge acquired on how to cope with constraints in attending work correlates with the actual coming to work.

To determine whether people retained the knowledge disseminated in the training program, the learning test was administered and scored 6 months and again 9 months subsequent to the training. The trainees had not been informed of the scoring of their answers. The coefficient alphas of the learning test were .74 and .80, respectively, for the 6- and 9-month administrations.

The alpha for the replication sample calculated 3 months subsequent to training was .78. This compares favorably with the alpha of .82 obtained after 3 months in the original study.

The test–retest reliability of the questionnaire between months 3 and 9 was .81 for the original training group. The test–retest reliability between the premeasure and month 3 for the replication sample was .80. This, too, compares favorably with the reliability estimate of .85 obtained in the original study.

TABLE 11.1
Means and Standard Deviations of Learning Measure
by Training and Control Group

Group	Time Measured									
	Pretraining		3 Months		6 Months		9 Months		12 Months	
	M	SD	M	SD	M	SD	M	SD	M	SD
Training	15.60	4.2	29.95	7.0	28.65	6.1	28.92	10.1	27.90	8.6
Control	16.20	4.3	15.70	4.6	16.10	3.8	15.40	5.6	28.90	7.3

Note: The 12 months score is a 1-year followup for the training group and a 3-month followup for the newly trained control group.

A repeated measures analysis of variance revealed no significant differences across months 3 through 9. Thus, the knowledge acquired in the training did not diminish over time. Moreover, an analysis of variance revealed no significant difference between the replication sample's 3-month scores and the original training group's 3-month scores. The respective means and standard deviations are shown in Table 11.1.

Attendance Employee absenteeism was defined by the organization as falling into one of 11 categories (e.g., holiday leave, sick leave, vacation leave, jury leave, bereavement leave, etc.). Because 49.8% of the absenteeism was recorded as sick leave, this measure was used in this study. This measure was operationalized as the number of sick leave hours taken per employee each week. Attendance was defined as the number of hours the employees were scheduled to be at work that they were actually on the job. The total number of hours the person could work on the job each week was 40. Overtime was not permitted. As noted previously, these two measures permitted multiple operationalism of the dependent variable of primary interest, namely, employee presence at the work site.

The test–retest reliabilities (stability) of the recording of sick leave assessed over a 52-week period ($n = 40$) prior to conducting the study was .38. This was done on the basis of employee time cards. The correlation was in sharp contrast to the reliability of the weekly measures of attendance, namely .90. The test–retest reliability of the recording of sick leave assessed over the 12 weeks subsequent to this study was .42; the test–retest reliability of the attendance measure was .92. The correlation between the 12-week measure of sick leave and attendance was − .64.

In the follow-up study, the test–retest reliability (stability) of the attendance measure from month 3 until month 12 (36 weekly measures) for the 40 employees was .91. Again, this is in sharp contrast with the stability of the sick leave categorization, namely .39. The correlation between these two measures was − .62.

A repeated measures multivariate analysis of variance based on 12 weeks of data on these two dependent variables revealed a significant difference

TABLE 11.2
Means and Standard Deviations of Attendance[a] Measure
by Training and Control Groups

| Group | Time Measured | | | | | | | | | |
| | Pretraining | | 3 Months | | 6 Months | | 9 Months | | 12 Months | |
	M	SD	M	SD	M	SD	M	SD	M	SD
Training	33.1	5.6	35.7	4.2	38.6	1.4	38.2	2.4	38.4	3.8
Control	32.3	7.6	30.0	4.9	31.6	4.3	30.9	3.3	34.9	4.3

Note: The 12-months score is a 1-year followup for the training group and a 3-month followup for the newly trained control group.
[a]Attendance is number of hours present per 40-hour scheduled work week.

between the training and the control group ($T[2, 37] = 6.67$, $p < .05$). Univariate F tests revealed a significant difference between the training ($\overline{X} = 458.4$, $SD = 32.7$) and the control group ($\overline{X} = 403.2$, $SD = 22.8$) for the measure of attendance ($F[1, 38] = 5.52$, $p < .05$). However, the F test was only marginally significant ($F[1, 38] = 1.84$ $p < .10$) for the measure of sick leave ($\overline{X} = 69.6$, $SD = 12.3$, $\overline{X} = 83.1$, $SD = 18.5$, training and control group, respectively). This latter finding undoubtedly reflects the lack of stability in this absenteeism measure due to criterion contamination relative to the measure of job attendance. The accuracy of the measure of sick leave was dependent on self-report.

Similarly, in the follow-up study across 9 months, a repeated measures multivariate analysis of variance on these two dependent variables revealed a significant difference between the training and the control group based on data collected in months 3, 6, and 9 ($T[2, 37] = 9.84$, $p < .05$). Univariate repeated measures analysis of variance revealed a significant difference between the training and the control group for the attendance measure. Thus, the increase in job attendance as a result of training in self-management did not diminish significantly over time. However, as in the initial 3-month study, the F test was only marginally significant at the .10 level for the measure of sick leave.

A multivariate analysis of variance on the attendance and sick leave measures for the replication sample 3 months subsequent to their training, and the original training group 3 months subsequent to training, revealed no significant differences. Tables 11.2 and 11.3 show the means and standard deviations of the attendance and sick leave measures.

Intervening Variables

Of critical importance to this research was understanding why the training was effective from a psychological standpoint. Did training in self-

TABLE 11.3
Means and Standard Deviations of Sick Leave Absenteeism
by Training and Control Groups

Group	Time Measured									
	Pretraining		3 Months		6 Months		9 Months		12 Months	
	M	SD	M	SD	M	SD	M	SD	M	SD
Training	5.26	3.6	4.12	2.4	3.68	1.4	3.59	2.6	3.72	2.2
Control	4.96	2.2	5.03	3.6	5.14	2.8	5.11	3.9	4.01	2.4

Note: The 12-months score is a 1-year followup for the training group and a 3-month followup for the newly trained control group.

management affect the trainees' perceived self-efficacy and outcome expectancies? Do these variables predict job attendance?

Perceived self-efficacy and outcome expectancies were measured prior to the study, immediately after the study, and again 3 months later. The 15-item perceived self-efficacy scale followed the format used to measure self-efficacy with regard to refraining from smoking (Condiotte & Lichtenstein, 1981). Other items were based on comments received from supervisors ($n = 12$) and employees ($n = 10$) regarding obstacles affecting a person's coming to work. For each of the 15 job attendance situations described, the trainees indicted whether they felt that they would be able to come to work (efficacy level) and, if yes, their confidence level on a scale from 1 to 100 (efficacy strength). The coefficient alphas were .88, .91, and .89. The test–retest reliability between time 1 and time 3 was .92 and between time 2 and time 3 was .94.

Outcome expectancies (e.g., "I will not be able to meet family demands"; "I will increase my sense of accomplishment") were measured using a 15-item questionnaire that contained both positive and negative consequences for coming to work as perceived by the employee. These items were generated from informal interviews with supervisors and personnel officers prior to conducting the study. For each item, individuals were asked to designate on a 100-point probability scale (expressed in % units), ranging in 10-unit intervals, the probability that they would experience or achieve a particular outcome as a result of coming to work. The coefficient alphas were .67, .63, and .68. The test–retest reliability between time 1 and time 3 was .74, and between time 2 and time 3 was .76.

There was no significant difference between the training and control groups on the measure of perceived self-efficacy or outcome expectancies prior to the training. A 2×3 repeated measures analysis of variance for the self-efficacy scores revealed a significant F for groups ($F[1, 119] = 24.78$, $p < .05$), time, ($F[2, 119] = 16.71$, $p < .05$) and group by time interaction ($F[2, 119] = 46.02$, $p < .05$). The experimental group ($\overline{X} = 102.3$, $SD = 17.5$) not only expressed higher self-efficacy than the control group

TABLE 11.4
Means and Standard Deviations of Self-Efficacy Measure
by Training and Control Groups

Group	Time Measured									
	Pretraining		3 Months		6 Months		9 Months		12 Months	
	M	SD	M	SD	M	SD	M	SD	M	SD
Training	45.0	14.3	60.2	15.1	86.6	11.3	87.5	10.2	85.9	8.6
Control	46.4	13.2	45.8	14.3	46.0	12.7	44.9	13.8	63.6	12.3

Note: The 12-months score is a 1-year follow-up for the training group and a 3-month follow-up for the newly trained control group.

($\overline{X} = 81.1$, $SD = 12.4$), but the relationships between perceived self-efficacy taken immediately after training, and subsequent job attendance and sick leave, were significant ($r = .49$, $r = -.40$, $p < .05$, respectively).

The analysis with regard to outcome expectancies did not yield any statistically significant findings. This may be because outcome expectancies were uniformly high prior to conducting the study. Consequently, they were not measured in the follow-up or replication studies.

In the replication sample, the alpha for the self-efficacy measure taken 3 months after the training was .87. The test–retest reliability over 3 months was .89.

The means and standard deviations for the measures of the trainees' self-efficacy are shown in Table 11.4. A repeated measures analysis of variance revealed a significant difference ($F[1, 119] = 27.22$, $p < .001$) across months 3, 6, and 9. The means indicate that perceived self-efficacy increased. Moreover, an analysis of variance revealed no significant difference between the original experimental and replication groups 3 months after the training of the replication group had been conducted.

The concurrent validity of the measure of self-efficacy with job attendance at month 3 was .45. The predictive validity of this measure with job attendance 9 months later was .48. Self-efficacy has been found to be at the root of relapse prevention (Marlatt & Gordon, 1985).

To understand from the employees' perspective why the training increased job attendance, employees in the original training group were assured confidentiality and then asked to state candidly to the second author their reasons for using sick leave. This occurred during week 2 of the training and again in months 3, 6, and 9. The procedure was not used with the replication sample because the trainer was an employee of the organization. The responses are shown in Table 11.5. It is interesting to note that the shift in reasons from pre to posttraining is predominantly one from situations in which psychological or personal control is required to a higher percentage of situations associated with physical illness, presumably beyond the individual's control.

TABLE 11.5
Self-Reported Reasons for Absenteeism
for Training Group

Classification	Time Measured			
	Pretraining	3 Months	6 Months	9 Months
Family problems	25%	12%	6%	5%
Co-worker problems	20%	10%	4%	5%
Transportation	15%	8%	5%	5%
Perceived employee privilege	12%	5%	5%	4%
Medical appointments	10%	28%	30%	32%
Legitimate illness	5%	36%	45%	42%
Alcohol/drug issues	8%	—	—	—
Job boredom	5%	—	—	—

Tardiness/Turnover/Generalizability

Data were collected on tardiness as well as voluntary and involuntary turnover to determine if the training program affected either of these behaviors adversely. No significant differences were found between the training and control groups throughout the study.

Interviews with supervisors ($n = 12$) revealed that they observed positive changes on the part of the trainees. They reported that the training taught the individuals effective strategies for maintaining schedules of job shop work orders as well as job completion. Several trainees were observed sharing viewpoints regarding effective ways of completing the work on time. One supervisor reported that his personal satisfaction with two of the trainees' job performance was so high that he had recommended both of them for a project start-up.

Another trainee, who had come to each session in a slovenly fashion, began taking interest in good grooming habits and appearance. This trainee stated that he had begun to feel better about himself as a result of his performance during the training and on the job.

Three individuals reported using the self-management techniques for problems other than sick leave, namely, weight loss, smoking, and stress reduction. They stated that they had members of their family (e.g., wife, son) serve as external verifiers of their progress in the program. In the 6-month follow-up interviews, one individual reported a 30-pound reduction in weight, another a reduction in smoking from 2.5 packs/week to .5 packs/week, and a third a significant improvement in a personal relationship as a result of effectively managing stressful situations. Two other individuals reported using the self-management techniques for implementing a body-building program and managing financial expenses, respectively. This anecdotal information is supportive of data on the generalizability of self-management techniques to other behaviors (Bandura, 1986).

DISCUSSION

The theoretical significance of this research is that it provides an explanation of why people come or do not come to work. As both Äs (1962) and Fichman (1984) have noted, absenteeism has been a social fact in need of a theory. Self-efficacy (Bandura, 1977b, 1982) is one such theory. People who come to work may be individuals who are able to overcome the personal obstacles, as well as the cultural and group norms that were identified by Chadwick-Jones et al. (1982), that affect their perceived ability to come to work. People who do not come to work may be unable to cope with these influences unless their efficacy is enhanced by providing them the skill to exercise control over these variables.

A self-efficacy-based theory of job attendance should not be viewed as being in conflict or in competition with Nicholson's social dynamics explanation of absenteeism. The discovery of group norms indigenous to absenteeism cultures that affects employee behavior within organizations was an important finding furthering the understanding of absenteeism. However, it would be questionable ethically to inculcate in employees the belief that a person is not responsible for his or her own behavior. Thus, the finding that increasing self-efficacy empowers employees to increase their job attendance is an equally important discovery as a control, specifically self-control, for minimizing absenteeism.

Of further theoretical significance is the finding that high-outcome expectancies alone will not result in employees coming to work if they judge themselves as inefficacious in overcoming personal and social obstacles to work attendance. This finding is in accord with other studies showing that low-perceived self-efficacy negates the motivating potential of outcome expectancies (Barling & Abel, 1983; Godding & Glasgow, 1985; Williams & Watson, 1985).

The practical significance of this study is eight-fold. First it showed the external validity of training in self-management for unionized workers employed by a state government. Until the present series of studies, training in self-management had been restricted primarily to people in clinical or educational settings.

Second, the present study showed the effectiveness of training in self-management on a dependent variable that had not been previously studied using this technique, namely, employee attendance. Employee attendance, as noted in the introduction to this chapter, has significant cost implications for organizations.

Third, the rival hypothesis that the effects of the training were trainer specific was rejected. Of special importance with regard to application was that the training in the replication study was conducted by a layperson in the organization's personnel department.

Fourth, employee attendance at work increased on the basis of a straightforward 12-hour training program. The concepts of goal setting and reinforcers are well known to most trainers. A unique aspect of this training is the emphasis on trainees developing a contract with themselves for self-administering reinforcers and punishers to facilitate goal commitment.

Fifth, the effectiveness of this training does not appear to extinguish with time. Reaction, learning, self-efficacy, and job attendance measures taken 9 months after the training showed that skill in self-management brings about a relatively permanent change in cognition, affect, and behavior.

Sixth, this study provided a stringent test of training in self-management. The control group, like the experimental group, was not only exposed to organizational rewards and penalties regarding attendance/absenteeism, but they had the desire to increase their attendance at work. Evidence of the latter is indicated by their attendance at the orientation session where people were randomly assigned to the experimental or the control group. Thus the rival hypothesis that the effects of this training were due to evaluation apprehension or attention was rejected.

Seventh, there appears to be no evidence of symptom substitution on the part of those who practice self-management techniques. This fact, plus the cost effectiveness of this training, casts significant doubt on the assertion of Nicholson and his colleagues (e.g., Chadwick-Jones et al., 1982) that the utility of behavioral interventions that focus on the individual are of questionable value.

Eighth, the study showed the importance of using attendance rather than a measure of absenteeism as the primary dependent variable. This point has been argued elsewhere (Latham & Frayne, 1987; Latham & Napier, 1984), but the superiority of the former measure for assessing the effects of an intervention had not been demonstrated empirically. Measures of absenteeism are typically nothing more than measures of the categorization behavior of recorders (Latham & Pursell, 1975, 1977); that is, an absence is sometimes classified as sick leave rather than as a vacation day as a reward for good performance (Goodman & Atkin, 1984). Thus, absenteeism measures are highly contaminated (Thorndike, 1949), and their reliability is typically quite low. Had only a measure of recorded sick leave been used in this study as the sole index of absenteeism, a Type II error would have been made. The results would have shown that training in self-management had only a marginal effect on employee absenteeism.

A limitation of both the attendance and the absenteeism measures is that they ignore the distinction between voluntary and involuntary absenteeism. Some people may take sick leave because they are too ill to come to work, whereas others may have negotiated with a supervisor to record a vacation day as sick leave. These two behaviors, illness and negotiation, are very different theoretically. This lack of sensitivity in the two measures provided a highly conservative test of the training program. To overcome this contamination in measurement, a researcher would have to observe each person who stayed away from work to determine whether illness was the valid reason. The practicality of involving medical experts and calculating subsequent interobserver reliability coefficients makes the likelihood of conducting this research relatively low.

As a small step toward the ethnographic stance, the second author, as noted previously, assured the trainees confidentiality in comments made to her. These interviews indicated that only 5% of the absenteeism prior to training was due to legitimate illness. Thus, the significance of these interviews is three-fold. First, they explain why absenteeism measures are usually highly contaminated. Employees candidly admit that they often do not tell the truth as to why they do not come to work. Thus, it would appear that researchers have little choice but to measure job attendance in addition to, if not in place of, organizationally categorized absences. Second, the relatively small percentage of people who reported that they missed work prior to this study because they were truly sick supports the notion of an absenteeism culture (Chadwick-Jones et al., 1982). Third, after the training in self-management, the follow-up reports indicate that absenteeism was no longer masquerading under labels of sickness. When sick leave was taken, it was actually due to illness.

ACKNOWLEDGMENTS

This chapter is based on an integration of papers written by Frayne and Latham (1987) and Latham and Frayne (1989). The authors wish to thank R. Pritchard for his helpful suggestions on an initial draft of this chapter and Dawn Winters for her editorial assistance. Preparation of this chapter was supported in part by the Ford Motor Company Affiliate Fund to the first author.

REFERENCES

Äs, D. (1962). Absenteeism: A social fact in need of a theory. *Acta Sociologica, 6*, 278–285.

Azrin, H. H. (1977). A strategy for applied research: Learning based but outcome oriented. *American Psychologist, 32*, 140–149.

Bandura, A. (1977a). *Social learning theory*. Englewood Cliffs, NJ: Prentice-Hall.

Bandura, A. (1977b). Self-efficacy: Toward a unifying theory of behavior change. *Psychological Review, 84*, 191–215.

Bandura, A. (1982). Self-efficacy mechanism in human agency. *American Psychologist, 37*, 122–147.

Bandura, A. (1986). *Social foundations of thought and action: A social cognitive theory*. Englewood Cliffs, NJ: Prentice-Hall.

Barling, J., & Abel, M. (1983). Self-efficacy beliefs and tennis performance. *Cognitive Therapy and Research, 7*, 265–272.

Campbell, J. P. (1982, August). *I/O psychology and the enhancement of productivity*. Paper presented at the annual meeting of the American Psychological Association, Washington, DC.

Chadwick-Jones, J. K., Nicholson, N., & Brown, C. A. (1982). *Social psychology of absenteeism*. New York: Praeger.

Condiotte, M. M., & Lichtenstein, E. C. (1981). Self-efficacy and relapse in smoking cessation programs. *Journal of Consulting and Clinical Psychology, 49*, 648–658.

Erez, M. (1977). Feedback, A necessary condition for the goal setting-performance relationship. *Journal of Applied Psychology, 62*, 69–78.

Fichman, M. (1984). A theoretical approach to understanding absence. In P. Goodman & R. Atkin (Eds.), *Absenteeism: New approaches to understanding, measuring, and managing employee absence* (pp. 1–46). San Francisco: Jossey-Bass.

Frayne, C. A., & Latham, G. P. (1987). The application of social learning theory to employee self-management of attendance. *Journal of Applied Psychology, 72*, 387–392.

Glynn, E. L. (1970). Classroom applications of self-determined reinforcement. *Journal of Applied Behavior Analysis, 3*, 123–132.

Godding, P. R., & Glasgow, R. E. (1985). Self-efficacy and outcome expectations as predictors of controlled smoking status. *Cognitive Therapy and Research, 9*, 583–590.

Goodman, P., & Atkin, R. (1984). Effects of absenteeism on individuals and organizations. In P. Goodman & R. Atkin (Eds.), *Absenteeism: New approaches to understanding, measuring, and managing employee absence* (pp. 276–321). San Francisco: Jossey-Bass.

Harris, S. N., & Ream, R. G. (1978). Follow-up strategies in the behavioral treatment of the overweight. *Behavior Research and Therapy, 13*, 167–172.

Ilgen, D. (1977). Attendance behavior. A reevaluation of Latham & Pursell's conclusions. *Journal of Applied Psychology, 62*, 230–233.

Johns, G. (1984). Unresolved issues in the study and management of absence from work. In P. S. Goodman & R. S. Atkin (Eds.), *Absenteeism: New approaches to understanding, measuring, and managing employee absence.* (pp. 360–390). San Francisco: Jossey-Bass.

Johns, G., & Nicholson, N. (1982). The meanings of absence: New strategies for theory and research. In B. M. Staw & L. L. Cummings (Eds.), *Research in organizational behavior* (Vol. 4, pp. 127–172). Greenwich, CT: JAI Press.

Kanfer, F. H. (1970). Self-regulation: Research, issues, and speculations. In C. Neuringer & J. L. Michael (Eds.), *Behavior modification in clinical psychology* (pp. 178–220). New York: Appleton-Century-Crofts.

Kanfer, F. H. (1974). Self-regulation: Research, issues, and speculations. In C. Neuringer & J. Michael (Eds.), *Behavior modification in clinical psychology* (pp. 178–220). New York: Appleton-Century-Crofts.

Kanfer, F. H. (1975). Self-management methods. In F. H. Kanfer (Ed.), *Helping people change.* (pp. 309–355). New York: Wiley.

Kanfer, F. H. (1980). Self-management methods. In F. H. Kanfer & A. P. Goldstein (Eds.), *Helping people change: A textbook of methods* (2nd ed.). (pp. 309–355). New York: Pergamon Press.

Kanfer, F. H. (1986). Implications of a self-regulation model of therapy for treatment of addictive behaviors. In W. R. Miller & N. Heather (Eds.), *The addictive behaviors: Vol. II. Process of change.* (pp. 117–153). New York: Plenum.

Kanfer, F. H., & Phillips, J. S. (1970). *Learning foundations of behavior therapy.* New York: Wiley.

Karoly, P., & Kanfer, F. H. (1982). *Self-management and behavior change: From theory to practice.* New York: Pergamon Press.

Kirkpatrick, D. L. (1976). Evaluation of training. In R. L. Craig (Ed.), *Training and development handbook: A guide to human resource development.* New York: McGraw-Hill.

Latham, G. P., & Finnegan, B. J. (August, 1987). The practicality of the situational interview.

In G. R. Ferris (Chair), *The employment interview: New research directions*. Symposium presented at the annual meeting of the academy of Management, New Orleans.

Latham, G. P., & Frayne, C. A. (1987, August). *The stability of job attendance of unionized workers*. Paper presented at the annual meeting of the Academy of Management Associations, New Orleans.

Latham, G. P., & Frayne, C. A. (1989). Self-management training for increasing job attendance; A followup and a replication. *Journal of Applied Psychology, 74*, 411–416.

Latham, G. P., Mitchell, T. R., & Dossett, D. L. (1978). Importance of participative goal setting and anticipated rewards on goal difficulty and job performance. *Journal of Applied Psychology, 63*, 163–171.

Latham, G. P., & Napier, N. K., (1984). Practical ways to increase employee attendance. In P. S. Goodman & R. S. Atkin (Eds.), *Absenteeism: New approaches to understanding, measuring, and managing employee absence*. (pp. 322–359). San Francisco: Jossey-Bass.

Latham, G. P., & Pursell, E. D. (1975). Measuring absenteeism from the opposite side of the coin. *Journal of Applied Psychology, 60*, 369–371.

Latham, G. P., & Pursell, E. D. (1977). Measuring attendance. A reply to Ilgen. *Journal of Applied Psychology, 62*, 239–246.

Latham, G. P., & Saari, L. M. (1984). Do people do what they say? Further studies on the situational interview. *Journal of Applied Psychology, 69*, 569–573.

Latham, G. P., Saari, L. M., Pursell, E. D., & Campion, M. A. (1980). The situational interview. *Journal of Applied Psychology, 65*, 422–427.

Mahoney, M. J., Moura, N. G., & Wade, T. C. (1973). They relative efficacy of self-reward, self-punishment, and self-monitoring techniques for weight loss. *Journal of Consulting and Clinical Psychology, 40*, 404–407.

Marlatt, G., & Gordon, J. (Eds.). (1985). *Relapse prevention: Maintenance strategies in addictive behavior change*. New York: Guilford.

Nicholson, N., & Johns, G. (1982). *The absence culture and the psychological contract—Who's in charge of absence?* Paper presented at the 20th International Congress of Applied Psychology, Edinburgh, Scotland.

Richards, C. S. (1976). When self-control fails: Selective bibliography of research on the maintenance problems in self-control treatment programs. *JSAS Catalog of Selected Documents in Psychology, 8*, 67–68.

Ross, L. (1977). The intuitive psychologist and his shortcomings. Distortions in the attribution process. In L. Berkowitz (Ed.), *Advances in experimental social psychology* (Vol. 10, pp. 174–220). New York: Academic Press.

Simon, K. M. (1979). Self-evaluative reactions: The role of personal valuation of the activity. *Journal of Cognitive Therapy and Research, 9*, 111–116.

Steers, R. M., & Rhodes, S. R. (1984). Knowledge and speculation about absenteeism. In P. S. Goodman & R. S. Atkin (Eds.), *Absenteeism: New approaches to understanding, measuring, and managing employee absence* (pp. 229–275). San Francisco: Jossey-Bass.

Thorndike, R. L. (1949). *Personnel selection*. New York: Wiley.

Wexley, K. N., & Latham, G. P. (1981). *Developing and training human resources in organizations*. Glenview, IL: Scott, Foresman.

Williams, S. L., & Watson, N. (1985). Perceived danger and perceived self-efficacy as cognitive mediators of acrophobic behavior. *Behavior Therapy, 16*, 136–146.

Part III

Development and Change in Motivation

As with other psychological states and processes work motivation changes over time. Such changes can be stimulated or promoted as for instance through quality circles. On the other side these changes can also occur unintentionally and unplanned through job loss affecting central aspects of motivation. Other important aspects of work motivation such as individual values change under the influence of organizational culture and value change under the influence of organizational culture and value systems of society. The analysis of such changes is the content of the last part. The first chapter deals with the quality circles, which have become powerful tools to improve work motivation. Matsui and Onglatco report on experiences in Japanese companies and provide empirical findings that participation in quality circles contributes to the development of motivation.

Feather looks at changes of motivation from another perspective. His study focuses on adolescents who are facing the situation of not finding a job and being unable to help themselves to get out of this situation. The variety of his findings challenges us to develop equally influential techniques as quality circles to stop the demotivation process experienced in jobless people and to strengthen the motivation to be persistent.

The change of the motivation pattern of adolescents moving from the educational institutions into employment systems is the issue in the study of Coetsier and Claes. On the basis of their findings they develop recommendations with regard to counseling, taking into account motivational variables. They stress the importance of supporting the helping behavior with the adolescent's immediate reference groups.

The chapter of Herman on motivation in organizations discusses the change of a value system, that is shared by the members of the organization. He explains why a strengthened goal commitment is a necessary condition for developing an accepted organizational culture. Furthermore, he shows that a sharing of common values (does) only lead to high levels of motivation, if the goals of the employees themselves are respected and taken into account. Ruiz-Quintanilla studied the interrelated uses of the dimensions of work related value systems by using cluster-analyses. He reports and compares findings for an American, a Japanese, and a German sample with respect to the three central dimensions; work-centrality, working goals, and social norms.

12

Relationships Between Employee Quality Circle Involvement and Need Fulfillment in Work As Moderated By Work Type: A Compensatory Or a Spillover Model?

Tamao Matsui
Surugadai University, Saitama, Japan

Mary Lou Uy Onglatco
The National University of Singapore, Singapore

Many studies have found that quality circle activities of employees contribute to the improvement of organizational effectiveness. Onglatco and Matsui (1984) found, based on a cross-lagged correlational analysis, that quality circle activities improved the efficiency of bank operations. Gunatilake (1984) found that the efficiency of processing medical records in a hospital was significantly improved by quality circle activities. Mohrman and Novelli (1985) reported that quality circle activities in a warehouse improved the productivity of loading. Onglatco (1988) reported a case where the changes in work-shift schedule during lunchtime that was made based on the suggestions from a quality circle in a bank reduced the time spent per transaction from 8 min 54 sec to 5 min 44 sec.

Although these findings suggest that well-organized quality circle activities contribute to the improvement of productivity, Marks, Mirvis, Hackett, and Grady (1986) examined the impact of quality circle involvement on employee as well as organizational outcomes. They found that participants of circle activities showed higher job satisfaction and decreased absenteeism compared to nonparticipants. This suggests the possibility that quality circle activities may benefit employees in terms of increased need fulfillment in work.

Quality circle activities introduce complexity into the work process. Circle members choose problem areas to be improved in their day-to-day work, collect data and analyze them to identify the causes of the problems, set improvement goals, test the effectiveness of the measures that they develop to solve problems, and recommend work method changes to managers. In conducting these activities, circle members often use a variety of techniques like Pareto charts, cause-and-effect diagrams, graphs, and so forth (Onglatco,

1988). Thus, the activities provide employees with chances to utilize a variety of skills and abilities, to perform a whole task, to exhibit their autonomy, to get feedback on their achievements, to initiate changes in work methods, and so forth. Hackman and Lawler (1971) and Hackman and Oldham (1976) found that jobs whose work processes involve higher levels of skill variety, task identity, task significance, autonomy, and feedback led to improved higher order need fulfillment. Thus, it is expected that quality circle activities enhance the fulfillment of higher order needs in work.

Quality circle activities also enrich the work process with increased peer interactions. Quality circles are formed based on work units. The employees belonging to the same circles periodically meet and discuss common interests. They cooperate with one another to accomplish their goals. They present their solutions as a team to managers and to members of other circles, and in some cases to a company-wide convention. These activities increase peer interactions and provide increased opportunities to fulfill social needs.

Based on the nature of quality circle activities described previously this study predicted that quality circle involvement would improve higher order need fulfillment and social need fulfillment in work, assuming the work itself does not provide adequate opportunity to fulfill such needs.

METHOD

Research Site

The study was conducted in 46 branches of a Japanese nation-wide commercial bank. This bank started the circle activities 7 years ago. The branches have nine work units (e.g., sales, loan, deposit, foreign exchange, and so forth), each forming one or two quality circles. Assistant branch managers take general charge of the circle activities in their branches. Supervisors advise the circle activities in their work unit.

All nonsupervisory employees are required to participate in the circles of their work units. The circles consist of three to 11 clerical employees depending on the size of the work units. Circle members choose circle leaders among themselves. Most of the circle activities are conducted during working hours. Employees receive overtime pay when they engage in these activities after working hours. Circles have meetings once a week or every 2 weeks, which last 30 minutes to an hour. Circles are required to achieve a goal, at least every 3 months. Circle suggestions are implemented with the branch managers' approval. Circles present their solutions in their branches. Circles that reach excellent solutions present their solutions in the company-wide quality circle convention held annually, and the best circles receive awards from the company president.

This study used the nonsupervisory employees belonging to sales and deposit work units as subjects. This was done because the largest number of employees belonged to these two work units, and because preliminary interviews suggested that the activities of the two work units are quite different. Sales employees work individually outside the office. They visit their customers to increase deposits to enhance the competitive edge of the bank. The work requires individual initiative and is quite challenging but provides little opportunity to interact with peers.

In contrast, deposit employees work as teams in the office. They handle customer transaction based on standardized procedures. This work is quite routine but provides many opportunities to interact with peers.

Subjects

Subjects consisted of nonsupervisory 292 sales employees and 135 deposit, clerical employees. All the sales subjects were males, because the sales units consisted of only males. About 93% of sales subjects were high school graduates, the remainder being university graduates. Mean age was 25.5 years, and mean length of service, 7.1 years. Of the deposit subjects, 88% were females. About 95% of the deposit subjects were high school graduates; the remainders were college graduates. Mean age was 21.5 years and mean length of service was 3.5 years.

Measures

Subjects were asked to respond to a questionnaire that measured job-motivating potential, peer interactions, higher order need fulfillment, and social need fulfillment in work. They were asked to write the name of the circle to which they belonged and the code number assigned to them for the study. Subjects were assured that their answers would be confidential.

Motivating Potential. Subjects were asked to describe their job with the use of the Japanese version of Hackman and Oldham's (1974) *Job Diagnostic Survey (Short Form)*. This questionnaire involves 15 items for the descriptions of jobs based on five core dimensions (i.e., skill variety, task identity, task significance, autonomy, and feedback). It uses a 7-point scale for each item. The motivating potential score was calculated based on Hackman and Oldham's (1974) formulation; i.e., motivating potential score = (skill variety + task identity + task significance)/3 × autonomy × feedback. The validity of the Japanese version was documented by Matsui (1983). Cronbach's alpha reliability coefficient was .72 for sales and .70 for deposit. Means and standard deviations are shown in Table 12.1.

TABLE 12.1
Means and Standard Deviations of Main Variables for Sales and Deposit

Variable	Sales (n = 292)	Deposit (n = 135)	t(425)
Job-motivating potential			
M	106.0	87.9	3.62*
SD	53.34	33.52	
Peer interaction			
M	3.4	3.8	5.46*
SD	0.63	0.64	
QC involvement			
M	13.4	13.3	0.64
SD	2.23	2.24	
Higher order need fulfillment			
M	5.7	4.3	13.07*
SD	1.01	1.01	
Social need fulfillment			
M	5.2	5.4	1.27
SD	0.98	1.11	

*$p < .01$.

Interactions Among Peers.   Subjects were asked to indicate the extent to which they interacted with peers in work with the use of five items. The items used were: "I talk about the work with peers during worktime," "My peers consider only about their own performance" (with reversed scoring), "My peers make up the delay made by others," "My peers help others when they finish their own work earlier," and "My peers are familiar with one another." Response alternative ranged from *never*(1) to *always*(5). The average of the five-item scores served as the index of interaction. Cronbach's alpha coefficient was .61 for sales, and .60 for deposit. Means and standard deviations are shown in Table 12.1.

Higher Order Need Fulfillment.   Subjects were given a list of six higher order need items and asked to indicate the extent to which each need was fulfilled in work. The items were adopted from the higher order need satisfaction scales of the *Job Diagnostic Survey* and were slightly modified to adjust to the bank situation. These items were: "utilizing one's ability," "accomplishing something worthwhile," "learning new things," "demonstrating one's best skill," "doing something interesting," and "implementing something as planned by oneself." The scale ranged from *not at all fulfilled*(1) to *highly fulfilled*(7). The average was used as the higher order need fulfillment index. Cronbach's alpha coefficient was .78 for sales and .70 for deposit. Means and standard deviations are shown in Table 12.1. The higher order need fulfillment score correlated .28 ($p < .01$) with the job-motivating potential score for the total samples.

Social Need Fulfillment.   Subjects were given a list of four social need items and asked to indicate the extent of need fulfillment in work. The items were: "discussing work with peers," "being respected by peers," "a feeling that one's peers and oneself belong to the same team," and "recognition form one's superior." The scale ranged from *not at all fulfilled* (1) to *highly fulfilled*(7). The average of the four items was used as the social need fulfillment index. Cronbach's alpha coefficient was .90 for sales and .89 for deposit. Means and standard deviations are shown in Table 12.1. The social need fulfillment score correlated .37 ($p < .01$) with the peer interaction score for the total sample.

Quality Circle Involvement.   Circle leaders were not asked to fill out the questionnaire. Instead, they were asked to indicate the extent to which each member was enthusiastic in circle activities using four items. They were assured that their answers would be confidential. Although all the clerical employees are required to participate in the circles, circle leaders rated the frequencies of attendance of each member in circle meetings, because preliminary interviews indicated that some members who were unenthusiastic in the activities sometimes ignored the meetings with the excuse of being busy in their own work. The items used were: "the number of problems he/she submitted to the circle in a year" (*one or less*[1] and *five or more*[5]), "the frequency of his/her attendance in circle meetings" (*never*[1] and *always*[5]), "the levels of his/her participation in discussion in circle meetings" (*very low*[1] and *very high*[5]), and "the general enthusiasm exhibited by him/her in circle activities" (*not at all enthusiastic*[1] and *highly enthusiastic*[5]). The sum of the scores formed the quality circle involvement (QC involvement) index of the subject. Cronbach's alpha coefficient was .60 for sales and .61 for deposit. Means and standard deviations are shown in Table 12.1.

RESULTS

Table 12.1 shows means and standard deviations of relevant variables for sales and deposit. It indicates that job-motivating potential is significantly higher for sales than for deposit, whereas peer interaction is significantly higher for deposit than for sales. Similarly, higher order need fulfillment is significantly higher for sales than for deposit, whereas social need fulfillment is higher for deposit than for sales. In addition, higher order need fulfillment is significantly higher ($t(291) = 11.85$, $p < .01$) than social need fulfillment for sales, whereas social need fulfillment is significantly higher ($t(134) = 16.35$, $p < .01$) than higher order need fulfillment for deposit.

TABLE 12.2
Intercorrelations Among QC Involvement, Higher Order Need and Social
Need Fulfillment for Sales and Deposit

Variable	Sales (n = 292)			Deposit (n = 135)		
	1	2	3	1	2	3
1. QC involvement	—			—		
2. Higher order need fulfillment	.19*	—		.31**	—	
3. Social need fulfillment	.39**	.78**	—	.15	.76**	—

*p < .05.
**p < .01.

These findings reflect the facts that were observed in the preliminary interviews: Sales subjects engage in challenging tasks but work individually outside the office. Thus, they fulfill social needs less than higher order needs in work. In contrast, deposit subjects work as teams in the office, but they engage in routine tasks. Thus, they fulfill higher order needs less than social needs in work.

To determine the relationships between QC involvement and need fulfillment in work, the correlations between QC involvement and the two types of need fulfillment were computed for the two types of work and are shown in Table 12.2. The table indicates that the correlation between QC involvement and higher order need fulfillment is higher for deposit members than for sales members, although the significance level for the difference between the two correlations is insignificant. The correlation between QC involvement and social need fulfillment, on the other hand, is significantly higher $(z(421) = 2.48, p < .01)$ for sales than deposit. Within-group comparison of correlations indicated that for sales the correlation of QC involvement was significantly higher $(t(289) = 5.68, p < .01)$ for social than for higher order need fulfillment, whereas for deposit the correlation was significantly higher $(t(132) = 2.82, p < .01)$ for higher order need than for social need fulfillment. Thus, as predicted, the relationships between QC involvement and need fulfillment in work is higher if the job does not provide sufficient opportunities to fulfill the needs than if the job provides sufficient opportunities to fulfill the needs.

The preceding findings were confirmed by estimating a 2 (QC involvement) 2 (work type) analysis of variance for the two types of need fulfillment. Sales and deposit subjects were divided into high- and low-QC involvement groups based on the mean of QC involvement scores across the total sample. Means of higher order need and social need fulfillment then were computed for the resulting four groups. Table 12.3 shows the cell means of higher order need fulfillment, whereas Table 12.4 summarizes the results of analysis of variance.

As seen in Table 12.3, mean difference between high- and low-QC in-

TABLE 12.3
Means and Standard Deviations of Higher Order Need Fulfillment for Two
Levels of QC Involvement and Two Work Types

	QC Involvement	
	High	Low
Sales		
n =	147	145
M =	5.8	5.6
SD =	0.89	1.10
Deposit		
n =	66	69
M =	4.7	4.0
SD =	1.01	0.89

TABLE 12.4
Summary of Analysis of Variance for Higher Order Need Fulfillment

Source	df	MS	F
QC involvement (A)	1	19.16	19.59**
Work type (B)	1	172.08	175.99**
A × B	1	5.84	5.98*

$*p < .05.$
$**p < .01.$

volvement groups is greater for deposit than for sales. Analysis of variance yields a significant interaction between QC involvement and work type. Thus, work type moderates the relationships between QC involvement and higher order need fulfillment in work.

Table 12.5 shows cell means of social need fulfillment for the four groups. Table 12.6 summarizes the results of analysis of variance. As seen in Table 12.5, mean difference between high- and low-QC involvement

TABLE 12.5
Means and Standard Deviations of Social Need Fulfillment for Two Levels
of QC Involvement and Two Work Types

	QC Involvement	
	High	Low
Sales		
n =	147	145
M =	5.5	4.9
SD =	0.86	1.00
Deposit		
n =	66	69
M =	5.5	5.2
SD =	1.10	1.12

TABLE 12.6
Summary of Analysis of Variance for Social Need Fulfillment

Source	df	MS	F
QC involvement (A)	1	16.80	16.95**
Work type (B)	1	1.81	1.83
A × B	1	3.97	4.01*

*p < .05.
**p < .01.

groups is greater for sales than for deposit. Table 12.6 shows a significant interaction between QC involvement and work type. Thus, work type also moderates the relationships between QC involvement and social need fulfillment in work.

DISCUSSION

This study found that job-motivating potential and higher order need fulfillment in work were higher for sales than for deposit, whereas peer interaction and social need fulfillment in work were higher for deposit than for sales. Correlational analyses indicated that the relationship between quality circle involvement and higher order need fulfillment in work was higher for deposit than for sales, whereas the relationship between quality circle involvement and social need fulfillment in work was higher for sales than for deposit. Analysis of variance indicated that work type moderated the relationships between quality circle involvement and higher order need fulfillment or social need fulfillment in work. Thus, the findings support the notion that the relationship between quality circle involvement and need fulfillment in work would be higher if the job does not provide sufficient opportunities to fulfill the needs than if the job provides sufficient opportunities to fulfill the needs.

As the present findings are based on concurrent relationships between quality circle involvement and need fulfillment in work, they tell nothing about the causal relationships between the two variables. Thus, two models are possible for the relationships observed between the two variables. One is a compensatory model. This model postulates that quality circle involvement enhanced the fulfillment of the needs that were not sufficiently fulfilled in work. The other model is a spillover model. It postulates that subjects who were high in need fulfillment in work became more involved in quality circle activities. Although further research is needed to determine which model is more appropriate for the present findings, the authors support the compensatory model. The difficulty of the spillover model is that it cannot explain why sales subjects who sufficiently fulfilled social need in work were more involved in quality circle activities that fulfilled social need. Such activities should have been obviously redundant for these sales subjects. In a similar vein, the model cannot explain why deposit subjects who sufficiently fulfilled higher order need in work became more involved in QC circle activities that fulfilled the same need.

Finally, sales subjects consisted of only males, and most of deposit subjects were females. Thus, the present study fails to separate the effects of sex differences from work-type differences for the relationships between quality circle involvement and need fulfillment. Although the solution of this problem is needed before establishing the conclusion, the authors do not consider the possible bias due to sex differences large. There are no reasons to believe that increased peer interaction leads to increased social need fulfillment *only* for males, and that the enrichment of work process leads to increased higher order need fulfillment *only* for females.

ACKNOWLEDGMENTS

This chapter is based on a portion of the dissertation study conducted by the second author under the supervision of the first author.

REFERENCES

Gunatilake, S. (1984). *An exploratory study of quality circles and team building in two hospital settings*. Unpublished dissertation, University of Hawaii.

Hackman, J., & Lawler, E. E. (1971). Employee reactions to job characteristics. *Journal of Applied Psychology Monograph, 55*, 259–286.

Hackman, J., & Oldham, G. R. (1974). *Job Diagnostic Survey* (Short form). New Haven, CT: Yale University.

Hackman, J., & Oldham, G. R. (1976). Motivation through the design of work: Test of a theory. *Organizational Behavior and Human Performance, 16*, 250–279.

Marks, M. L., Mirvis, P. H., Hackett, E. J., & Grady, J. F. (1986). Employee participation in a quality circle program: Impact on quality of work life, productivity, and absenteeism. *Journal of Applied Psychology, 71* (1), 61–69.

Matsui, T. (1983). *Motivation* (in Japanese). Tokyo: Daiyamondo-Sha.

Mohrman, S. A., & Novelli, L. (1985). Beyond testimonials: Learning from a quality circles programme. *Journal of Occupational Behavior, 6*, 93–110.

Onglatco, M. L. U. (1988). *Japanese quality circles: Features, effects and problems*. Tokyo: The Asian Productivity Organization.

Onglatco, M. L. U., & Matsui, T. (1984). Organizational and motivational correlates of quality control circle involvement: A case study in a Japanese bank. *Journal of Applied Sociology*, Rikkyo University, *25*, 155–178.

13
The Effects of Unemployment on Work Values and Motivation

N. T. Feather
The Flinders University of South Australia

My aim in this chapter is not to review the vast literature on the psychological impact of unemployment but rather to focus on some recent contributions from my own research program that provide information about the effects of unemployment on work values and on motivation to seek employment. A much more detailed description of this program appears in my forthcoming book (Feather, 1989b) where I also consider other research into the psychological impact of unemployment in the light of relevant theoretical approaches.

There already exist extensive reviews of studies that deal with the psychological effects of unemployment during the Great Depression and during the 1970s and 1980s. Unemployment was an important topic of research in the 1930s, and the influential studies by Jahoda, Lazarsfeld, and Zeisel (1933), Bakke (1940a, 1940b), and Komarovsky (1940) are well known, especially the frequently cited study of unemployment in the Austrian village of Marienthal (Jahoda et al., 1933). Some of the early research was reviewed by Eisenberg and Lazarsfeld (1938), and more recently Jahoda (1979, 1981, 1982) has referred to these earlier studies again and compared the effects of unemployment in the 1930s with its impact in the 1970s, noting that one cannot assume that the same effects will occur given the many social and economic changes that have taken place over the last 50 years, and differences that have occurred in the unemployed themselves when compared with the unemployed in the 1930s. Elder and his colleagues have looked at the long-term effects of the Great Depression on those who were children or adolescents at the time (Elder, 1974; Elder & Likert, 1982; Elder & Rockwell, 1979). Kelvin and Jarrett (1985), Fryer (1988), Hartley and Fryer (1984), O'Brien (1986), Warr (1984, 1987a, 1987b), and Fryer and

Payne (1986) also provide useful and informative summaries that refer to some of the earlier work in the context of more recent developments. These more recent reviews are critical of the simple generalizations that are frequently drawn from the Great Depression literature (e.g., the assumption that the unemployed move through a sequence of stages in their responses to the unemployment condition). They also indicate features of the 1930s' literature that are often overlooked (e.g., the emphasis on the adverse effects of poverty and economic hardship, the mediating effects of past job experiences).

The major focus of the more recent reviews, however, has been on the psychological impact of unemployment in the 1970s and 1980s, with particular emphasis on health and psychological well-being. Warr's (1984, 1987a, 1987b) most recent statements draw attention to the significant negative consequences of unemployment, exhibited in feelings of distress, anxiety, depression, psychosomatic symptoms, and family strain. He notes also that there are individual differences in responses to unemployment that relate to variations in personal and family circumstances and also to more enduring personal characteristics that can mediate the effects of being unemployed. Among the mediating variables that have been considered are employment commitment or the degree to which people are personally strongly committed to being in paid employment, age, length of unemployment, financial strain, level of activity, social class, personal vulnerability, and gender. To these we can add the degree to which people are active copers, seeking new goals and adapting positively to changed circumstances (Fryer & Payne, 1986), and a person's past experience with employment, including the nature of past employment and the interest and opportunities for control that past employment provided.

Jahoda (1982) likewise stresses the difficulty of coming to any conclusions about the psychological impact of unemployment that are not also accompanied by qualifying statements that take account of different groups and different circumstances. She comments that the results of unemployment research indicate that "the comparison looks somewhat different for every individual affected, depending on a whole host of personal circumstances" (p. 48). Different groups experience different sets of problems, a point that Warr (1987a, 1987b) also emphasizes. How young people, men, managers, and professional personnel react to unemployment, for example, would be expected to differ from how middle-aged people, women, and unskilled workers react to unemployment. These various groups differ in a wide range of personal and background characteristics.

Despite the fact that it is difficult to generalize to different segments of the population, Warr (1983) believes that the evidence indicates that "the psychological health of unemployed people is significantly below that of people in jobs" (p. 306). He recognizes, however, that there is both good and bad employment (Warr, 1983, 1987a, 1987b). Employment differs in the degree to which it provides people with opportunities for exerting personal control and the use of skill, goals and task demands, variety, environmental clarity, financial rewards, physical security, opportunities for interpersonal contact, and social status. Similarly, unemployment may provide for different levels of these factors. Some unemployed people, for example, may still find opportunities for personal control in their lives and may have physical security, personal contacts, and higher levels on some of the other factors that Warr (1987a, 1987b) mentions when compared with other unemployed people. Comparisons between groups may involve different combinations of these factors, deficiencies in which are assumed to have negative consequences. An overabundance of some of these factors may also have negative consequences according to Warr's (1987b) "vitamin" model. One requires a close analysis of how well either employment or unemployment satisfies these various factors prior to predicting the effects of employment or unemployment on health and psychological well-being.

I have digressed somewhat mainly to make the point that the primary emphasis in current unemployment research has been on psychological and physical health, justifiably so because the health of its members is an important consideration for any society. Not so evident are studies of the impact of unemployment on values and motivation. My research program at Flinders University has included measures of values and motivation, and it is to a description of these measures that I now turn.

RELEVANT MEASURES

I have included a fairly wide range of variables concerned with values and with motivation in the studies that I have been involved with over the past 10 years (see Table 13.1). Many of these variables have involved single items with 1 to 5 or 1 to 7 rating scales; others have involved multiitem scales that I developed on the basis of factor analysis and other scales in common use that have been constructed by others. Most of the research has been concerned with young employed and unemployed people and with students in their final years of secondary school. Let me first list the main measures of values that I have used.

1. A 19-item Measure of the Work Ethic Developed by Mirels and Garrett (1971) and Based on Weber's (1976) Classic Analysis of the Protestant Ethic.   Items in this scale emphasize the virtues of industriousness, asceticism, and individualism (e.g., "If one works hard enough he/she is likely to make a good life for himself/herself"). I included this measure because it is often assumed that unemployment, particularly if prolonged, will erode the work ethic; that is, unemployed people will begin to devalue effort and hard

TABLE 13.1
Measures Relating to Values and Motivation

Variables	
Value Variables	*Motivation Variables*
Protestant ethic values	Job confidence (expectancy of success)
Employment value	Helplessness and perceived control
Desired work values	External locus of control
Skill-utilization	Hopelessness or pessimism
Variety	Causal attributions
Influence	For own unemployment
	For youth unemployment
	Job need
	Affective responses
	Helplessness
	Guilt
	Anger
	Depression
	Disappointment
	Time structure

work if they have been without a job for a long period of time. Note, however, that Kelvin and Jarrett (1985) are sceptical about the importance of the work ethic. In an interesting historical analysis they argue that "for the vast majority of people work is, and always has been, a matter of labouring 'for the necessities of life.' Work may be a *norm*, but it is not an *ethic*" (p. 109). Furnham (1984) has recently reviewed the psychological literature on the protestant work ethic.

2. A Measure of Employment Value. This measure has been used in a number of studies in the Flinders program (e.g., Feather, 1983, 1986a; Feather & Barber, 1983; Feather & Bond, 1983; Feather & Davenport, 1981; Feather & O'Brien, 1986a, 1986b). In most cases the measure has involved three items: "Should a job mean more to a person than just money?" "Does most of the satisfaction in a person's life come from his/her work?" and "How much should people be interested in their work?" This measure resembles Warr's (1987a, 1987b) employment commitment but it uses fewer items.

3. Measures of Desired Work Values Relating to Skill-Utilization, Variety, and Influence in a Person's Ideal Job. These scales were developed in previous studies by O'Brien, Dowling, and Kabanoff (1978; see also O'Brien, 1980; O'Brien & Dowling, 1980). Respondents are asked to indicate how much opportunity for skill-use, variety, or influence they would like to have in their ideal job. For example, in the desired skill-utilization scale the four items that were included concerned opportunities for learning new jobs, working in the way you think best, using abilities, and using education and experience.

The main measures of motivation that I have used constitute a rather more diverse set. They followed from a continuing interest that I have had for many years in expectancy-value theories of motivation, a theoretical approach to the analysis of motivated behavior that has wide currency (Feather, 1982a, 1986b). This theory of motivation relates action to the perceived attractiveness (positive valence) or aversiveness (negative valence) of expected outcomes. A person's behavior is assumed to be related to the expectations that the person holds and to the subjective values or valences of the possible outcomes. The expectations involve both beliefs about one's capabilities to perform the action to some defined standard that denotes a successful outcome and beliefs about the consequences that might occur as a result of the action. This form of analysis has been used in many different areas of psychology, various theorists having argued that expectations and valences have an important status in theories of action (Feather, 1959, 1982a, 1986b, 1988).

The motivational variables involved in my unemployment research can therefore be seen as relating to expectations and to valences (or subjective values). Some of the measures have been refined and redefined over the years. Next is a list of the major ones.

Three Measures of Job Confidence or Expectancy of Success in Relation to Getting a Job. In recent studies (Feather & O'Brien, 1986a, 1986b, 1987) the items used for young unemployed people were as follows: "Think back to the time immediately before you left school. How confident were you then about finding a job? Now think over your current situation. How confident are you about finding the job you really want in the near future? How confident are you about finding any kind of job at all in the near future?"

Feelings of Helplessness and Control That One Would Also Expect to be Related to Expectations About Finding Employment. In recent studies (Feather & O'Brien, 1986a, 1987) these items were: "How helpless do you feel about your unemployment? Can you do anything to change the cause of your unemployment? Can any other person or any group change the cause of your unemployment?"

A Shortened Version of the Rotter (1966) Internal-External Control Scale. This scale consists of nine items chosen on the basis of the results of a previous factor analysis of student data conducted by O'Brien and Kabanoff (1981). It provided a general measure of the extent to which subjects saw personal outcomes as due to external agents such as social forces, luck or fate, as opposed to internal factors such as effort, personal action, and ability.

A Measure of Hopelessness Developed by Beck, Weissman, Lester, and Trexler (1974). This 20-item scale provided a global measure of self-reported pessimism.

Some Items Concerned with Causal Attributions for Unemployment. In one procedure used recently (Feather & O'Brien, 1986a, 1986b) we requested respondents to write what they believed to be the major cause of their unemployment and then to rate this cause on scales concerned with internality, stability, globality, personal uncontrollability, and external uncontrollability, following the procedure used in attributional style questionnaires (e.g., Feather & Tiggemann, 1984; Peterson & Seligman, 1984). In a second procedure used in a number of studies (e.g., Feather, 1985a; Feather & Davenport, 1981; Feather & O'Brien, 1986a, 1986b), respondents were presented with a large number of possible explanations of youth unemployement and asked to rate each explanation for importance. On the basis of results from a factor analysis, one can construct scales that refer to different kinds of explanation. Our most recent research provided separate scales, in which unemployment was blamed on the economic recession, on lack of motivation, on competence deficiency, and on appearance/interview inadequacy (Feather & O'Brien, 1986a, 1986b). Other single-item measures of internal attribution have also been used (e.g., Feather, 1983; Feather & Davenport, 1981). For example, in the Feather and Davenport (1981) study we asked young unemployed respondents: "How much do you think that your unemployment is your own fault?" I have included attributional variables in my research program because of a long-standing interest in the attribution area and because some motivational approaches assign causal attributions a key status within the expectancy-value framework (Weiner, 1985, 1986).

Measures Concerned with Need for a Job and with Affective Reactions. A need item that has been commonly used is: "How much do you feel that you need a job?" The items assessing affective responses to unemployment have concerned helplessness (already described), guilt ("How guilty do you feel about your unemployment?"), anger ("How angry do you feel about your unemployment?"), depression ("How depressed do you feel about your unemployment?"), and disappointment ("When you think about being unemployed, or the possibility of being unemployed, how does it make you feel? Really glad/really depressed). These items and related ones have been used in questionnaires that have been completed by children still at school and by young people who were either employed or unemployed at the time (e.g., Feather, 1983, 1986a; Feather & Barber, 1983; Feather &

Bond, 1983; Feather & Davenport, 1981; Feather & O'Brien, 1986a, 1986b, 1987).

A Measure Developed to Assess the Degree to Which People See Their Use of Time as Structured and Purposive (Feather & Bond, 1983).   Jahoda (1982) argues that an important function of employment is to provide activities that fill the day and that give individuals a sense of purpose.

There are other variables that I have included in my research program that I do not describe in detail because they are less related to values, expectations, and valences than the ones that I have mentioned (see Feather, 1989b). Some of these other variables were global and componential measures of the self-concept (both global measures and measures of separate components), depressive symptoms, life satisfaction, and stress symptoms. All studies have also provided for assessment of background variables such as social class, age, and gender. Questions have also been included dealing with length of unemployment, number of job applications, and frequency of job search. We come back to these later. Finally, the items have varied somewhat in their statement depending on whether respondents were at school or had entered the workforce and were either employed or unemployed. The reader is referred to the specific articles for these details and also for the format of the items.

FACTOR ANALYSES

Given this long list of variables, many of them single items, is it possible to combine some of them to create scales? The results of two factor analyses show that this can be done. Table 13.2 presents the results of a factor analysis of the intercorrelations between 10 variables that were included in a questionnaire that was answered by 334 students in Year 11 classes in five high schools in metropolitan Adelaide in 1983 (Feather, 1986a). Also presented in Table 13.2 are the loadings on two factors that emerged among others from a factor analysis of the intercorrelations between a large number of variables that were included in a longitudinal investigation conducted by Feather and O'Brien (1986a, 1986b, 1987). The data analyzed in this second study came from a sample of 320 young unemployed people who were tested in 1982. Only the variables that defined each factor are included in Table 13.2. The factor analyses in both studies involved the principal factor solution with iterated communalities followed by varimax rotation for factors with eigenvalues greater than 1 (the PA/2 solution in Nie, Hull, Jenkins, Steinbrenner, & Bent, 1975).

Both sets of findings provide evidence for a dimension concerned with job valence or the subjective value of having employment, and a dimension concerned with optimism and control (or its reverse—pessimism and help-

TABLE 13.2
Factors from Two Studies Defining Job Valence and Optimism-Control (or
Pessimism–Helplessness)

	Feather (1986a)			Feather O'Brien (1987)	
Variables	Job Valence	Pessimism–Helplessness	Variables	Job Valence	Optimism-Control
Work interest	.50	—	Job need	.65	—
Job satisfaction	.40	—	Unemployment disappointment	.69	—
Job need	.70	—			
Job want	.83	—	Unemployment depression	.40	—
Unemployment disappointment	.65	—	Unemployment helplessness	—	– .35
Job confidence	—	– .69	Confidence–desired job	—	.75
Job difficulty	—	– .65			
Unemployment time	—	.53	Confidence–any job	—	.73
Helplessness	—	.54	Stable cause	—	– .33
Uncontrollability	—	.47	Personal uncontrollable cause	—	– .38

Adapted by courtesy of the author(s), the Australian Psychological Society, and the British Psychological Society.

lessness). Thus, in the Feather (1986a) study variables were linked together that concerned how much the respondent wanted a job, needed a job, would feel depressed or disappointed about not having a job, felt that most of the satisfaction in a person's life comes from having a job, and felt that people should be interested in their work. Similarly, in the Feather and O'Brien (1987) study with a different sample, job need, unemployment disappointment, and unemployment depression were grouped together. I have assumed that these kinds of variables measure job valence. The concept of valence was introduced by Lewin many years ago to refer to the perceived attractiveness or aversiveness of regions of the psychological environment. Lewin (1938, pp. 106–107) assumed that valences could be related to psychological needs and tension systems and to the perceived nature of the object or activity to which the valence applies. I have recently argued that valences are closely tied to the affective system and that anticipated affect is a key indicator of the strength of positive and negative valences (Feather, 1986b). It is interesting to note that Table 13.2 shows that variables concerned with need and affect defined the job valence factor.

The second factor that emerged from the Feather (1986a) study linked together a cluster of variables involving low confidence about finding a job, a belief that finding a job would not be easy and would take a long time, and feelings of helplessness and lack of control over whether one would find a job or not. This factor clearly relates to low expectations and lack of perceived control. The second factor emerging from the Feather and O'Brien (1987) study is an equivalent factor except that it is reflected in the reverse direction. Confidence about finding one's desired job or any job, low feelings of helplessness about unemployment, and beliefs that the cause of unemployment would not be stable and could be changed all combined to define a factor concerned with optimism and control. This factor demonstrates that beliefs about control and perceived self-efficacy become fused with feelings of hopefulness and optimism about outcomes in the context of our unemployment research. In this sense, the concept of expectation has multiple facets (see also Bandura, 1986; Feather, 1982a, 1988; Heckhausen, 1977).

Is there any evidence to show that the more global measures of values come together to define particular dimensions? Indeed there is. The results of the factor analysis reported by Feather and O'Brien (1987) showed two factors, one defining work values and the other defining the internal work ethic. Table 13.3 presents the relevant factor loadings.

The first factor brings together three scales that were concerned with desired work values—how much skill-utilization, variety, and influence one would wish for in one's ideal job. The second factor involved a cluster of variables relating to the Protestant work ethic, employment value, internal control and internality, a tendency to attribute youth unemployment to lack of motivation, and feelings of guilt about being unemployed. This pattern of variables defines a value dimension. Note that the internal work ethic was linked to internal attributions for one's failure to find employment and also to feelings of guilt. These linkages are consistent with some of those investigated by Weiner (1986) in his attributional analysis of motivation and emotion.

EMPLOYED VERSUS UNEMPLOYED DIFFERENCES

I now describe some results that have been obtained from studies in my research program that have included one or more of the measures that I have described. Initially, my focus is on differences between employed and unemployed groups, using cross-sectional data collected at the same time. Subsequently, I describe results obtained from a major longitudinal study in which students were tested on a wide range of variables and then followed up as they entered the workforce and either obtained jobs or became unemployed.

Cross-Sectional Studies

In one study differences in depressive symptoms, self-esteem, Protestant Ethic values, attributional style, and general interest (or lack of apathy) were investigated in two samples of young male and female respondents who were either employed or unemployed (Feather, 1982c). Depressive

TABLE 13.3
Factors Defining Desired Work Values and Internal Work Ethic

Variables	Feather and O'Brien (1987)	
	Desired Work Values	Internal Work Ethic
Skill utilization	.77	—
Variety	.45	—
Influence	.55	—
Work ethic	—	.61
Employment value	—	.41
External control	—	−.25
Unemployment guilt	—	.36
Lack of motivation	—	.32
Internality	—	.29

Adapted by courtesy of the author and the British Psychological Society.

symptoms were assessed by using the long form of the Beck Depression Inventory (BDI), covering a range of symptoms such as sadness, pessimism, social withdrawal, and somatic preoccupation (Beck, 1967). Global self-esteem was assessed by using the Rosenberg (1965) self-esteem scale as adapted by Bachman, O'Malley, and Johnston (1978). Protestant Ethic (PE) values were assessed by using the Mirels and Garrett (1971) PE scale. Attributional style was assessed by using a measure of attributional style developed by Feather (1982c) and described by Feather and Tiggemann (1984). Table 13.4 presents the mean scores on the depressive symptoms, self-esteem, and work ethic variables. The corresponding results for the attributional style variable are not included because easily interpretable find-

TABLE 13.4
Means Scores for BDI, Self-esteem, and Protestant Ethic Values for Employed and Unemployed Samples (Feather, 1982)

Variable	Group (Employed/Unemployed)				F Values for		
	Males		Females				
	Employed (N = 39)	Unemployed (N = 32)	Employed (N = 39)	Unemployed (N = 37)	Group Effect	Gender Effect	Group x Gender Effect
Depressive symptoms	5.21	11.84	6.36	10.73	21.04***	.01	.91
Self-esteem	40.92	37.16	38.54	35.76	9.05**	3.17	.21
PE values	82.72	72.41	82.62	84.65	2.27	4.76*	5.44*

*$p < .05$.
**$p < .01$.
***$p < .001$.
Adapted by courtesy of the author and the Australian Psychological Society.

ings were not obtained for this general measure of how individuals attribute causality for positive and negative outcomes.

Table 13.4 shows that the unemployed samples had higher depression scores on the BDI and lower self-esteem scores when compared with the employed groups. These differences occurred for both sexes and the respective overall means for the employed and unemployed samples were 5.78 versus 11.25 for the BDI scores, and 39.73 versus 36.41 for the self-esteem scores. Note, however, that the differences between groups were not statistically significant in regard to the Protestant Ethic scores but the Group by Gender interaction did achieve statistical significance. The PE scores were lower on the average for the male unemployed group than for the male employed group, but there was very little difference between the mean PE scores for unemployed female subjects when compared with employed female subjects.

A further cross-sectional study was conducted by Feather and Bond (1983). In this case it was possible to compare employed and unemployed university graduates from Flinders University on the extent to which they found their use of time to be structured and purposeful, following the emphasis given to this variable by Jahoda (1979, 1981, 1982). The measure of time structure was especially constructed for this study and it involved questions such as: "Do you often find that your life is aimless, with no definite purpose?" "Looking at a typical day in your life, do you think that most things you do have some purpose?" "Do you ever have trouble organizing the things you have to do?" We also included the Rosenberg (1965) measure of self-esteem as adapted by Bachman et al. (1978), the short form of the Beck Depression Inventory (Beck & Beck, 1972), and the three-item measure of employment value described previously.

The results of this study are presented in Table 13.5. Notice that the unemployed sample had higher depression scores on the short form of the BDI and lower use of time scores on the time structure scale. They also had lower self-esteem scores based on the negative items of the self-esteem scale. Note, however, that differences between the employed and unemployed groups were not statistically significant in regard to total self-esteem, self-esteem based on the positive items, and employment value.

The correlations obtained from this study are also of interest (see Feather & Bond, 1983, for details). In particular, the correlations between employment value and the structured and purposeful use of time were positive for the employed group ($r = .23$, $p < .001$) but negative for the unemployed group ($r = -.50$, $p < .001$). Thus, those *employed* people who saw employment as important to themselves were more likely to report more organization and purpose in their use of time when compared with those employed people who had low employment value scores; those *unemployed* people who saw employment as important to themselves were especially likely to report a lack of organization and purpose in their use of time when com-

TABLE 13.5
Mean Scores for Employed and Unemployed Samples and Results of
Analysis of Variance (Feather & Bond, 1983)

| | Group | | F Values for Main Effect of Group |
	Employed (N = 255)	Unemployed (N = 43)	
Use of time	79.30	74.49	4.17*
Self-esteem			
Total	41.93	40.43	1.32
Positive items	25.04	24.86	.02
Negative items	16.91	15.57	5.18*
Depressive symptoms	2.57	5.44	16.05***
Employment value	16.33	16.16	1.75

*$p < .05$.
**$p < .01$.
***$p < .001$.
Adapted by courtesy of the authors and the British Psychological Society.

pared with those unemployed people with low employment value scores. Note also, that the structured and purposeful use of time was positively associated with self-esteem and negatively associated with depression. These relations have recently been replicated in a wide-ranging study of the correlates of time structure scores (Bond & Feather, 1988). Finally, a further aspect of the Feather and Bond (1983) study was to investigate differences in the willingness of the fulltime employed, partly employed, and unemployed graduates to support a hypothetical organization called the Campaign to Assist Unemployed Youth (Feather & Bond, 1984). These results, however, are beyond the scope of this review.

Longitudinal Studies

The two studies that I have described used cross-sectional designs, collecting information from different samples at the one point in time. Such studies can be useful for identifying differences that then have to be explained, but the findings are always difficult to interpret in causal terms. For example, if respondents from an unemployed sample displayed more symptoms of depression, or lower self-esteem, or less commitment to the work ethic than respondents from an employed sample, one cannot attribute these differences to the unemployed state. It could be the case that those people in the unemployed group were more depressed, or had lower self-esteem, or had a lower work ethic to begin with, and that these initial differences may have contributed to their difficulties in finding a job. Alternatively, those with employment may have found it easier to obtain a job because of lower depression, higher self-esteem, or a stronger work ethic. Furthermore, the experience of employment may have reduced depression and heightened both self-esteem and work values. Clearly, one is on tricky ground when attempting to interpret differences that have been obtained from cross-sectional research. To be on firmer ground one needs to conduct longitudinal studies, investigating people who more either from employment to unemployment or the reverse, or tracking young people who leave school and who either find or fail to find jobs. Such detailed longitudinal studies are much rarer in the literature of unemployment than are the many cross-sectional studies. They take up a lot of research time, are expensive to conduct, difficult to control, and lead one into complex statistical analyses given the fact that one usually loses subjects over longer periods of time, and that one also has to control for a variety of extraneous variables that might affect the dependent variables in which one is mainly interested. Despite these problems, longitudinal studies are an essential part of any causal enquiry into the psychological impact of unemployment.

Some longitudinal studies of the effects of employment and unemployment have been conducted in recent years (see Feather, 1985b; O'Brien, 1986; Warr, 1987a, 1987b, for reviews). Once more I focus on a study from my own program of research that involved a selection from the list of variables that I described previously. Again, I am mainly concerned with those variables relating to values and to aspects of motivation.

The study that I describe was conducted in collaboration with my colleague, Gordon O'Brien. It involved over 3,000 subjects who were drawn from year 10, 11, and 12 classes in 15 State high schools in metropolitan Adelaide. These are the last 3 years of high school in South Australia with the age of most subjects ranging from 15 to 18. We first tested these students in 1980 while they were at school and then followed them up subsequently using mailed questionnaires when they were either employed, unemployed, still at school, or in further education (e.g., tertiary studies). Testing extended over a 2-year period from 1980 to 1982, and additional samples were recruited in 1981 and 1982 to control for the possible effects of testing procedures and societal influences (see Feather & O'Brien, 1986a, 1986b).

Table 13.6 presents a sample of the results that were obtained. Table 13.6 concerns respondents who were either employed or unemployed in 1982 and compares their responses to the major variables with those they provided when they were at school in 1981.

To attribute an effect on a variable to employment or unemployment, one needs to demonstrate patterns of change in that variable over time that differ depending on whether subjects subsequently became employed or unemployed. The crucial term in the analysis is the employment status by time interaction effect because it takes account of these relative changes. A significant employment status by time interaction effect might or might not be accompanied by a statistically significant main effect of employment status. If a significant main effect of employment status were found and if

TABLE 13.6
Results of Longitudinal Analyses for Respondents Who Were Employed or Unemployed in 1982 (Feather & O'Brien, 1986b)

	At school in 1981		Employed or unemployed		F values		
	Employed in 1982	Unemployed in 1982	Employed in 1982	Unemployed in 1982		Employment	
Variable	Mean	Mean	Mean	Mean	Time (T)	Status (E)	T × E
Self-concept measures							
Competence	45.36	43.62	46.98	42.42	11.15***	19.72***	13.66***
Positive attitude	16.68	16.60	16.88	16.56	2.35	1.92	.91
Depressive affect	12.95	13.77	12.56	14.55	.59	13.09***	7.48**
Potency	17.36	17.33	17.33	16.86	.89	.44	1.68
Activity	15.36	14.73	15.62	14.17	.52	16.30***	8.87***
Anger	7.31	7.20	7.24	7.80	.70	1.44	8.19**
Value measures							
Skill-utilization	15.88	15.69	16.08	15.84	3.74	.85	.02
Variety	13.10	13.05	13.39	13.29	7.61**	.28	.04
Influence	16.22	16.62	16.44	16.28	2.97	.61	.41
Protestant ethic	74.34	72.48	74.26	71.30	.62	5.24*	1.11
Employment value	15.87	14.95	15.73	14.97	.72	14.49***	.15
Affective measures							
Stress symptoms	60.76	55.78	61.18	56.29	1.48	17.09***	.02
Life satisfaction	48.38	46.90	50.59	45.48	12.45***	15.70***	15.29***
Unemployment disappointment	5.51	5.32	5.62	5.38	2.70	6.91**	.09
Job need	5.90	5.52	5.85	5.63	.06	9.37**	1.19
External control	5.02	5.39	5.25	5.89	14.97***	9.78**	1.96
Unemployment attributions							
Economic recession	23.16	23.02	23.06	23.78	.28	.31	4.84*
Lack of motivation	13.61	13.70	14.11	12.92	2.44	3.79	12.88***
Competence deficiency	14.61	15.10	14.63	15.12	.02	2.91	.09
Appearance/interview inadequacy	7.68	7.69	7.74	7.98	2.00	.58	.95

Note: Due to missing cases on variables ns for employed subjects ranged from 426 to 479; ns for unemployed subjects ranged from 107 to 132. Lower scores on the stress symptoms scale denote higher stress.
*p < .05. **p < .01. ***p < .001.
Adapted by courtesy of the authors and the British Psychological Society.

this main effect was not accompanied by a statistically significant interaction effect, it would suggest that differences between employed and unemployed groups were present on both occasions (e.g., when subjects were at school and subsequently), and that any changes that occurred across time were similar for both groups and not influenced by the employment or unemployment experience.

The results in Table 13.6 show that the employment status by time interaction effect was statistically significant for the following variables: competence, depressive affect, activity, anger, life satisfaction, economic recession, and lack of motivation. The results tend to indicate reverse or different patterns of change in these variables for those subjects who subsequently became employed, when compared with those who became unemployed, although the changes that followed employment were generally less obvious and less consistent over all data analyses than those that followed unemployment. Thus, self-rated competence, activity, and life satisfaction scores increased for those who found a job but decreased for those who became unemployed after they left school. Self-rated anger and depressive affect decreased for those who became employed but increased for those who became unemployed. These results demonstrate both the positive effects of employment and the negative effects of unemployment.

Note also that the analysis of causal attributions for youth unemployment, using the scales previously described, showed consistent patterns of change (see Table 13.6). Those who became employed showed a slight decrease in the tendency to blame youth unemployment on factors relating to economic recession, but scores on the economic recession variable increased over time for those subjects who became unemployed. In marked contrast, employment led to an increased tendency to blame youth unemployment on lack of motivation, whereas unemployment led to a reduced tendency to endorse lack of motivation as a reason for youth unemployment.

There were also some statistically significant main effects of employment status and main effects of time that emerged from the analyses. These indicated consistent differences between employed and unemployed groups that occurred irrespective of when they were tested (e.g., at school or subsequently), and consistent differences across time that occurred irrespective of which group (employed or unemployed) was involved. The reader is referred to the detailed articles for discussion of these findings (Feather & O'Brien, 1987a, 1987b).

Finally, note that there was no evidence from this longitudinal study that the value measures were affected by employment or unemployment (see Table 13.6), or that there were widespread effects on those variables that were assumed to be related to motivation. For example, although different patterns of change occurred in some of these variables (e.g., depressive affect, activity, attributions for youth unemployment), other variables such as job need did not show similar differences. There were group differences to be sure. For example, those who subsequently became employed had higher Protestant Ethic scores, higher employment value scores, and higher job need scores when compared with those who became unemployed, but these differences were also present when they were at school and could not be attributed to their subsequent experience of employment or unemployment.

A further detailed analysis of data from the longitudinal study was conducted with a view to examining the effects of different patterns of employment and unemployment on the variables listed in Table 13.6. Hence, in this case, the analysis was not concerned with comparing the scores obtained from employed and unemployed groups on the list of variables in Table 13.6 with the scores they provided on these variables when these same respondents were at school. Rather, the analysis was concerned with the scores provided by respondents who reported that they were employed in 1981 and in 1982, unemployed in 1981 and in 1982, employed in 1981 but unemployed in 1982, and unemployed in 1982 but employed in 1982 (Feather & O'Brien, 1986a). The form of analysis was modeled on studies by Jackson, Stafford, Banks, and Warr (1983) and by Warr and Jackson (1985). It involved a 2 by 2 by 2 analysis of variance with sex of subject (male, female) as the first factor in the analysis, employment status in 1981 (employed, unemployed) as the second factor, and whether or not a respondent had changed status from 1981 to 1982 (same, different) as the third factor.

In general, the results of this analysis revealed very few statistically significant interaction effects that would support the prediction that change to a different employment status from 1981 to 1982 would be positive for measures related to psychological well-being (e.g, fewer stress symptoms, more life satisfaction) when the change was from unemployment to employment, and negative (e.g., more stress symptoms, less life satisfaction) when the change was from employment to unemployment (see Table 13.7). A change from employment to unemployment was accompanied by an increased attribution of youth unemployment to socioeconomic causes and decreased attributions to lack to motivation and appearance/interview inadequacy. A change from unemployment to employment was accompanied by the reverse pattern. Respondents in this subgroup were less likely to attribute youth unemployment to socioeconomic causes and more likely to blame it on lack of motivation and appearance/interview inadequacy. These findings are similar to those reported in Table 13.6.

Protestant Ethic scores, life satisfaction scores, and unemployment disappointment scores tended to decrease with a shift from employment to unemployment and to increase with a shift from unemployment to employment. In these cases, however, significance levels for the interaction term ($p < .10$) only approached conventional levels of statistical significance.

These results are weaker than those reported in Table 13.6 where the tran-

TABLE 13.7
Results of ANOVA of Change Scores (Feather & O'Brien, 1986a)

| | Mean Change Scores for Subgroups | | | | d.f. | F Values |
| | Employed in 1981 | | Unemployed in 1981 | | | |
Variable	Same Status in 1982 E–E	Different Status in 1982 E–U	Same Status in 1982 U–U	Different Status in 1982 U–E		Initial Status x Status Change Interaction
Self-concept measures						
Competence	0.36	−0.74	2.42	0.67	1,485	0.04
Positive attitude	−0.00	0.08	−0.35	−0.02	1,500	0.10
Depressive affect	0.43	0.54	0.74	0.66	1,494	0.02
Potency	0.26	0.13	0.08	−0.12	1,498	0.01
Activity	−0.22	−1.17	0.55	0.71	1,499	1.59
Anger	0.21	0.92	0.13	0.12	1,499	0.92
Value measures						
Skill utilization	0.03	0.50	0.08	0.05	1,496	0.43
Variety	0.21	1.13	0.03	−0.02	1,494	0.95
Influence	0.40	1.25	−0.08	0.15	1,486	0.27
Protestant Ethic	0.48	−2.90	2.41	4.62	1,446	3.30*
Employment value	0.05	−0.79	0.52	−0.53	1,483	0.01
Affective measures						
Stress symptoms	−0.83	1.52	−0.92	−0.51	1,432	0.44
Life satisfaction	−0.58	−2.24	−2.25	1.14	1,473	3.06*
Unemployment disappointment	0.07	−0.46	0.20	0.41	1,491	3.45*
Job need	0.11	0.08	0.24	0.15	1,487	0.07
External control	−0.01	0.57	0.23	−0.03	1,460	1.76
Unemployment attributions						
Economic recession	0.23	1.25	0.67	−1.05	1,468	5.12**
Lack of motivation	0.29	−2.23	0.21	1.63	1,479	16.28****
Competence deficiency	−0.07	−0.71	0.56	0.46	1,483	0.31
Appearance/interview inadequacy	−0.14	−0.54	0.02	0.82	1,485	4.04**

Note: A negative change on the stress symptoms scale denote increased stress. Ns are provided in the detailed report.
$*p < 0.10$. $**p < 0.05$. $***p < 0.001$.
Adapted by courtesy of the authors and the British Psychological Society.

sition was from school to employment or from school to unemployment. Moreover, unlike Jackson et al. (1983), we found no evidence that variables assumed to reflect the importance of finding employment had a moderating effect on aspects of psychological well-being, depending on whether a person was employed or unemployed (see Feather & O'Brien, 1986a, Table 5, for details). Such effects would be observed if there was a positive correlation between employment importance and psychological well-being for employed subjects but a negative correlation between these variables for unemployed subjects. Neither the longitudinal analysis nor the cross-sectional analyses provided any consistent evidence of such moderating effects. For example, life satisfaction scores were not both positively correlated with job need, Protestant Ethic values, and employment value for the employed group and negatively correlated with these variables for the unemployed group. Instead the correlations were positive and statistically significant for both groups. As noted previously, we did find some evidence for these effects in an earlier study that involved employed and unemployed university graduates when the dependent variable was time structure (Feather & Bond, 1983). However, the results from the Sheffield group in regard to the moderating effects of employment commitment on psychological well-being in relation to employment and unemployment are not entirely consistent, as is evident when one compares findings from the Jackson et al. (1983) study with those from the Warr and Jackson (1985) study. Clearly, we need more conceptual analysis of what is meant by psychological well-being and employment commitment, as well as detailed analysis of the scales that have been used to measure these variables.

JOB-SEEKING BEHAVIOR

Earlier in this chapter, I reported the results of factor analyses that did provide information about the structure of relations among variables. In the longitudinal study that I have been discussing the factor analysis was based on data obtained from 320 unemployed subjects who were tested in 1982 in the final part of the study. The full range of variables for which we had measures is described in the detailed report (Feather & O'Brien, 1987). These variables overlap considerably with those listed in Tables 13.6 and 13.7, but with the addition of some measures of job confidence and further specific measures of affective responses to unemployment and attributions concerning each person's own unemployment. Ten factors emerged from the factor analysis and four of these factors have been described in Tables 13.2 and 13.3. Three of these factors are of particular interest in relation to the analysis that follows.

One of these factors was assumed to reflect differences in respondents' expectations of finding a job and we called this factor *control-optimism*. A second factor was assumed to reflect differences in the valence or perceived attractiveness of employment. We called this factor *job valence*. The results of the factor analysis described in Table 13.2 enabled us to define subscales that were assumed to measure each of these factors and that were based on the variables with the highest factor loadings. The third factor, *internal work ethic*, was defined by scores on the Protestant Ethic scale (Mirels & Garrett, 1971) because the scale had the highest loading on the factor.

The increased sophistication in measurement was combined with the conceptual framework of expectancy-value (or expectancy-valence) theory that I referred to earlier to enable us to test predictions about job-seeking behavior in two samples from our longitudinal study, subjects who were unemployed in 1981 and subjects who were unemployed in 1982. We predicted that: (a) Frequency of job-seeking behavior will be positively related to an unemployed persons's expectation of finding employment; (b) frequency of job-seeking behavior will be positively related to the extent to which an unemployed person sees employment as attractive or positively valent; and (c) measures of expectation and valence will provide better prediction of job-seeking behavior than either measure alone.

We also tested a number of predictions that concerned other variables in the study. These hypotheses were as follows: (a) An unemployed person's expectation of finding employment will be negatively related to the number of previous unsuccessful attempts to find a job; (b) an unemployed person's expectation of finding employment will be negatively related to length of unemployment; (c) an unemployed person's expectation of finding employment will be related to the degree of social support that person receives; and (d) the perceived attractiveness of employment will be a positive function of the strength of the unemployed person's work ethic or Protestant Ethic (PE) values. In regard to the latter prediction, it was assumed that general values may be assumed to be a class of variables that influences specific valences (Feather, 1982b, 1986b, 1988). Just as food is more attractive when a person is hungry, or a successful outcome in a skill situation is more attractive for a person with a strong achievement motive, so getting a job should have higher positive valence for a person with strong PE values.

Note that this study was an attempt to analyze an important real-life activity (viz., job-seeking behavior by young unemployed people) in terms of a well-known motivational approach, expectancy-value theory. I undertook this analysis in the firm belief that progress in the area of unemployment research will depend both on greater attention to the measurement of basic variables and recognition of the need to link these variables to theoretical frameworks. In this way, one might be able to bring some order into diverse and sometimes confusing patterns of results (see also Feather, 1989b).

How was job-seeking defined? We used an item that had been included in a previous study of unemployment (Feather, 1982c). Subjects were asked: "How frequently do you look for a job?" They checked a 6-point Likert scale labeled "Not looking for a job," "When I feel like it," "Monthly," "Weekly," "Every couple of days," and "Daily." We also asked subjects how long (in weeks) they had been looking for work, how many jobs they had applied for since they became unemployed, and questions about how much support they received from their parents.

The detailed findings are presented in Feather and O'Brien (1987). Table 13.8 presents the correlations for the two samples who were involved in the study, and Fig. 13.1 shows the results of a path analysis that explored the structure of relations for the 1982 sample. Some of the main findings based on the correlations reported in Table 13.8 were as follows: (a) Job-seeking behavior was positively related to job valence but unrelated to control-optimism; (b) job-seeking behavior was positively related both to the length of time unemployed and the number of unsuccessful job applications; (c) job valence was positively related to the work ethic; (d) control-optimism was negatively related to the length of time unemployed (both samples) and to the number of unsuccessful job applications (1982 sample only); (e) control-optimism was positively related to support received from parents (1982 sample only); (f) number of unsuccessful job applications was positively related to length of time unemployed; (g) support from parents was higher for female subjects when compared with male subjects; (h) job-seeking behavior was positively related to a general measure of negative affect associated with unemployment. Note that some of these relations between variables were reduced in magnitude by the path analysis.

Table 13.9 presents the results of a hierarchical multiple regression analysis for both samples in which a wider range of variables was considered in relation to job-seeking behavior. The measure of social class was based on the levels of education that subjects reported for both parents and also on the status of the occupation of the father. Academic potential was based on teachers' ratings obtained when subjects were at school, and they involved teachers assigning students to the top 33%, the middle 33%, or the bottom 33% as far as academic potential was concerned. We also added an interaction term to the regression equation involving the product of control-optimism and job valence.

The results of the hierarchical multiple regression analysis reinforce the other findings that I have reported. Only two variables significantly added to the variance accounted for in job-seeking behavior: a history of job-seeking in the past and job valence. Note that the interaction term did not add significantly to the variance accounted for in the dependent variable. Job-seeking behavior was not better predicted from a combination of measures of expectation and valence (additive or multiplicative) than from either measure alone. When all the variables were entered in the equation, it was possible to account for around 20% of the variance in job-seeking behavior. So 80% of the variance was not accounted for.

Taken as a whole, the results of this study are only partially consistent with the expectancy-valence analysis because the measure of valence pre-

TABLE 13.8
Correlations Between Variables for 1981 and 1982 Unemployed Respondents (Feather & O'Brien, 1987)

Variable	Control-Optimism	Job Valence	Support	Duration Unemployed	Job Applications	Sex of Respondent	Work Ethic	Job Seeking
Control-optimism	—	-0.26***	0.12*	-0.26***	-0.20***	-0.04	0.06	-0.07
Job valence	-0.04	—	0.07*	0.11**	0.16**	-0.00	0.19***	0.40***
Support	0.14	0.20*	—	-0.08	-0.01	0.16**	0.12*	0.04
Duration unemployed	-0.19*	0.14	-0.09	—	0.45***	0.01	0.03	0.15**
Job applications	-0.13	0.08	-0.13	0.28**	—	0.06	-0.06	0.28***
Sex of respondent	-0.01	0.23**	0.21*	0.10	0.08	—	-0.06	-0.02
Work ethic	0.27**	0.31***	0.17	-0.13	-0.10	0.12	—	0.11*
Job seeking	-0.17	0.30***	-0.11	0.18*	0.26**	0.04	-0.06	—

Note: Tests of significance are two-tailed. Sex of respondent was coded 1 = male, 2 = female. Correlations for the 1982 sample are above the diagonal; correlations for the 1981 sample are below the diagonal. Ns are provided in the detailed report. Adapted by courtesy of the authors and the British Psychological Society.

*p < 0.05.
**p < 0.01.
***p < 0.001.

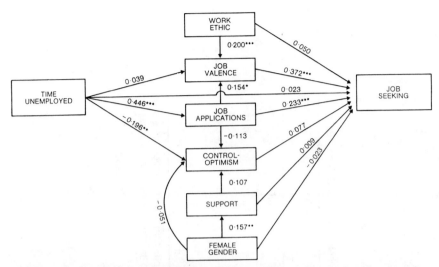

FIG. 13.1   Path diagram linking job-seeking behavior with other variables. The numbers on the lines are standardized beta coefficients. *p < .05. **p < .01. ***p < .001. Adapted by courtesy of the authors and the British Psychological Society.

dicted job seeking but the measure of expectation did not. We provide a number of possible explanations for this failure to find the hypothesized relation between control-optimism and job-seeking behavior in the published report (Feather & O'Brien, 1987). Some of these explanations concern the level at which the variables were measured (e.g., whether it might have been more appropriate to develop more specific measures of the expectation variable). Generally, however, it may be the case that relations between control-optimism and behavior are more complicated than we assumed, especially when real-life events are concerned (see also Mineka & Hendersen, 1985). For example, external forces such as pressure from parents may impel young unemployed people to look for a job even though they are pessimistic about their chances and feel that they have little control over the outcome. On the positive side, however, there was firm evidence that the measure of job valence was positively related to job-seeking behavior as predicted and that job valence itself was positively related to the work ethic as predicted. Furthermore, most of the other predictions were supported. As we conclude in our report (Feather & O'Brien, 1987), "the present findings take us a little further toward understanding a relatively neglected aspect of unemployment, viz., job-seeking behavior. They also raise issues concerning the applicability of the expectancy-valence framework to real-life settings and, more generally, they support the general strategy of relating research in unemployment to theoretical frameworks" (p. 270).

TABLE 13.9
Multiple Correlations and Proportions of Variance Explained from Hierarchical Multiple Regression Analyses
(Feather & O'Brien, 1987)

Step	Independent Variable	Job Seeking: 1982 Sample			Job Seeking: 1981 Sample		
		R	R²	R² Change	R	R²	R² Change
1	Social class + academic potential + age + sex	0.089	0.008	0.008	0.085	0.007	0.007
2	Support	0.101	0.010	0.002	0.136	0.019	0.011
3	Work ethic	0.143	0.020	0.010	0.143	0.020	0.002
4	Duration unemployed + job applications	0.330	0.109	0.088***	0.292	0.086	0.065*
5	Control-optimism	0.330	0.109	0.000	0.315	0.099	0.014
6	Job valence	0.471	0.222	0.113***	0.440	0.194	0.094**
7	Control-optimism × job valence	0.477	0.228	0.006	0.445	0.198	0.004

*$p < 0.05$.
**$p < 0.01$.
***$p < 0.001$.
Adapted by courtesy of the authors and the British Psychological Society.

CONCLUDING COMMENTS

I conclude with some general comments that refer to the various studies that I have reviewed.

There was little evidence that values were affected by employment or unemployment. The results of the longitudinal study indicated that what differences there were between employed and unemployed subjects in regard to values such as the work ethic were already present when these young people were at school. It is interesting to note also that a further analysis of the longitudinal data showed that those students who subsequently became unemployed had lower self-rated confidence of finding a job when they were at school and lower teachers' ratings of academic potential when compared with those students who obtained employment (Feather & O'Brien, 1986b). Table 13.6 indicates other group differences as well that were there at the beginning.

The results did indicate that unemployment had negative effects in regard to some variables; of these, some concerned psychological well-being (e.g., life satisfaction), some concerned self-perceptions (e.g., perceived competence, depressive affect, activity, anger), and some involved cognitive variables (e.g., causal attributions). There was also evidence to suggest that increasing length of unemployment determined decreases in expectations and feelings of control (diminished control-optimism; Table 13.8). Feather and Davenport (1981) also found evidence that expectations of finding a job were reduced in a sample of young unemployed people compared to how confident they were about finding a job immediately before leaving school.

Some variables may be less amenable to change because they represent relatively stable aspects of self. Other variables may be more sensitive to change because they are keyed to a person's immediate life situation. The relatively stable variables (e.g., self-concepts, values) may change as a result of life experiences but these changes may be more gradual, requiring longer time periods to identify. For example, our findings showed that shifts from employment to unemployment or vice versa led to predictable changes in the degree to which current youth unemployment was attributed to the economic recession, to lack of motivation, and to appearance/interview inadequacies. These kinds of changes would tend to preserve a positive view of self because those moving to employment became more internal in their attributions and those moving to unemployment became more external. If, however, a person remained unemployed over a long period of time, despite repeated efforts to find a job, and if that person saw that most others who were similar in many ways to self were ultimately successful in finding a job, then that person's own causal attributions for being unemployed may shift from external to internal, and self may be seen as deficient in competence and ability. One might then expect to find self-esteem deficits, associated depressive symptoms and feelings of hopelessness and helplessness

(Feather & Barber, 1983). A negative view of self might also develop when the unemployed come to believe that others despise and deprecate them for their failure to find to job (Breakwell, Collie, Harrison, & Propper, 1984). Other cognitive changes might also occur that lead to a realignment of value priorities as the person adjusts both to external realities and internal dynamics.

In my studies I have consistently included variables that relate to the expectancy-value (valence) framework of motivational theory. The recent study of job-seeking behavior (Feather & O'Brien, 1987) goes further than the previous studies by attempting to use these variables in a conceptual analysis of a person's motivation to seek employment. My earlier studies of depressive affect and depressive symptoms in samples of young unemployed people were also based on theoretical analyses that used the expectancy-value (valence) framework of ideas (Feather & Barber, 1983; Feather & Davenport, 1981). I believe that such attempts to relate employment and unemployment studies to conceptual schemes mark an important advance in that they provide a coherent framework for research and take one beyond particularities to wider perspectives.

There is a need in future studies to look in more detail at the nature of employment and unemployment experiences. Warr (1987a, 1987b) cogently draws our attention to the fact that unemployment means different things for different groups (e.g., young versus middle aged; single women versus married women; "blue-collar" workers versus professionals; see also Rowley & Feather, 1987). So too, the experience of employment varies. Not all employment would be expected to enhance self-esteem, reduce stress and depression, increase life satisfaction, or positively affect other aspects of psychological well-being. Mundane, routine, and tiring jobs may have negative effects on well-being when they provide low income and poor working conditions and where there is little opportunity to exercise one's skills, to experience variety, or to exert influence and control in day-to-day activities in the workplace (Feather & O'Brien, 1986b; O'Brien, 1986).

We need to go beyond studies of youth employment and unemployment to investigate different groups across the life cycle. Some studies of middle-aged and older groups have already been conducted (e.g., Feather, 1989a; Jackson & Warr, 1984; Rowley & Feather, 1987; Warr & Jackson, 1985), and it is already apparent that the effects of unemployment are somewhat different for these groups when compared with the findings obtained for young people. These studies would profit from more attention to the literature from developmental psychology that is concerned with life-span development.

We need more research and theoretical analysis into the effects of unemployment duration. It is possible, for example, that job-seeking behavior might increase with increasing length of unemployment as a person learns about and explores different avenues for finding employment but then declines as the range of options is exhausted. Expectations of finding a job would then fall to very low levels and feelings of helplessness might also develop. These changes could vary depending on the unemployed group that is investigated (e.g., young versus middle aged). For example, Rowley and Feather (1987) found that length of unemployment was positively related to use of more job-search methods in a young sample but the corresponding relation was negative in a middle-aged sample.

Finally, there is a need to look at employment and unemployment effects cross-culturally. There is no guarantee that results found in one culture (e.g., Britain) will automatically transfer to another culture (e.g., Australia), given the different ways in which governments deal with the problem of unemployment and given the many other differences that may occur (e.g., in values and attitudes, social organization, economic resources, climate, living standards, leisure activities, social support, family structures, ethnic groups, and the legacy of a nation's history). Clearly, such research will call for multidisciplinary collaboration.

These various comments indicate that there are many directions that can be taken in future research into the impact of both employment and unemployment on values and motivation. The agenda is a large one, but the research that follows has social as well as theoretical relevance.

REFERENCES

Bakke, E. W. (1940a). *The unemployed worker*. New Haven, CT: Yale University Press.

Bakke, E. W. (1940b). *Citizens without work*. New Haven, CT: Yale University Press.

Bachman, J. G., O'Malley, P. M., & Johnston, J. (1978). *Adolescence to adulthood*. Ann Arbor, MI: Institute for Social Research.

Bandura, A. (1986). *Social foundations of thought and action*. Englewood Cliffs, NJ: Prentice-Hall.

Beck, A. T. (1967). *Depression: Clinical, experimental, and theoretical aspects*. New York: Harper & Row.

Beck, A. T., & Beck, R. W. (1972). Screening depressed patients in family practice: A rapid technic. *Postgraduate Medicine, 52*, 81–85.

Beck, A. T., Weissman, A., Lester, D., & Trexler, L. (1974). The measurement of pessimism. *Journal of Consulting and Clinical Psychology, 42*, 861–865.

Bond, M. J., & Feather, N. T. (1988). Some correlates of structure and purpose in the use of time. *Journal of Personality and Social Psychology, 55*, 321–329.

Breakwell, G. M., Collie, A., Harrison, B., & Propper, C. (1984). Attitudes towards the unemployed: Effects of threatened identity. *British Journal of Social Psychology, 23*, 87–88.

Eisenberg, P., & Lazarsfeld, P. F. (1938). The psychological effects of unemployment. *Psychological Bulletin, 35*, 358–390.

Elder, G. H. (1974). Children of the Great Depression. Chicago: University of Chicago Press.

Elder, G., & Likert, J. K. (1982). Hard times in women's lives: Historical influences across forty years. *American Journal of Sociology, 88*, 241–269.

Elder, G. H., & Rockwell, R. C. (1979). Economic depression and postwar opportunities in men's lives: A study of life patterns and health. In R. G. Simmons (Ed.), *Research in community and mental health* (Vol. 1, pp. 249–303). Greenwich, CT: JAI Press.

Feather, N. T. (1959). Subjective probability and decision under uncertainty. *Psychological Review, 66*, 150–164.

Feather, N. T. (Ed.). (1982a). *Expectations and actions: Expectancy-value models in psychology.* Hillsdale, NJ: Lawrence Erlbaum Associates.

Feather, N. T. (1982b). Human values and the prediction of action: An expectancy-valence analysis. In N. T. Feather (Ed.), *Expectations and actions: Expectancy-value models in psychology* (pp. 263–289). Hillsdale, NJ: Lawrence Erlbaum Associates.

Feather, N. T. (1982c). Unemployment and its psychological correlates: A study of depressive symptoms, self-esteem, protestant ethic values, attributional style, and apathy. *Australian Journal of Psychology, 34*, 309–323.

Feather, N. T. (1983). Causal attributions and beliefs about work and unemployment among adolescents in state and independent secondary schools. *Australian Journal of Psychology, 35*, 211–232.

Feather, N. T. (1985a). Attitudes, values, and attributions: Explanations of unemployment. *Journal of Personality and Social Psychology, 48*, 876–889.

Feather, N. T. (1985b). The psychological impact of unemployment: Empirical findings and theoretical approaches. In N. T. Feather (Ed.), *Australian psychology: Review of research* (pp. 265–295). Sydney: George Allen & Unwin.

Feather, N. T. (1986a). Employment importance and helplessness about potential unemployment among students in secondary schools. *Australian Journal of Psychology, 38*, 33–44.

Feather, N. T. (1986b). Human values, valences, expectations and affect: Theoretical issues emerging from recent applications of the expectancy-value model. In D. R. Brown & J. Veroff (Eds.), *Frontiers of motivational psychology: Essays in honor of John W. Atkinson* (pp. 146–172). New York: Springer-Verlag.

Feather, N. T. (1988). From values to actions: Recent applications of the expectancy-value model. *Australian Journal of Psychology, 40*, 105–124.

Feather, N. T. (1989a). Reported changes in behavior after job loss in a sample of older unemployed men. *Australian Journal of Psychology*, in press.

Feather, N. T. (1989b). *The psychological impact of unemployment.* New York: Springer-Verlag.

Feather, N. T., & Barber, J. G. (1983). Depressive reactions and unemployment. *Journal of Abnormal Psychology, 92*, 185–195.

Feather, N. T., & Bond, M. J. (1983). Time structure and purposeful activity among employed and unemployed university graduates. *Journal of Occupational Psychology, 56*, 241–254.

Feather, N. T., & Bond, M. J. (1984). Potential social action as a function of expectation-outcome discrepancies among employed and unemployed university graduates. *Australian Journal of Psychology, 36*, 205–217.

Feather, N. T., & Davenport, P. R. (1981). Unemployment and depressive affect: A motivational and attributional analysis. *Journal of Personality and Social Psychology, 41*, 422–436.

Feather, N. T., & O'Brien, G. E. (1986a). A longitudinal analysis of the effects of different patterns of employment and unemployment on school-leavers. *British Journal of Psychology, 77*, 459–479.

Feather, N. T., & O'Brien, G. E. (1986b). A longitudinal study of the effects of employment and unemployment on school-leavers. *Journal of Occupational Psychology, 59*, 121–144.

Feather, N. T., & O'Brien, G. E. (1987). Looking for employment: An expectancy-valence analysis of job-seeking behaviour among young people. *British Journal of Psychology, 78*, 251–272.

Feather, N. T., & Tiggemann, M. (1984). A balanced measure of attributional style. *Australian Journal of Psychology, 36*, 267–283.

Fryer, D. (1988). The experience of unemployment in social context. In S. Fisher & J. Reason (Eds.), *Handbook of life stress, cognition and health* (pp. 211–238). Chichester, England: Wiley.

Fryer, D., & Payne, R. (1986). Being unemployed: A review of the literature on the psychological experience of unemployment. In C. L. Cooper & I. Robertson (Eds.), *International review of industrial and organizational psychology*, (pp. 235–278). New York: Wiley.

Furnham, A. (1984). The Protestant work ethic: A review of the psychological literature. *European Journal of Social Psychology, 14*, 87–104.

Hartley, J. F., & Fryer, D. (1984). The psychology of unemployment: A critical appraisal. In G. M. Stephenson & J. H. Davis (Eds.), *Progress in applied social psychology* (Vol. 2, pp. 3–30). Chichester, England: Wiley.

Heckhausen, H. (1977). Achievement motivation and its constructs. *Motivation and Emotion, 1*, 283–329.

Jackson, P. R., Stafford, E. M., Banks, M. H., & Warr, P. B. (1983). Unemployment and psychological distress in young people: The moderating role of employment commitment. *Journal of Applied Psychology, 68*, 525–535.

Jackson, P. R., & Warr, P. B. (1984). Unemployment and psychological ill-health: The moderating effect of duration and age. *Psychological Medicine, 14*, 605–614.

Jahoda, M. (1979). The impact of unemployment in the 1930s and the 1970s. *Bulletin of the British Psychological Society, 32*, 309–314.

Jahoda, M. (1981). Work, employment, and unemployment: Values, theories, and approaches in social research. *American Psychologist, 36*, 184–191.

Jahoda, M. (1982). *Employment and unemployment: A social-psychological analysis*. Cambridge, England: Cambridge University Press.

Jahoda, M., Lazarsfeld, P. F., & Zeisel, H. (1933). *Marienthal: The sociography of an unemployed community* (English translation, 1972), London: Tavistock Publications.

Kelvin, P., & Jarrett, J. (1985). *The social psychological effects of unemployment*. Cambridge, England: Cambridge University Press.

Komarovsky, M. (1940). *The unemployed man and his family*. New York: Dryden.

Lewin, K. (1938). The conceptual representation and the measurement of psychological forces. *Contributions to psychological theory* (1). New York: Johnson Reprint Company.

Mineka, S., & Hendersen, R. W. (1985). Controllability and predictability in acquired motivation. *Annual Review of Psychology, 36*, 495–529.

Mirels, H., & Garrett, J. B. (1971). The protestant ethic as a personality variable. *Journal of Consulting and Clinical Psychology, 36*, 40–44.

Nie, N. H., Hull, C. H., Jenkins, J. G., Steinbrenner, K., & Bent, D. H. (1975). *SPSS statistical package for the social sciences*. New York: McGraw-Hill.

O'Brien, G. E. (1980). The centrality of skill-utilization for job design. In K. Duncan, M. Gruneberg, & D. Wallis (Eds.), *Changes in working life* (pp. 167–187). Chichester, England: Wiley.

O'Brien, G. E. (1986). *Psychology of work and unemployment: The psychology of employment, underemployment, and unemployment*. New York: Wiley.

O'Brien, G. E., & Dowling, P. (1980). The effects of congruency between perceived and desired job attributes upon job satisfaction. *Journal of Occupational Psychology, 53*, 121–130.

O'Brien, G. E., Dowling, P., & Kabanoff, B. (1978). *Work, health, and leisure*. Working paper 28, National Institute of Labour Studies, Flinders University of South Australia.

O'Brien, G. E., & Kabanoff, B. (1981). Australian norms and factor analysis of Rotter's internal–external control scale. *Australian Psychologist, 16*, 184–202.

Peterson, C., & Seligman, M. E. P. (1984). Causal explanations as a risk factor for depression: Theory and evidence. *Psychological Review*, 347–374.

Rosenberg, M. (1965). *Society and the adolescent self-image*. Princeton, NJ: Princeton University Press.

Rotter, J. B. (1966). Generalized expectancies for internal versus external control of reinforcement. *Psychological Monographs, 80*, 1–28.

Rowley, K. M., & Feather, N. T. (1987). The impact of unemployment in relation to age and length of unemployment. *Journal of Occupational Psychology, 60*, 323-332.

Warr, P. B. (1983). Work, jobs, and unemployment. *Bulletin of the British Psychological Society, 36*, 305-311.

Warr, P. B. (1984). Job loss, unemployment and psychological well-being. In V. Allen & E. van de Vliert (Eds.), *Role transitions* (pp. 263-286). New York: Plenum.

Warr, P. B. (Ed.) (1987a). *Psychology at work* (3rd Ed.). Harmondsworth: Penguin.

Warr, P. B. (Ed.) (1987b). *Work, unemployment, and mental health*. Oxford: Oxford University Press.

Warr, P. B., & Jackson, P. R. (1985). Factors influencing the psychological impact of prolonged unemployment and of reemployment. *Psychological Medicine, 15*, 795-807.

Weber, M. (1976). *The Protestant Ethic and the spirit of capitalism* (T. Parsons, Trans.). London: Allen & Unwin (Original work published 1904-1905).

Weiner, B. (1985). An attributional theory of achievement motivation. *Psychological Review, 92*, 548-573.

Weiner, B. (1986). *An attributional theory of motivation and emotion*. New York: Springer-Verlag.

14

Work Motivation of Youngsters Entering the Labor Market

P. Coetsier
R. Claes
State University Ghent, Belgium

INTRODUCTION

Studies on the entry into the labor market (e.g., Osterman, 1980; Silberman, 1982), as well as studies on the failure to enter the labor market (e.g., Frese & Mohr, 1978; Fryer & Payne, 1986; O'Brien, 1986), point out that the transition from school to work influences the social integration of young people. Nowadays, this transition is problematic as demonstrated by the high rate of youth unemployment.

Technological innovations do have effects on the quantity and quality of work, although it is not yet clear exactly what these effects are. However, it may reasonably be expected that the necessity, and readiness, for mobility in the labor market will increase. Tomorrow's work force, especially young people, should be prepared for such mobility, which implies that they should allocate work a more or less central place in their lives.

In the first section of this chapter we examine the motivation of young people to have paid work at the time of their entering the labor market, and the stability of work motivation over time. Next, we investigate, on the basis of reports from the youngsters themselves, whether their work motivation is actually being "translated" into job-searching behavior. Finally, some implications of the research findings are formulated.

The data used in this study are based on an international research project on the Meaning of Work (MOW, 1981, 1987), and from a Belgian pilot study that is part of another international research project called WOSY (Work Socialization of Youth; Coetsier, Claes, & Berings, 1987).

In the MOW-project (started in 1979) social scientists from Belgium, West Germany, Great Britain, Israel, Japan, the Netherlands, the United

States, and Yugoslavia are studying the psychological meaning of work (paid employment) as perceived by various social, professional, and age groups in their respective countries. In each country, MOW-samples comprise representative samples from the work force and 10 target groups (Unemployed, Retired, Chemical Engineers, Teachers, Self-employed, Tool- and Diemakers, Textile Workers, White-collar Workers, Temporary Workers, Students). The total number of respondents in the MOW-study amounts to nearly 15,000.

The WOSY-project (started in 1985) was set up by an international team of vocational and organizational psychologists from 10 countries and is still in its starting phase. Its objective is to make a comparative study of the quantitative and qualitative changes that take place in individuals (between 18 and 25 years of age) when they enter the world of (paid) work.

Because the international WOSY-data are not yet available, Belgian MOW-data is used here; international MOW-findings are occasionally referred to.

The empirical structure of the various meanings of work reveals that their contents can be divided into three overall categories (MOW, 1987):

1.   The role of work in a person's life: Assigning a central role to work implies that one's values are primarily orientated towards working (Lawler & Hall, 1970; Lodahl & Kejner, 1965; Maurer, 1968) and that one's decisions and behavior are oriented towards preferred life spheres, i.e., work (Barker, 1968; Dubin, 1956; Heider, 1958).

2.   Societal norms pertaining to work: These include normative statements about work and working in terms of entitlements (that is, what one should expect from working; Locke & Schweiger, 1979; Perlman, 1976), as well as in terms of obligations (that is, what should be expected from one in working; Parson & Shils, 1952).

3.   The value attached to work outcomes: What do people want from work and what do they feel the functions of working are (Cragin, 1983)?

These are the three categories of meanings of work, here labeled *work motivation* or *the meaning of work*, that are examined next.

METHOD

Samples, Data Collection, Research Variables, Statistical Analyses

The MOW-target group of Students is defined as follows (MOW, 1981): "50% males, attending technical training colleges; 50% females, attending full-time clerical–secretarial courses. Although students may have part-time jobs, the target group should consist of students who are supposed to enter the labor market immediately after finishing their training." The total number of respondents in the target group of Students is 592 (Great Britain didn't take part in the target group part of the MOW-study, whereas Yugoslavia was not able to collect data for the target group Students). Data were collected by means of a standardized questionnaire administered to small groups of students during school hours. Data collection in the various participating countries took place between 1980 and 1983, in Belgium in 1981.

The Belgian WOSY-pilot sample consisted of 627 students in their final school year. Two months before they left school, a standardized questionnaire was administered to small groups of students during school hours. In-depth, retrospective interviews with the students took place at their homes about 6 to 9 months after they had left school. Simultaneously, they were asked to fill out a questionnaire concerning personality characteristics. Here, 212 young people were included. They were "ready and available for the labor market" and neither attending any additional vocational training nor doing their military/civil service. Data collection for the Belgian WOSY-pilot study took place in 1985–1986.

The research variables involved are centrality of work, agreement with societal norms pertaining to work, value attached to work outcomes, channels used to find a job, and selectiveness before accepting a first job. The first three variables cover the meaning of work as perceived by young people; their measurements in the MOW-study and in the WOSY-project were similar. The questionnaire can be found in the Appendix.

The statistical analyses performed were mainly t-tests between means. Only results at the $p \leq .05$ level of significance are accepted. These can be checked in the Appendix.

RESULTS

Centrality of Work

In the MOW-study, questions 29 and 30 were used to investigate the centrality of work. For all individuals in the samples from all participating countries, the two indicators of "centrality of work" are moderately related ($r = .29$), but not identical. The data on "centrality of work" are presented here as an index of centrality of work at the individual level. This index is obtained by adding up the T-scores (standardized across countries) on both questions and dividing the outcome by 2.

Figure 14.1 illustrates the centrality of work for Belgian Students as compared to the same target group in the other countries and the other nine Belgian target groups.

The Students' scores on centrality of work are lower than the overall mean index score (50). Students in Belgium score significantly lower than Students in the other four countries (see left side of Fig. 14.1 and t-tests in

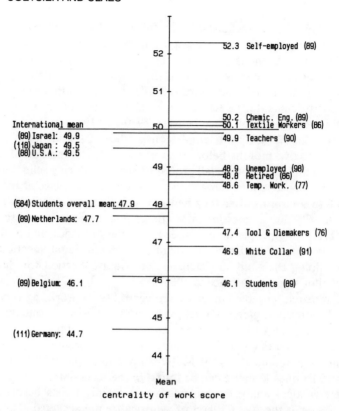

FIG.14.1.   Centrality of work of Belgian Students as compared to students in other countries (left) and to other Belgian target groups (right). (Size of samples given in brackets.)

the Appendix). Of all target groups, Belgian Students score lowest on work centrality (see right side of Fig. 14.1 and Appendix for t-tests). They score significantly lower on centrality of work than seven other target groups. The students do not yet have any working experience and in this group, contrary to the other target groups, the "worker" role is not yet dominant. Belgian Students share this low centrality of work with Tool and Diemakers and White-collar Workers. This finding is not really surprising, considering the fact that the Students' training—technical for males, clerical for females—strongly resembles that of the Tool and Diemakers and White-collar Workers, respectively.

Societal Norms Pertaining to Work

The measurement of the norms pertaining to rights and duties is based on the extent to which respondent agree with the 10 normative statements about these rights and duties listed in MOW-question 47. The "rights" index and the "duties" index are calculated by means of a number of princi-

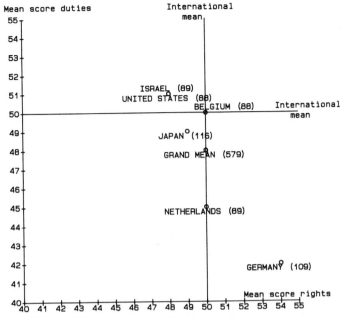

FIG. 14.2.   Position of Students per country. (Size of samples given in brackets.)

pal components analyses performed on the responses to the 10 statements of question 47. Both indices are expressed in T-scores (standardized across countries).

The mean scores on the two indices are used to position each country's target group of Students within the overall societal norms space and to position the Belgian Students relative to the other nine Belgian target groups in the overall societal norms space.

In the MOW-study (MOW, 1987) we found that a country's position in the overall societal norms space is strongly associated with the relative positions of most of its target groups. For example, in Belgium and Germany the levels of agreement with the two norms are slightly out of balance, with "rights" scoring somewhat higher than "duties" in both countries. In the Netherlands, to take another example, the difference between the levels of agreement with these two norms is larger: Agreement is relatively much higher on "rights" and much lower on "duties." So, when considering the Students' position in Fig. 14.2 and 14.3, we must bear in mind a country's position in the societal norms space does have consequences.

Figure 14.2 clearly shows that the Belgian Students could not have expressed a more balanced degree of agreement with the "rights" and "duties" of working: On both indices their mean target group score is 50. On the basis of the agreement expressed on the individual items of question 47, the actual work ethic of Belgian Students could be described as follows.

People have a right to work, but they also have duties. Everyone is enti-

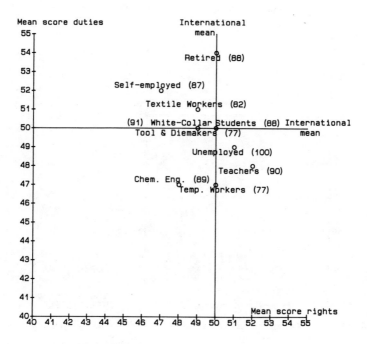

FIG.14.3.   Position of Belgian target groups. (Size of samples given in brackets.)

tled to have an interesting and a meaningful work: Dirty or unskilled labor is unacceptable. The educational system should prepare people for a good job and later on employers are responsible for retraining or re-employing workers whose skills have become obsolete. On the one hand, workers should be allowed to participate in decision making when working methods have to be reviewed, but on the other hand they may be expected to think of ways of doing their jobs more effectively.

With their balanced position in the societal norms space, Belgian Students differ from Students in Israel, Germany, the Netherlands, and the United States (see t-tests in the Appendix). These findings correspond with the position of Belgium as a country relative to that of the other four countries.

Figure 14.3 and t-tests in the Appendix show that, within Belgium, Students agree with both societal norms to the same degree as the Unemployed and two of the employed groups: The Tool and Diemakers and the White-collar Workers. Obviously, being a nonworking group, the Students resemble the Unemployed; the Students' resemblance to the Tool and Diemakers and the White-collar Workers is associated with the resemblance between the Students vocational training and the occupations of the latter two target groups.

The Value of Work Outcomes

MOW question 28 lists six broadly defined work outcomes. Respondents were asked to rate these outcomes by giving points to each of them according to the value they attach to them. The total number of points should not exceed 100.

In MOW (1987) it was found that neither countries nor target groups differ greatly in the order in which the three most important work outcomes are ranked: income, interpersonal contacts, intrinsic value of work. It further became clear that the other three work outcomes are far less important in all countries and in all target groups.

Belgian Students, however, give significantly more points to "income" than Teachers and significantly fewer points than the remaining eight target groups. Belgian Students value "interpersonal contact" to the same extent as Teachers and Temporary Workers but significantly more than the other seven target groups. Finally, Students assign the same number of points to the "intrinsic (or self-expressive)" value as Unemployed, Retired, Textile Workers, and Temporary Workers. Students assign significantly more points to this outcome than Tool and Diemakers and less than Chemical Engineers, Teachers, Self-employed, and White-collar Workers. We refer to the Appendix for the relevant t-tests.

The meaning of work for Belgian Students as revealed by the MOW data can be characterized as follows: Students score low on "centrality of work", they mostly agree with the rights and duties involved in working that are alive in society; compared to other target groups, they attach relatively less importance to "income" and relatively more importance to "interpersonal contacts."

Comparing the meaning of work as perceived by the Belgian MOW-target group of Students with the meaning of work as perceived by the WOSY-respondents just before leaving school (the latter were asked the same questions), certain shifts become apparent. These shifts are due to differences between the sample groups (the MOW-target group involves a more limited range of training courses than the WOSY-sample) and to the time interval (1981 and 1985, respectively).

For "centrality of work" the mean index score rises from 46 to 50 ($t = -5.18$, $df = 697$) and for "income" as valued work outcome there is a rise in mean points from 27 to 36 ($t = -5.24$, $df = 702$). However, the appreciation of "interpersonal contacts" declines significantly from 23 down to 17 mean points ($t = 4.09$, $df = 705$). Agreement with societal norms pertaining to work remains quite stable from one study to the other.

It appears, then, that young people are changing their view of the meaning of work: Apparently, work is becoming a more central interest in their lives and the value they attach to it is becoming increasingly instrumental. These changes also put young people/students more in tune with other occupational groups. Both tendencies can be very well understood in the light of the economic crisis and the rise of youth unemployment.

HOW YOUNG PEOPLE ENTER THE LABOR MARKET

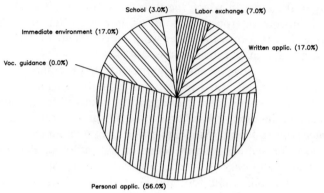

FIG.14.4.   Channels used in job searching ($N = 212$).

Between 6 to 9 months after they left school, the Belgian youngsters were interviewed individually at their homes by the WOSY-researchers. The interviews concerned the channels they used to find their first jobs and the relative popularity of each of these channels. Figure 14.4 shows what role some of the socializing agencies play in the job-searching behavior of young people.

The youngsters' main approach apparently is that of the personal application (either in response to advertisements or on their own initiative). Written applications and help from their immediate environment (family, friends) are the next two major channels used by youngsters wishing to enter the labor market. The Labor Exchange is used only in a rather passive manner ("getting registered as unemployed should do"); the youngsters do not seem to be very familiar with the kinds of activity undertaken by the Exchange offices. The school system only plays a minor role in their job-searching behavior. It is, however, astonishing that none of the youngsters reported having turned to one of the vocational guidance centers, of which there are so many in Belgium.

So, the job-searching behavior reported, with its strong focus on personal initiative, may indicate that work is gaining a central position in young people's lives. On the other hand, failure to utilize all available channels may be an indication of a low to average centrality of work in youngsters entering the labor market.

TABLE 14.1
Selectivity in Accepting Jobs Per Aspect (%) (*N* = 212)

Job Aspect	Not Important	Important if Choice	Condition for Acceptance
Job level	74	17	9
Kind of work	42	32	26
Physical work cond.	59	20	21
Statute	93	5	2
Pay	87	10	3
Work schedule	88	10	5
Geograph. region	94	5	1

To get an idea of the selectiveness exercised by young people before accepting their first job, the WOSY-respondents were asked to indicate to what extent certain job aspects influence their decision to accept or refuse a job. These aspects are divided into three categories.

Table 14.1 shows that, for the whole sample, only the aspects "kind of work" and "physical working conditions" are strong reasons for refusing a job. The former is associated with the relatively high value young people attach to the "intrinsic-expressive" function of work, the latter may be the result of the probably unrealistic picture they have of today's physical working conditions.

IMPLICATIONS

The low to moderate value young people appear to attach to the centrality of work in life may well cause problems in the future when, due to the declining birth rate, employment for all will be feasible again. Yet, the work force of tomorrow may be oriented to other life spheres than work. The youngsters' adherence to the rights as well as the duties involved in working implies that a redivision of employment may be necessary in the future.

Young people care relatively little about income as a valued work outcome and are quite ready to accept a job even if the pay is low. It would therefore seem useful to investigate the effects of providing all adults with a basic income (regardless of whether one is employed). It should be remembered, nevertheless, that young people also want their share of paid work, not primarily because of the pay, but rather because in our society it is the only way "work" is appraised.

The youngsters' job-searching behavior is not too bad. If guidance and counseling are to facilitate young people's entry into the world of work, then they should include the impact of supportive behavior in their immediate environment. The rather low selectiveness in accepting jobs indicates willingness to work and a certain degree of occupational mobility.

REFERENCES

Barker, R. (1968). *Ecological psychology*. Stanford, CA: Stanford University Press.

Coetsier, P., Claes, R., & Berings, D. (1987). *Socialisatie van jongeren met werken inzonderheid in verband met nieuwe technologieën* [Work Socialization of Youth, especially in view of new technologies]. Gent: Laboratorium en Seminarie voor Toegepaste Psychologie.

Cragin, J. (1983). The nature of importance perceptions: A test of a cognitive model. *Organizational Behavior and Human Performance, 31*, 262–276.

Dubin, R. (1956). Industrial workers worlds: A study of the "central life interest" of industrial workers. *Social Problems, 3*, 131–142.

Frese, M., & Mohr, G. (1978). Die psychopathologischen folgen des entzugs von arbeit: Der fall arbeitslosigkeit [Psychopathological consequences of unemployment]. In M. Frese, S. Greif, & N. Semmer (Eds.), *Industrielle psychopathologie* (pp. 282–320). Bern: Huber.

Fryer, D., & Payne, R. (1986). Being unemployed: A review of the literature on the psychological experience of unemployment. In C. Cooper & I. Robertson (Eds.), *International review of industrial and organizational psychology* (pp. 235–277). London: Wiley.

Heider, F. (1958). *The psychology of interpersonal relations*. New York: Wiley.

Lawler, E., & Hall, D. (1970). Relationships of job characteristics to job involvement, satisfaction and intrinsic motivation. *Journal of Applied Psychology, 54*, 305–312.

Locke, E., & Schweiger, D. (1979). Participating in decision-making: One more look. In B. Staw (Ed.), *Research in organization behavior* (pp. 265–339). Greenwich, CT: JAI Press.

Lodahl, T., & Kejner, M. (1965). The definition and measurement of work involvement. *Journal of Applied Psychology, 49*, 24–33.

Maurer, J. (1968). Work as a "central life interest" of industrial supervisors. *Academy of Management Journal, 11*, 329–339.

MOW-International Research Team (1981). The meaning of working. In C. Dlugos & K. Weirmair (Eds.), *Management under differing value systems—Managerial Philosophies and strategies in a changing world* (pp. 565–630). Berlin/New York: Walter De Gruyter.

MOW-International Research Team (1987). *The meaning of working*. London: Academic Press.

O'Brien, G. E. (1986). *Psychology of work and unemployment*. Chichester, England: Wiley.

Osterman, P. (1980). *Getting started: The youth labor market*. Cambridge, MA: MIT Press.

Parson, T., & Shils, E. (Eds.). (1952). *Toward a general theory of action*. Cambridge, MA: Harvard University Press.

Perlman, M. (1976). *Labor union theories in America*. Westport, CT: Greenwood Press.

Silberman, H. F. (Ed.). (1982). *Education and work. Eighty-first yearbook of the national society for the study of education*. Chicago: University of Chicago Press.

APPENDIX

Valued Working Outcomes (MOW & WOSY)

28. To help explain what *working means to you*, please assign a total of 100 points, in any combination you desire, to the following six statements. The more a statement expresses your thinking, the more points you

should assign to it. Please read all the statements before assigning points.

a)_____Working give you status and prestige

b)_____Working provides you with an income that is needed

c)_____Working keeps you occupied

d)_____Working permits you to have interesting contacts with other people

e)_____Working is a useful way for you to serve society

f)_____Working itself is basically interesting and satisfying to you

(100 Total)

Centrality of Work (MOW & WOSY)

29. How important and significant is working in your *total* life?

One of the least important things in my life	1	2	3	4	5	6	7	One of the most important things in my life

Of medium importance in my life

30. Assign a total of 100 points to indicate how important the following areas are in your life at the present time.

a)_____My leisure (like hobbies, sports, recreation, and contacts with friends)

b)_____My community (like voluntary organizations, union and political organizations)

c)_____My work

d)_____My religion (like religious activities and beliefs)

e)_____My family

(100 Total)

Societal Norms About Working (MOW & WOSY)

47. On this page are some work-related statements that people might make. I would like you to decide whether you agree or disagree with each of these statements depending on your personal opinions. If you strongly agree with a statement, please circle the number 4; if you agree somewhat with the statement, circle the number 3; and so on.

	Strongly Disagree	Disagree	Agree	Strongly Agree
a) If a worker's skills become outdated, his employer should	1	2	3	4

be responsible for retraining
and reemployment.

b)	It is the duty of every able-bodied citizen to contribute to society by working	1	2	3	4
c)	The educational system in our society should prepare every person for a good job if they exert a reasonable amount of effort.	1	2	3	4
d)	Persons in our society should allocate a large portion of their regular income toward savings for their future.	1	2	3	4
e)	When a change in work methods must be made, a supervisor should be required to ask workers for their suggestions before deciding what to do.	1	2	3	4
f)	A worker should be expected to think up better ways to do his or her job.	1	2	3	4
g)	Every person in our society should be entitled to interesting and meaningful work.	1	2	3	4
h)	Monotonous, simplistic work is acceptable as long as the pay compensates fairly for it.	1	2	3	4
i)	A job should be provided to every individual who desires to work.	1	2	3	4
j)	A worker should value the work he or she does even if it is boring, dirty, or unskilled.	1	2	3	4

Job Search (WOSY)

How did you go about to find your first job? (open question)

Selectivity (WOSY)

Indicate for the following aspects how important these would be in accepting a job: Job level; Kind of work; Work conditions; Statute; Pay; Work schedule; Geographical region.

Use 0 to indicate: "It is not important to me."
> 1 to indicate: "I would take it into account if there were several jobs offered to me."
>
> 2 to indicate: "It would be a condition to accept the job."

Significant t-tests on the centrality of work for Belgian Students as compared to Students of other countries.

	M	SD	N	t-value	df
Belgium	46.06	6.8	89		
Israel	49.94	5.59	89	4.17	176
Japan	49.51	5.41	118	3.94	164
Netherl	47.66	6.1	89	1.66	176
USA	49.5	6.38	88	3.47	175

Significant t-tests on the centrality of work for Belgian Students as compared to other Belgian target groups.

	M	SD	N	t-value	df
Students	46.06	6.8	89		
Unempl	48.96	8.42	98	2.6	183
Retired	48.81	5.92	86	2.86	173
Chem. Eng	50.18	7.54	89	3.83	176
Teachers	49.89	5.87	90	4.04	177
Self Emp	52.28	7.8	89	5.68	176
Textile	50.09	6.45	86	4.03	173
Temp. Wo	48.64	7.47	77	2.33	164

Significant t-tests on the societal norms for Belgian Students as compared to Students of other countries.

Entitlements

	M	SD	N	t-value	df
Belgium	50.27	5.53	88		
Germany	53.86	5.13	109	−4.71	195
Israel	48.09	6.6	89	2.38	175

| USA | 48.26 | 5.46 | 88 | 2.43 | 174 |

Obligations

	M	SD	N	t-value	df
Belgium	49.66	5.87	88		
Germany	42.07	6.35	111	8.66	197
Israel	51.3	5.48	90	− 1.93	176
Netherl	45.27	5.86	90	5	176

Significant t-tests on the societal norms for Belgian Students as compared to other Belgian target groups.

Entitlements

	M	SD	N	t-value	df
Students	50.27	5.54	88		
Chem. Eng	48.33	5.84	89	− 2.27	175
Teachers	51.79	5.46	90	1.84	176
Self Emp	47.22	6.37	87	− 3.39	173

Obligations

	M	SD	N	t-value	df
Students	49.66	5.87	88		
Retired	53.53	5.83	88	4.39	174
Chem. Eng	47.41	6.23	87	− 2.45	173
Self Emp	51.72	6.77	87	2.16	173
Textile	51.14	5.45	85	1.72	171
Temp.Wo	46.53	5.98	77	− 3.38	163

Significant t-tests on income as valued working outcome for Belgian Students as compared to other Belgian target groups.

	M	SD	N	t-value	df
Students	26.8	15.68	90		
Unempl	35.91	23.49	100	3.17	174
Retired	31.88	19.79	88	1.89	166
Chem. Eng	34.14	18.77	90	2.85	173
Teachers	20.02	13.54	90	− 3.1	178
Self Emp	38.92	21.36	88	4.31	160
Tool-Die	49.98	24.75	80	7.19	131

Wh Col	37.04	21.45	91	3.67	165
Textile	37.12	21.67	85	3.59	152
Temp.Wo	34.25	19.47	81	2.74	154

Significant t-tests on contacts as valued working outcome for Belgian Students as compared to other Belgian target groups.

	M	*SD*	*N*	*t-value*	*df*
Students	22.71	11.17	90		
Unempl	17.03	12.59	100	− 3.27	188
Retired	15.67	14.56	88	− 3.61	163
Chem. Eng	14.26	11.07	90	− 5.1	178
Self Emp	15.49	13.88	88	− 3.82	167
Tool-Die	11	8.8	80	− 7.63	166
Wh Col	17.66	9.34	91	− 3.3	179
Textile	14.38	10.17	85	− 5.15	173

Significant t-tests on intrinsic as valued working outcome for Belgian Students as compared to other Belgian target groups.

	M	*SD*	*N*	*t-value*	*df*
Students	17.3	10.25	90		
Chem.Eng	28.79	17.25	90	5.43	145
Teachers	28.04	15.66	90	5.45	153
Self Emp	23.86	17.25	88	3.08	141
Tool-Die	13.43	11.44	80	− 2.33	168
Wh Col	21.85	15.92	91	2.29	154
Textile	15.13	12.06	85	− 1.29	173

15

Who Shares Whose Values: Identity and Motivation in Organizations

Hubert J.M. Hermans
University of Nijmegen
The Netherlands

After the publication of Peters and Waterman's *In Search of Excellence* (1982) and Deal and Kennedy's *Corporate Cultures* (1982), the many studies, discussions, and conferences about organizational or corporate culture have taken fashionable proportions (Frissen, 1986). For some serious scientists this could be a reason to drop the term *culture* from the map of theoretical concepts in organizational studies, which is more understandable because there is a tendency to attach highly divergent meanings to the concept of culture that are scarcely compatible with each other, as Schein (1985) recently argued. On the other hand, the concept of culture can be given the benefit of the doubt when we realize that it has renewed and deepened our interest in the irrational factors in corporate life, which is relevant not only for the achievements of organizations but also for the meaning people find in their daily work.

The topic of organizational culture became particularly heated when some studies (e.g., Ouchi, 1981; Pascale & Athos, 1981) suggested that Japanese enterprises were successful because of their cultural coherence. This "Japanese challenge" was a reason for Western studies to focus on the concept of "shared values." Peters and Waterman (1982) argued that the crucial aspect of management is "the promotion and protection of values", and that excellent concerns in particular are characterized by a strongly developed system of values that is shared by the members of the organization. Also Deal and Kennedy (1982) emphasized the central role of values in successful organizations that provide a "philosophy" shared by all levels of that organization and give "a sense of identity": "Values are the bedrock of any corporate culture. As the essence of a company's philosophy for achieving success, values provide a sense of common direction for all employees and guidelines for their day-to-day behavior" (p. 2).

From an anthropological perspective, however, the idea of shared culture, shared meanings, and shared values was criticized because it was based on a so-called "small-homogeneous-society metaphor" (Gregory, 1983). This metaphor leads researchers to contrast "strong," homogeneous cultures with "weak" heterogeneous cultures that deviate from management philosophy and are said to lack integration. However, this metaphor is often inappropriate to those organizations that are large, internally differentiated, rapidly changing, and only command part-time commitment from members. The robustness of any group as *a* culture, Gregory continues, is questionable. People participate in many groups and acquire culture in all experiences (e.g., as family members, residents, citizens, employees). Thus, people as culture bearers link groups simultaneously through joint membership and sequentially over their careers. Societies, and many organizations, can more correctly be viewed in terms of multiple, cross-cutting cultural contexts changing through time, rather than as stable, bounded, homogeneous cultures.

A MODEL OF SENDERS AND VALUES

The critique of the small-homogeneous-society metaphor questions the notion of shared values, as a central feature of organizational culture, as long as one does not know who shares whose values. This problem is particularly relevant when different reference figures or reference groups have different, contrasting, or conflicting value systems that come together in one person and ask for some kind of order, hierarchy, or choice. Departing from the question "who shares whose values?," I conceive for heuristic purposes the sharing of values as *a process of sending and receiving values*. In this conception it is supposed that there is a particular individual or group (A) who sends a value to another individual or group (B) who does or does not endorse the value emitted by A. In the case that it is endorsed, the value—as a desirable objective—is shared by A and B. When it is not endorsed, the value is apparently important for A but not for B and consequently is not shared by the two parties involved in the process. Conversely, whether or not B accepts the value emitted by A, B is in a position to send one or more values to A where A is in the position to endorse this value or not. In this process of sending, receiving, and endorsing of values, one or more values can emerge as common between A and B. In this conception every individual or group is both a sender *and* a receiver of values. This view permits a more differentiated analysis of the sharing of values, i.e., one can assess not only the sender and the receiver of a value but also, in the case of more than one value, which value is endorsed and thus shared and which is not; or, in the case of contrasting or conflicting values, which one is given priority. The model can be expanded by assuming more than two senders, which is the typical situation in organizations and in society in general. For example, a head of department (A) endorses a value he receives from his co-workers (B) and tries to convince management (C) who does not accept it. In this case a value (e.g., "a better product with more personnel") is shared by A and B but is not in common with C. With this model, which assumes a process where different senders emit and endorse different values, it is in principle possible to investigate which specific value is shared by which specific senders. At the same time this sharing may be different for different values: The main objective of a firm has more chance to be endorsed by various departments in an organization than an extravagant idea of a storyteller (although in a pub this may be different from a meeting).

The proposed model, based on earlier work on the process of valuation (Hermans, 1987a, 1987b), can be elaborated on in a matrix where rows represent values and columns represent senders. This representation assumes that there is more than one sender emitting more than one value. A cell in the matrix then represents the degree of importance a particular sender attaches to a particular value. In this way one can study the pattern or *profile* of values emitted by a particular sender (a column in the matrix), where one value has a higher degree of importance than another, and one can compare the profiles of various senders.

Presented in this open way the model allows for various applications where the choice and formulation of senders and values depends on the theoretical premises and questions of the investigator. On the basis of such premises and questions, various classifications of senders and values are possible. For example, when the researcher is interested in the interaction between an organization and its environment, then the classification in internal versus external *senders* is a relevant one. Given a set of values one can study the extent of endorsement by, for example, employees (internal) and clients (external), which gives an indication of the extent to which the two groups are interacting on the basis of a common set of values. Another classification of senders results when one wants to confine the study to the internal situation in an organization. Then the interaction between management and co-workers may be the focus of the investigation. On the other hand, the *values* can be classified in various ways as well. When, for example, the researcher wants to know if a certain group or organization has an individualistic or a collectivistic orientation, then a classification in individualistic values (e.g., freedom of behavior) versus collectivistic values (e.g., high consensus in decision making) may be relevant. In this way the proposed model serves, as a flexible scheme, the interests and questions of the researcher. In the following the model is illustrated by an application in two concerns with the focus on the interaction between management and co-workers.

Application of the Proposed Model in Hotel Business

The model was applied by comparing two hotel–restaurants situated in the same area of The Netherlands but strongly different from a cultural perspective. The two concerns were selected on the basis of three criteria. The first criterion refers to the observation that organizational culture develops through successive growth stages. As Schein (1985) described, a company that is in the first stage of growth may develop a strong innovative orientation where people share the enthusiasm of a new beginning. This may change into "organizational midlife," where different subcultures, each with their own commitments, emerge. In "organizational maturity" culture may assume a rigid character so that it puts constraints on innovations. The second criterion concerns the hero-like status of the leader. Deal and Kennedy (1982) explained: "Heroes" personify values and epitomize the strength of the organization. They function as "motivators" and show that the ideal of success lies within human capacity" (p. 37). Finally, the overall satisfaction of the employees was chosen as a third criterion in the selection process. When these criteria were applied to the two hotels, the following differences showed up:

1. Hotel (1) was a young, quickly growing concern that opened several new branches within the first 5 years of its existence. Hotel (2) was an old family concern where the present owner was of the fourth generation. There was no growth and there were no plans and possibilities to open new branches. In terms of Schein (1985) Hotel (1) typically was in a stage of first growth with a strongly innovative orientation, whereas Hotel (2) was rather in a stage of organizational maturity with constraints on innovation.

2. The leader (owner and general manager) of Hotel (1) could be described as a hero. He was the type of the highly successful and admired founder of a limited chain of hotels who was able to obtain large subsidies and licenses for a new business so that in a few years he provided work to almost 100 people. He was generally seen in and outside the concern as a highly qualified and very inspiring leader. The leader (owner and general manager) of Hotel (2) could not be described as a hero. He was not the founder of the hotel but worked in the tradition of his ancestors, and there were no special attributes or achievements that could give him a hero-like status.

3. In the interviews with both leaders, previous to the investigation, leader (1) had no complaints about his personnel, apart from some incidental problems with co-workers. Leader (2), however, expressed many complaints and explained that there was a "motivation-crisis" on the side of his personnel. In the later interviews I had with the personnel of Hotel (2), they ventilated many complaints about their manager and described him as an authoritarian leader who had no inspiring influence on them. This differ-

ence in dissatisfaction between the two hotels was in agreement with the differences in sickness rate: In the period of investigation Hotel (1) had a sickness rate of less than 1%, whereas in Hotel (2) this rate was 15%. Summarizing: When the three criteria, as just described, were applied to the hotels in question, Hotel (1) appeared as well functioning and Hotel (2) as less well functioning on each of the selected criteria.

The main research question was to compare within each of the two concerns the values of leader and co-workers with the expectation that there was more sharing of values between management and staff in the well-functioning Hotel (1) than in the less well-functioning Hotel (2).

The procedure was as follows. In a 1-hour interview I invited the leader to formulate the three main objectives that he considered of high importance to his concern and that he tried to convey to his co-workers. He was asked to phrase these objectives in terms that were clearly understandable to his personnel. Then, I included these objectives in a form that I presented to the co-workers. They were invited to rate the objectives as they saw them of importance in the eyes of the leader, the colleagues of their department as a group, the guests of the hotel, and also in the eyes of themselves as co-workers. They also were asked to fill in two objectives they found important for the concern as co-workers themselves. Also for their own objectives they rated the importance in the eyes of the leader, the colleagues of their department, the guests, and themselves as co-workers. A 0–5 scale was used to rate the degree of importance. The subjects were asked to base their ratings on the behavior of the different people they had to judge. In both hotels staff of all departments were represented in the investigation: the kitchen personnel, the waiters, the parlor maids, the cleaning personnel, and the technical people. All these groups were defined as co-workers and they filled in the forms: 44 of Hotel (1) and 38 of Hotel (2). For each cell of the matrix a mean score was calculated for all co-workers of Hotel (1) (Table 15.1) and for all co-workers of Hotel (2) (Table 15.2). Differences between mean scores were studied with t-tests.

On the basis of a comparison of the two concerns, the main results can be summarized as follows. The co-workers of the well-functioning concern (Hotel 1, Table 15.1) endorse the first-mentioned objective (Top quality of food) to a high degree (4.5), and they see this value of equal importance in the eyes of the leader (4.6), the colleagues of their own department (4.4), and the guests (4.8). The second-mentioned objective (Dutch hospitality) receives an overall lower degree of importance and the third one (Preservation of the atmosphere of the past) a much lower degree of importance with an exception for the guests. When we look at Hotel (2) (Table 15.2), which was less well functioning, it is striking to see that essentially the same picture arises: The co-workers endorse more or less the three objectives of the leader (4.8, 4.4, and 3.7, respectively) and they see these objectives as hav-

TABLE 15.1
Mean Ratings of Co-workers of Hotel (1) who Judged the Values of the
Leader and Their Own Values as Important in the Eyes of the Leader,
Themselves as Co-workers, their Colleagues as a Group, and the Guests

| | Senders | | | |
Values	Leader	Co-worker	Colleagues	Guests
Top quality of food (objective 1 of leader)	4.6	4.5	4.4	4.8
Dutch hospitality (objective 2 of leader)	4.4	3.9	3.6	4.6
Preservation of the atmosphere of the past (objective 3 of leader)	2.4	2.6	2.2	3.4
Objective 1 of co-worker	3.9	4.8	3.8	3.3
Objective 2 of co-worker	3.5	4.9	3.9	3.1

TABLE 15.2
Mean Ratings of Co-workers of Hotel (2) Who Judged the Values of the
Leader and Their Own Values as Important in the Eyes of the Leader,
Themselves as Co-workers, Their Colleagues as a Group, and the Guests

| | Senders | | | |
Values	Leader	Co-worker	Colleagues	Guests
Satisfied guests (objective 1 of leader)	4.9	4.8	4.0	4.8
Healthy team spirit (objective 2 of leader)	4.0	4.4	3.6	3.4
Personal management (objective 3 of leader)	4.4	3.7	2.7	3.8
Objective 1 of co-worker	2.1	4.6	3.6	2.4
Objective 2 of co-worker	1.8	4.9	3.6	2.6

ing considerable importance in the eyes of the leader, colleagues, and
guests. The finding of more or less equal endorsement by the two hotels is
striking when we recall the clear differences in heroship and motivational
problems. In fact, I was surprised to see that the co-workers of the less well-
functioning hotel endorsed the three objectives of the leader even at some
higher degree than was the case in the well-functioning hotel. This result
suggested that in Hotel (2) there was also a strong sharing of the values
emitted by the leader.

When we move from the upper to the lower part of Table 15.1 and Table
15.2, however, we see a dramatic difference between the two hotels when we
focus on the objectives of the co-workers. The co-workers of Hotel (1) have
the feeling that their own objectives (1 and 2) are also regarded as impor-

tant by the leader (3.9 and 3.5, respectively). This is quite different in Hotel (2), where the co-workers find that their own objectives are regarded as *unimportant* in the eyes of the leader (2.1 and 1.8, respectively). This means that the co-workers of Hotel (2) do not find their own values reflected in the eyes of the leader.

For a better understanding of the so-called objectives of the co-workers, I give some typical examples (objective 1) of Hotel (1) where the co-workers found their values reflected in the eyes of the leader: "autonomy in the work," "good fellowship," "appreciation of each other's work," "enthusiastic work sphere," "listening to complaints," and "a good promotion of the concern." Some typical examples of objectives (1) of co-workers of Hotel (2), which they did not find reflected in the eyes of the leader, are these: "better listening to complaints," "contact with colleagues," "opportunity to express opinions," "payment according to achievement," "better social understanding," and "good planning of activities."

As a summary of the results the following can be concluded: The co-workers of each of the two hotels endorsed the main objectives as formulated by their leaders. The difference was that the staff of Hotel (1) found their own values reflected by the leader, whereas this was not the case in Hotel (2). In other words, in the experiences of the co-workers there was a one-way mirroring of values in the latter case and a two-way mirroring in the former case. The question is now what is the meaning of this difference?

IDENTITY AND MOTIVATION: DISCUSSION

Our data suggest that the existence of shared values is an inadequate concept as a differentiating criterion for the well functioning of groups and organizations, as long as one does not know whose values are shared and by whom they are shared. At first sight it was un unveiling datum that the staff of the less well-functioning hotel strongly stressed the importance of the main objectives of the concern as they were formulated by management, at least as strongly as the staff did in the well-functioning hotel. The differentiating criterion was not the co-workers' support of the values of the leader, but their judgment of the leader's support of their own values. The meaning of this result can be clarified when we make a distinction between two concepts that are closely related on the level of the individual and on the level of the group and the organization: identity and motivation. As Deal and Kennedy (1982) said, the sharing of values in an organization gives "a sense of identity." The people, although they may work at different departments and often do not know each other, have a common direction. They know these values for themselves and suppose that they are present in their fellow-workers. And besides a sense of direction, the sharing of values gives a sense of continuity in this way, because the common direction provides a continuous orientation towards a set of goals that do not need to be formulated each day again. Identity then can be described in terms of values insofar as there is a common orientation towards the main objectives of a concern, objectives that are primarily incorporated in the figure of the leader. Identity in organizations is a necessary precondition for motivation but it never can be equalized with it. There is motivation for working hard, or a "high motivation," when people feel their own values reflected in the values of management that represents the main objectives of the concern. When this happens, people typically say: "I can find myself in the goals of my leader" or "I can find myself in the way he or she is doing it." There is no motivation without identity because a common goal is a precondition to coordinated work; on the other hand, motivation is more than identity because there can only be motivation when the common goals are invested by energy derived from the value orientations of the co-workers. So I propose to differentiate the concept of "shared values" in terms of identity and motivation. For identity a one-way mirroring of values suffices, that is, the co-workers support the objectives of the leader as the first representative of the concern or department. For a high motivation a two-way mirroring of values is required, that is, the co-workers do not only support the values of the leader but, moreover, they feel that their own values are congruent with the leader's values. In this view the realization of goals can be compared with car driving: The leader serves the wheel giving direction, the co-workers provide the fuel necessary for the movement, assuming that they agree with the direction.

In this chapter the concept of shared values was translated as an organized system of values on the assumption that, in the process of sending and receiving values, more than one value and also more than one sender is involved. This multiplicity of various senders emitting a complexity of values always results in some ordering or organization of values in profiles that may be different or contrasting for various senders. The question of change of values or of shared values can, on the same lines, be described as a reordering or reorganization of the system of values. The problem of change far exceeds the scope of this chapter, but one suggestion follows directly from the preceding argumentation. When one wants to increase or enhance the sharing of values in an organization with the intention of promoting production or efficiency "in search of excellence," it is a naive supposition that the common support of the main objectives by staff and management is a sufficient condition in realizing that promotion. As argued in this chapter, this one-way sharing is at best a necessary precondition, but never a sufficient one. The sharing of values only leads to a high motivation when the goals of the staff itself are taken into account as a part of a two-way mirroring of values.

ACKNOWLEDGMENTS

I thank Willem van Gilst for writing the computer programs, Fred Nulens for his help in the translation of this chapter, and Gerard Koene for his stimulating advice and help in the beginning of this study.

REFERENCES

Deal, T. E., & Kennedy, A. A. (1982). *Corporate cultures. The rites and rituals of corporate life*. Reading, MA: Addison-Wesley.

Frissen, P. (1986). Organisatiecultuur: Een overzicht van benaderingen [Organizational culture: A survey of approaches]. *Mens en Onderneming*, November-December, 532–544.

Gregory, K. L. (1983). Native-view paradigms: Multiple cultures and culture conflicts in organizations. *Administrative Science Quarterly, 28*, 359–376.

Hermans, H. J. M. (1987a). Self as organized system of valuations: Toward a dialogue with the person. *Journal of Counseling Psychology, 34*, 10–19.

Hermans, H. J. M. (1987b). The dream in the process of valuation: A method of interpretation. *Journal of Personality and Social Psychology, 53*, 163–175.

Ouchi, W. G. (1981). *Theory Z: How American business can meet the Japanese challenge*. Reading, MA: Addison-Wesley.

Pascale, R. T., & Athos, A. G. (1981). *The art of Japanese management*. New York: Simon & Schuster.

Peters, Th.J., & Waterman, R. H. (1982). *In search of excellence. Lessons from America's best-run companies*. New York: Harper & Row.

Schein, E. H. (1985). *Organizational culture and leadership: A dynamic view*. San Francisco: Jossey-Bass.

16

Major Work Meaning Patterns Toward A Holistic Picture

S. Antonio Ruiz Quintanilla
Berlin University of Technology

THE MEANING OF WORKING LIFE
AS A FIELD OF STUDY

Living in a "work society" means that the daily, weekly, and yearly and even life-long time table is structured by work and nonwork periods for most adults. Although individuals can influence the time exposed to the work domain up to a certain degree, only few become independent from the overarching schedule.

It is also trivial to state that the majority of adults derive the major part of their economic well-being from income generated by their work activities. Besides this economic function there are other motives or needs that are fulfilled or frustrated through working. Working can offer the possibility for contacts (social dimension) and can in itself be experienced as interesting and satisfying or boring and dull (intrinsic/expressive dimension). Most studies comparing occupational groups have shown systematic occupational differences in the importance rating of work goals (Friedlander, 1965; Hofstede, 1972). Finally, the fact that members with similar work experience develop a common set of work orientations has been discussed as an aspect of the socializing influence of work (Kohn & Schooler, 1983).

Besides these more scientific reasons, the topic of meaning of working is important from a practical viewpoint as well. Industrialized countries are faced with unemployment, growing international competition, and technological changes. The work society has become a topic in question. To formulate alternatives or to learn from other countries, a better understanding of the subjective function that working fulfills for individuals is needed. The work meanings and values and the intergenerational differences, if

257

there are any, have to be taken into account in company employment or labor market policies.

Last but not least, the sample chosen for the analysis (F.R. Germany, United States, Japan) is of special interest. The success of the Japanese on the world market lets Western academics and managers strive for an identification of organizational or procedural causes for this achievement. To remain internationally competitive, "Japanese" management and organizational practices are proposed to be transferred to Western organizations (e.g., Schonberger, 1982). What is often neglected are the specific psychological and social circumstances (e.g., work meanings and their antecedents and consequences), which make the practice at issue (i.e., Quality Circles, just-in-time-production) successful in Japan but perhaps not in a Western environment. To be able to decide on their adaptability, a better understanding of the similarities and differences within and between countries is needed. To compare countries on single work-meaning dimensions in a descriptive way, one by one, as it is done later in a forthcoming section, explores differences and similarities but does not offer much explanation. Thus, in the second section we show that the complex construct of work meanings can be better treated by using a more complex analysis technique like cluster analysis. Cluster analysis identifies typical patterns of relations among meaning of work dimension for individuals. The last section shows groups of individuals sharing a meaning of work pattern who can then be characterized according to antecedents variables (i.e., personal characteristics, quality of work) to arrive at causal hypotheses for further research.

THE MEANING OF WORKING (MOW) STUDY—
AN INTERNATIONAL COMPARISON

In response to the forementioned scientific and practical reasons, social scientists from eight countries[1] jointly designed and conducted a comparative study to explore the empirical structure of work meanings of individuals from different social, professional, and national backgrounds (MOW 1981, 1987).

In a first step a heuristic research model was developed on the basis of various important theoretical assumptions. The model defines three major components as core concepts.

Work centrality is defined as the degree of importance that working has in the life of an individual. The method of measurement is a combination of an absolute assessment of the importance of working in one's life on a

---

[1]Belgium, F. R. Germany, Great Britain, Israel, Japan, Netherlands, United States, and Yugoslavia.

Likert-scale *and* a relative judgment of the importance of working in one's life as compared to the importance of other life domains (e.g., leisure, family). The centrality index aims to answer the question: How central or important is the role of working in one's life?

Work goals is defined as the relative importance of 11 work goals that individuals prefer or look for in their work life. The goals ranked were opportunity to learn, good interpersonal relations, opportunity for promotion, convenient work hours, variety, interesting work, job security, match between job requirements and abilities, pay, physical working conditions, and autonomy. For the purpose of estimating the differences and similarities between the countries on a more general level, two dimensions were derived through factor analysis by country. Comparable loadings in the countries led to a general *economic work-goal dimension* (pay, job security) and a general *expressive work-goal dimension* (autonomy, interesting work, good match). The question behind this concept is: Which goals motivate individuals in the work domain?

Societal norms about working is defined as beliefs and expectations concerning specific rights and duties attached to working. The MOW project focused on two dimensions as measured by an individual's agreement or disagreement with 10 normative statements. Factor analysis revealed two normative dimensions: the *obligation norm*, representing the underlying duties of all individuals to a society with respect to working. This includes the notion that everyone has to contribute to society by working, should save money from his/her income for the future, and have the duty to value his/her work independent of its nature. The *entitlement norm* is represented by statements expressing the underlying work rights of individuals and the work-related equitable responsibilities of organizations and the society towards all individuals working or willing to work. Included are notions that all members of a society are entitled to have meaningful and interesting work, are entitled to retraining when it is needed, and have the right to participate in work-method decisions. At issue are the normative (obligation/entitlement) feelings individuals have concerning their rights and duties in respect to the world of work.

The results presented and discussed in this chapter use part of the database of the Meaning of Working study. The procedure used for data collection was an intensive interview on the basis of a questionnaire. Whereas the Mow-study included both representative samples of the work force ($N = 8749$) and 10 identical target groups ($N = 5895$) selected on the basis of their centrality or marginality to the labor market of the eight countries, this contribution restricts itself to the representation of data from the representative work force samples of only three countries (F. R. Germany, United States, Japan). Choosing these countries allows us to concentrate on more comprehensive analyses of the data than could be done for the first international documentation of the MOW results, which included all coun-

TABLE 16.1
Description of the National Representative Samples
(N's for FRG = 1278; Japan = 3226; USA = 1002).

		FRG	JAPAN	USA
Sex	% Male	65	66	54
Age	% 16–19	6	2	3
	% 20–29	23	18	30
	% 30–39	21	27	31
	% 40–49	25	29	18
	% 50–59	18	16	13
	% over 60	7	8	5
Highest level of education				
	% Primary	17	2	5
	% Secondary	65	57	35
	% some College	8	14	30
	% Univ. Degree	10	27	30
Number of hours worked/week		40	49	43
Net income/month		DM 1735	Y 340000	$1394

tries (MOW, 1987). At the same time, Germany, the United States, and Japan have the advantage of representing most of the variance from the total international sample. Table 16.1 gives an overview on the composition of the samples.

Looking at the sample characteristics, there are some differences between the countries. For the purpose of a country comparison, these are "true national" differences insofar as they reflect the labor force composition at the time (1982/1983) the interviews were conducted.

COUNTRY SAMPLES COMPARED IN IMPORTANT WORK MEANING DIMENSIONS

Work Centrality

Figure 16.1 shows the mean scores of the combined work centrality measure, which has a theoretical range possibility between 2 and 10. The country scores differ significantly (.05). The Japanese show the highest value, the United States a moderate one, and Germany the lowest. Looking at the absolute component of the work centrality index alone (Table 16.2) reveals that differences stem mainly from the very important pole of the 7-point scale.

For nearly half of the Japanese work force, working is one of the most important things in their life (score 7) compared to one-third in the United

States sample and one-seventh of the German sample. The magnitude of these statistical differences speak for fundamental differences between the work forces of the three countries regarding working as a life role. A different but possibly related dimension to our measure of work centrality could be the number of hours worked (cf. Table 16.1). Thus we are able to point to a quantitative correlate of perceived work centrality. To explore the qualitative side, let us take a closer look at the prominent work goals of individuals in the three countries under study.

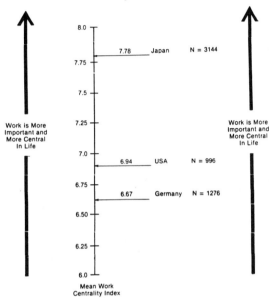

FIG. 16.1   Mean score of the Work Centrality Index for representative samples of FRG, USA, and Japan (adapted from MOW, 1987, p. 83).

TABLE 16.2
Work Centrality Component I.
Percentage Distribution of the German, Japanese, and United State's
Workforce Samples

How important and significant is working in your total life?								
One of the least important things in my life	1	2	3	4	5	6	7	One of the most important things in my life
FRG	2.0	4.0	8.3	21.4	25.8	24.3	14.0	
USA	0.9	0.9	2.5	14.5	27.3	23.7	30.2	
Japan	0.4	0.3	1.4	22.4	14.0	16.3	44.3	

TABLE 16.3
Mean Ranks and Intracountry Importance Ranks of Work Goals
(National Sample Data: Adapted from MOW, 1987, 122)

Work Goals	FRG (N = 1248)		USA (N = 988)		Japan (N = 2897)	
Interesting work	7.26	3	7.41	1	7.38	2
Good pay	7.73	1	6.82	2	6.56	5
Good interpersonal relations	6.43	4	6.08	7	6.39	6
Good job security	7.57	2	6.30	3	6.71	4
A good match between you and your job	6.09	5	6.19	4	7.83	1
A lot of autonomy	5.66	8	5.79	8	6.89	3
Opportunity to learn	4.97	9	6.16	5	6.26	7
A lot of variety	5.71	6	6.10	6	5.05	9
Convenient work hours	5.71	6	5.25	9	5.46	8
Good physical working conditions	4.39	11	4.84	11	4.18	10
Good opportunity for upgrading or promotion	4.48	10	5.08	10	3.33	11

Work Goals

Table 16.3 gives the relative importance ranks of the 11 work goals for the three country samples. In comparing the similarities and differences on specific work goals, we focus on the first three ranks in each country. Among the three most important ranks we find "interesting work" in all three countries, "good pay" and "job security" in two of them (not in Japan), and "a good match between you and your job" and "a lot of autonomy" in Japan only. First, it can be stated that the German and the American work force—in terms of work goals—are more similar to each other than to the Japanese. Second, the economic goals have a more prominent place in the labor force of Germany and the United States compared to Japan. In scrutinizing general differences and similarities concerning the relative importance of economic and expressive work-goal dimensions, we again find important differences between the work force of our three countries (Fig. 16.2).

In Germany economic goals are rated more important than expressive ones, in the Unites States both dimensions are rated about equal, and in Japan expressive work goals are rated more important than economic work

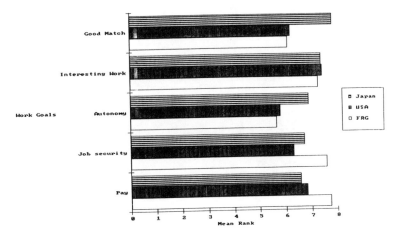

FIG. 16.2.   Mean importance ranks of economic and expressive work goals in the FRG, USA, and Japan (National sample data).

goals. Comparisons across the three countries show that in Germany economic work goals are rated more important than in the other two countries, and expressive work goals have about the same importance in the United States and Germany whereas they are rated more highly in Japan.

Societal Norms about Working

Figure 16.3 shows the location of the three countries in the societal norm space formed by the two dimensions of obligation and entitlement norms.

Note that there are entitlement differences between all three countries with the United States having low values, Germany the highest, and Japan in between, nearer to the United States. However, differences in the obligation norm are found between the United States on the one hand and the other two countries on the other, the United State's sample showing a higher obligation norm.

A MORE COMPLEX ANALYTICAL APPROACH

The descriptive results just presented show significant differences between the three countries on the MOW-dimensions. A further exploration of these results might try to analyze the antecedents and consequent variables (correlates) of each of the single MOW-dimensions as has been done elsewhere (MOW, 1987). This has the disadvantage that the major work-meaning dimensions are treated as operating independently within the individual. As we stated in the beginning, although necessary as a first step, such a procedure has its drawbacks.

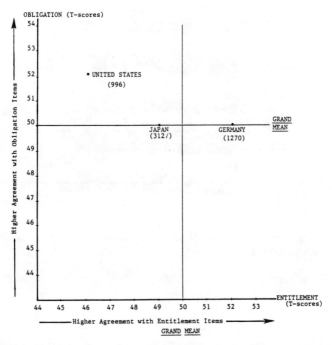

FIG. 16.3. Representative samples in the Societal Norms space (adapted from MOW, 1987, p. 96).

To move towards a more holistic view of how the work meanings are interrelated within the individual, typical (frequent) patterns of work meanings have to be identified. A cluster analysis was conducted using the five work-meaning indices previously discussed, so that individuals within a cluster were maximally similar to each other in terms of the work-meaning indices whereas different clusters were maximally different from each other. The method used on the combined three-country sample ($N = 2940$) was Ward's hierarchical clustering method (Ward, 1963). The combined sample was taken to allow an identification of frequent patterns independent of the nationality. All indices were expressed as standardized T-scores with a mean of 50 and a standard deviation of 10. Considering the optimal ratio between loss of variance (error coefficient) and number of clusters, eight work-meaning clusters was the optimal solution. The results of a multiple discriminant analysis showed that 64 to 85% of the respondents were correctly classified using their discriminant functions' scores.

Results: Description of the Patterns

In a first step we describe the eight meanings of work patterns (cluster) in terms of the central MOW-indices. Table 16.4 presents the combination of

TABLE 16.4
Characteristic Scores Within the Meaning of Working Patterns
(Combined Labor Force Samples in the FRG, USA, and Japan, N = 2938).

MOW Pattern	Below Average	Above Average
A	Work Centrality Economic Index Obligation Index	
B	Work Centrality Expressive Index	Obligation Index
C	Obligation Index Expressive Index	Economic Index
D	Expressive Index	Economic Index Obligation Index Entitlement Index
E	Economic Index Obligation Index Entitlement Index	
F	Economic Index	Work Centrality Expressive Index Obligation Index
G	Economic Index Obligation Index	Work Centrality Expressive Index Entitlement Index
H		Work Centrality Economic Index Expressive Index

work-meaning index scores, which are found frequently over all countries. For the description we consider the three most characteristic work-meaning index scores in each of the eight clusters of individuals.

Roughly the eight patterns can be categorized as two with low work centrality (A,B), three with a work centrality around the mean (C,D,E), one with a moderately high work centrality (F), and two with high work centrality (G,H). The following differentiated observation shows how these different levels of centrality go together with the other work-meaning dimensions for the eight patterns.

Low Centrality Pattern. Pattern A members have the lowest work centrality scores among the eight groups. They have low economic work values and the lowest obligation scores. Their evaluation of working itself and their normative entitlement beliefs are not significantly different from the total sample. To characterize this group we label them *nonwork-centered, nonduty-oriented, noneconomic workers.*

Pattern B members have a very low work centrality score (over one standard deviation below the overall mean). They have low expressive work values and above-average obligation scores. We label this group as *nonwork-centered, duty-oriented workers*.

Recall that individuals with a low work centrality are those who evaluate working as a life role as being absolutely or relatively seen of lower importance to other activities. Members of pattern A (the nonwork-centered, nonduty-oriented, noneconomic workers) fit into this picture. Economic goals like high income, opportunities for promotion, and good job security are for them of less importance, and they feel free from any obligation to work. We would predict this group as having a low quality of work and a low occupational satisfaction. Trying to raise their motivation towards work by means of improving their work according to their slightly above-mean expressive goals might thus be successful.

Pattern B members (the nonwork-centered, duty-oriented workers) give about the same evaluation of the importance of work as a life role but show quite a different mixture on the other MOW-dimensions: a low expressive goal orientation and an obligation norm above the mean. It might be safe to assume that this group is among the most difficult to be further motivated.

Average Work Centrality Pattern.   Pattern C workers have about average work centrality scores and relatively low obligation scores. The strongest distinguishing characteristics of this group, however, are their very high economic values and their very low expressive values (in both cases above one standard deviation from the overall average). As this pattern clearly represents a very strong economic orientation to work, we label this group as the *economic workers*.

Pattern D workers have about average work centrality scores. The most salient features of the pattern are high economic work values and very high levels of obligation norms and entitlement norms, both one standard deviation above the overall averages. This group clearly represents strong normative obligation and entitlement beliefs about working as well as a strong economic orientation. We label the group as *high rights and duties, economic workers*.

Pattern E seems to be a difficult pattern to interpret. Members of it have average work centrality scores, relatively low economic values, relatively low obligation norms, and extremely low entitlement norms (more than 1.7 standard deviations below the overall average). Similar to pattern A all major defining characteristics of this pattern are lower than the overall average. We label this pattern *low rights and duties, noneconomic worker* pattern.

Pattern C (economic workers) and D (high rights and duties economic workers) share a high economic orientation in combination with a low expressive one. Whereas the economic factors seemed to be the main source for the motivation of pattern C members, pattern D members also are strongly influenced by societal norms. Due to this we would expect pattern D members to have a slightly higher occupational satisfaction than pattern C members.

As to pattern E members (low rights and duties, noneconomic workers), besides a similar evaluation of working as a life role, they show nearly the opposite picture on the other dimensions compared to pattern D. For now it seems difficult to explain why this group does not evaluate working as of low importance.

High Work Centrality Pattern. Finally we come to the pattern with moderately high or high evaluation of working in their life. Pattern F members have a moderately high work centrality level, a very low level of economic values, and a moderately high level of expressive values. Their obligation index scores are significantly above the average and are considerably higher than their average level entitlement scores. We label this group as *moderately work-centered, duty-oriented, noneconomic workers.*

Pattern G workers have high work centrality scores, very low economic values, and very high expressive work values. Their obligation norm score is below average whereas their entitlement norm score is about average. We label this group *work-centered, expressive workers.*

Pattern H members have high work centrality scores and relatively high economic and expressive values. Their obligation and entitlement scores are close to average and about equal. We label this group as *work-centered and balanced-work values workers.*

All three patterns share a higher than average expressive goal orientation, which if being fulfilled to some degree in their working conditions would let us predict occupational satisfaction above the average. Pattern H (work-centered and balanced-work values workers) is the only group that is open for the whole range of economic and expressive motivators and also shares the societal norms in an average degree.

Country Differences

Looking at Fig. 16.4 on the distribution of the eight patterns over the three countries (Japan, USA, and FRG), we see that none of the patterns is country specific. All patterns are found in all countries, but there are considerable differences regarding respective frequencies. Japan has a big portion of highly work-centered workers (G,H), the Federal Republic of Germany has the most economic workers (C,D), and the United States relatively more duty-oriented workers (B). This picture presents a first answer for the question: Which individuals are found in which pattern? Hence, we are left to answer the next: What are the biographical and situational characteristics of the members of the different patterns?

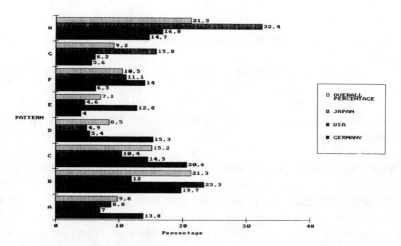

FIG. 16.4. Work meaning patterns in the FRG, USA, and Japan (Percentage distribution; $N = 2938$).

TABLE 16.5
Demographic Characteristics of Pattern Members of the Combined Labor
Force Samples in the FRG, USA, and Japan ($N = 2938$)

Correlates	Percentage Per Pattern:								Overall
	A	B	C	D	E	F	G	H	Mean
Age (years)									
under 30	47.8	34.9	34.3	26.3	26.8	23.4	29.9	21.8	30.3
30–50	40.8	45.3	45.7	48.2	51.7	47.7	55.7	55.7	49.0
over 50	11.4	19.7	20.0	25.1	21.5	28.9	14.0	22.6	20.6
Gender									
Male	51.9	53.4	61.0	66.5	61.2	62.3	63.1	72.6	62.0
Education									
primary									
school	10.0	10.0	11.7	11.2	7.7	5.5	3.0	5.1	8.0
secondary									
school	51.2	52.1	60.5	66.9	32.5	49.4	45.4	51.4	52.1
some									
college	14.2	20.2	16.4	12.7	23.0	16.6	13.7	16.3	16.8
university									
degree	24.6	17.4	11.0	9.2	35.9	28.2	37.6	27.0	22.8
Country									
FRG	46.7	35.8	45.3	59.8	18.7	20.1	20.3	23.0	33.4
USA	23.5	42.3	31.8	21.1	59.8	44.5	22.5	26.2	33.3
Japan	29.8	21.9	22.9	19.1	21.5	35.4	57.2	50.7	33.4
N's	289	539	446	251	209	308	271	625	

CHARACTERISTICS OF PATTERN MEMBERS

Personal Characteristics

In the following we describe the patterns in terms of the personal characteristics of its members.

Pattern A: Nonwork-centered Nonduty-oriented, Noneconomic. Forty eight percent of pattern A members belong to the age group under 30 compared to an average of 30% in all groups. Females make up 47% of this pattern as compared to an overall average of 38%. The educational distribution is like the one of the total sample. Nearly half the members of this pattern are West German citizens.

Pattern B: Nonwork-Centered, Duty-Oriented.   Members of this pattern have an average age distribution, and females are over-represented (47% vs. an average of 38%). The educational level is near average, only there is a slightly lower percentage of college graduates than average. Most of the members are from the United States (42.3%) or from the Federal Republic of Germany (35.8%).

Pattern C: Economic.   This pattern has an age and sex distribution similar to the total group. In their educational level primary and secondary levels are over-represented. Again, members of this pattern come mainly from the Federal Republic (43.5%) and the United States (31.8%).

Pattern D: High Rights and Duties, Economic.   In this pattern the over-50 age group is over-represented (25.1% vs. 20.6% overall average). There is a slightly higher than average percentage of males and also a slightly higher than average percentage of primary and secondary educational levels. About 60% of this pattern are of West German origin.

Pattern E: Low Rights and Duties, Noneconomic.   This group has a slightly higher than average age distribution (about 1 year older), an average sex distribution, and a high proportion of college graduates (35.9% vs. an overall average of 22.8%). Over half the members (59.8%) are American.

Pattern F: Moderately Work-Centered, Duty-Oriented, Noneconomic. Members of this pattern are about 2 years older than the overall average and are particularly under-represented in the under-30 age group and over-represented in the above-50 age group. They have an average sex distribution and slightly above-average educational level. Most of the members are either American (44.5%) or Japanese (35.4%).

Pattern G: Work-Centered Expressive.   Pattern G members are about 1 year younger than the overall average age but have about a 7% over-representation in the 30–50-year age group. There is an average sex distribution and it contains the highest percentage of college graduates of all eight groups (39.5% vs. an overall average of 22.8%). Over half (57.2%) the pattern members are Japanese.

Pattern H: Work-Centered and Balanced Work Values.   Members of Pattern H are under-represented in the under-30 age group and over-represented in the 30–50-year age group by 7–8%. They have the highest percentage of males of all eight groups (72.6% vs. an overall average of 62%) and have a near-average educational distribution. Again about half (50.7% the members are Japanese.

If in summarizing we take into account only the most salient personal characteristic of each pattern, we see that females are more frequent in the two nonwork-centered patterns and to a lesser degree in pattern H (work-centered, balanced work values). Most of the individuals with a high work centrality are between 30–50 years old, i.e., in the middle of their working career. Individuals of the age group under 30 are often found in pattern A (nonwork-centered, nonduty-oriented, noneconomic). Furthermore there seems to be a tendency that a higher educational level goes together with at least an average or high work centrality.

Quality of Work

Finally, have a closer look at the quality of the work situation and the occupational satisfaction of the pattern members. Table 16.6 gives an overview of the patterns on five measures of the characteristics of the work situation: variety, autonomy, responsibility, possibilities to learn, and supervisory status.

If one distinguishes between values above the mean and below the mean, members of pattern A to D characterize their quality as low and members of pattern E to H as high, on all four dimensions. Only on the supervisory status, pattern D and G are in an average position. In summary we find, that the patterns with a low or average work centrality have a work quality below average. The only exception is pattern E (low rights and duties, noneconomic workers). This relatively better evaluation of working conditions helps us to explain their general average evaluation of the importance of working as a life role.

Occupational Satisfaction

Two questions were used to measure the occupational satisfaction. In the first question we asked a person if she/he would choose the same occupation again. The second was the so-called "lottery question," where people are asked to express what they would do if they had won enough money to live comfortably without the need to work.

TABLE 16.6
Quality of Work and Occupational Satisfaction of Pattern Members of the
Combined Labor Force Samples in the FRG, USA, and Japan (N = 2938)

| Correlates | Percentage Per Pattern: | | | | | | | | Overall |
	A	B	C	D	E	F	G	H	Mean
Quality of work									
Wide variety	31.8	31.2	24.7	30.3	49.8	46.8	50.9	43.0	37.5
Own decision making	19.0	22.4	13.0	20.3	34.0	25.3	22.1	21.8	21.4
Serious consequences of mistakes	17.6	24.7	23.3	25.1	36.4	27.3	17.0	22.2	23.7
Learning many things	20.8	31.2	26.7	17.5	52.2	51.0	47.2	35.7	34.3
Nonsupervisory position	37.7	44.2	36.8	24.3	42.1	40.3	48.3	43.7	40.4
Occupational satisfaction									
Choose same occupation again	36.7	37.8	39.2	50.6	48.8	43.5	31.7	31.8	38.6
Lottery question									
stop working	23.2	21.5	24.2	19.5	15.8	7.8	2.6	7.7	15.4
continue same	34.3	36.4	37.7	36.7	46.9	60.1	57.9	52.8	45.1
continue different	42.6	41.4	37.9	43.8	37.3	31.5	39.1	39.0	39.1
N's	289	539	446	251	209	308	271	625	

We find that members of pattern A to C have values below the mean on both items: Less persons than average would choose the same occupation again or continue it if they would have enough money, and more than average would stop working if they were able to. Looking at pattern F to H members we find above-average values for choosing the same occupation again and continuing; and only a low percentage of persons would stop working.

CONCLUSIONS

The large majority of members of the workforces in the Federal Republic of Germany, the United States, and Japan can be classified as members of one out of eight cluster analytically derived work-meaning patterns. Out of the eight patterns found, none was country specific: All patterns were found in all three countries. The description of the national workforces in terms of the frequencies of pattern membership shows that Japan has about twice as many (about 50%) work-centered individuals (pattern G and H) than Germany and the United States. However, this still implies that the high work orientation of Japanese workers is only true for half its workforce.

Analyses of the patterns in terms of individual and work-setting characteristics showed that members of patterns with a relatively low work quality generally also show a low occupational satisfaction. This is not necessarily true for individuals who have a strong affiliation towards societal norms (pattern D). Individuals with work-quality settings above average evaluate working as a life role in terms of medium or higher importance, depending on their work-goal orientations and their agreement/disagreement with common societal norms. This seems to indicate that some of the work-meaning dimensions appear to function in compensatory ways.

Although this analysis serves only as a first step in understanding the meaning of work in its complexity, the results discussed allow us to formulate interesting hypotheses about intraindividual relations of work meanings, about the relations between personal, biographic, and situational characteristics and shared work-meaning patterns, as well as about the characteristic composition of workforces in terms of pattern membership frequency.

ACKNOWLEDGMENTS

This contribution has benefited much from the discussions with Professor G. W. England, of the United States. The author would like to express thanks to him and to Professor Jyuji Misumi of Japan for use of their national data.

REFERENCES

Friedlander, F. (1965). Relationships between the importance and satisfaction of various environmental factors. *Journal of Applied Psychology, 49*, 160–164.

Hofstede, G. (1972). The color of collars. *Columbia Journal of World Business, 7*, 72–80.

Kohn, M., & Schooler, C. (1983). *Work personality*. An inquiry into the impact of social stratification. Norwood, NJ: Ablex.

MOW-Meaning of Working International Research Team (1987). *The meaning of working*. London: Academic Press.

Schonberger, R. J. (1982). *Japanese manufacturing techniques*. New York: Free Press.

Ward, J. (1963). Hierarchical grouping to optimize an objective function. *Journal of the American Statistical Association, 58*, 236–244.

Author Index

Subject Index